MILLFIELD

MILLFIELD

A SCHOOL FOR ALL SEASONS

A Collection of Anecdotes
Compiled and Collected by

CHRISTOPHER MARTIN

ABSOLUTE DESIGN PUBLISHING

First published 2007 by Absolute Design Publishing, Betham House, 164 Oldfield Lane, Greenford UB6 9JT

A catalogue record of this book is available from the British Library.

ISBN 978-0-9555056-0-7

Cover photo courtesy of John Davies
Designed and typeset by Absolute Design.

CONTENTS

FOREWORD

Do we remember the past in terms more of places or of the people who inhabited them? Do buildings or faces monopolise our memory? And since childhood memories live longest in our increasingly ageing minds, and since we all went to school, was it the general experience of being young within a set framework, or the people with whom we shared it that subsequently stand most clearly in our mind?

If I thought I knew the answers to these questions when I embarked on this collection of memoirs, the responses I received consistently confirmed my view. People represent, of course, the most formative influences in our lives, perhaps at any stage but certainly when we are young. A school can therefore be seen primarily as a setting, perhaps even as no more than a backdrop, against which people interact in various ways, positive and negative, creative and destructive, good and bad. The richer the mix of old and young, boys and girls, from different backgrounds and countries and cultures, with different expectations, gifts, skills, attributes, failings, the richer should be the sum total for everyone of these inter-relationships. This, in short, is the Millfield mix. Vive la différence! In a school like ours, where almost two thousand people work in various capacities, tens of thousands of verbal transactions will take place every day, some trivial, others significant, but all tending to generate a feeling, ultimately a bond between people which brings the place alive for them at the time, and characterises their memory of it subsequently.

The range and quality of the buildings which constitute the framework for these exchanges do, of course, help, but they do not ultimately forge the strength of feeling which creates the best educational experience. Those OMs who learnt in the Nissen huts do not feel their schooling was blighted by an environment which would certainly be considered unacceptable today. All the heat and light generated by national discussions on curricular matters, important though these may be, would and indeed do founder if

1

teachers can't and pupils won't perform. I have seen in Africa dynamic classes of passionately engaged youngsters who outnumber the teacher by 60 to 1 with no textbook in sight, but where no observer could doubt the significance of the experience for everyone in the room. Everything comes down eventually to the teachers and the taught. People.

We are told by L.P. Hartley that the past is a foreign country and that they do things differently there. This may be true in other contexts, but the many contributors to this collection tend to convey individually and collectively a different view. Again and again I have been struck by the extent to which people view their time at Millfield, not as some bolt-on extra, but as a viscerally integral part of their current life. We can all draw some satisfaction from each individual recollection imbued with the affection which characterises so many of the contributions in these pages.

When Adrian White, as Chairman of the school's Governors, suggested that the story of Millfield might emerge most colourfully from the memories of those who have, over the last 70 years, effectively *been* the school, I knew that compiling such a collection would be fun. It is an original approach, possibly a unique one, and I am extremely grateful to all those OMs who have taken the trouble to let me have their stories, together with John Davies and his valiant assistant Kate who have pushed the project along so helpfully.

This is not, of course, a history. Our history has already been extensively documented by Barry Hobson, to whose work this kaleidoscope of anecdotes claims only to add illustration. Some of my own recollections, drawn from diaries written at the time, are included here and there in italics, but the substance here, as indeed in the school itself, is as usual down to the pupils. It's your book about your school.

Christopher Martin
Millfield 1990 – 1998

FOREWORD

I feel honoured to be asked to write a few words to help kick off this interesting collection of Millfield anecdotes.

It is perhaps inevitable that local perceptions of the school concentrate on the incredible building programme, especially over the last 20 years or so. As all teachers will agree, although modern buildings have helped to improve our teaching, it is people who really make a school. It is most gratifying to see that the relationships between tutors and pupils and amongst pupils themselves are as healthy and friendly now as they ever were.

These relationships are never more rewarding than when dealing with the unexpected. Some 30 years ago, Ted Bullard, oscillating between Judo coaching and ordering school supplies in the Domestic Bursar's Department, came across a requisition form, possibly in a foreign language, offering cut-price lavatory rolls. With his mind possibly on other things, Ted placed the figure 3 not, as intended, in the column headed 'Large Boxes containing 10,000 rolls', but instead in the column headed 'Pantechnicon Loads'.

And so it was, soon after dawn a few days later, that three heavyweight Dutch lorries arrived at Millfield House, each one packed to the brim with these essential toilet necessities. The lead driver saw a man who, at such an hour, could only be the School Caretaker, leaned out of his cab and yelled "Where do you want this lot, Guv?" The 'caretaker' was, of course, Founder Headmaster R.J.O.Meyer who was very often an early riser. Sadly, Boss's actual reply was not recorded but no doubt it would have been appropriate and caustic.

The stories in this book may remind us of the enormous variety of activities – academic, artistic or sporting - which abound in this amazing school. I hope they rekindle fond memories and give as much pleasure to the readers as they surely must have given to the writers.

Brian Gaskell
Millfield, 1965 – 1990

FOREWORD

When CSM told me that I was taking over the best job in education, I felt it was a bold statement: how could he say that with such confidence? I would wait and see ...He was right of course, as he was in so many things he told me about Millfield. Now I keep telling people that I have the best job in education. The fear of sounding pleased with myself did not last long. These days I just say it rather smugly and enjoy the moment.

I hope that those who read this book will understand and forgive this self-indulgence. They will have a feel for the place, born of their own experiences or sense it through the memories of others and will understand the reasons for my enthusiasm. Many will be sad that the original Nissen huts have gone, the elms have died, the rooms they lived in have been changed (some might say improved!), great teachers have passed on, buns are not served at break, swimming takes place in a pool not a pond, girls no longer wear hot-pants and pipe smoking is not, shall we say, encouraged. If they met the current pupils, spent a few hours in the School and felt the warmth of the welcome and the enthusiasm of the staff they would know that they were in the right place: one altered, developed, dare I say enhanced, but not changed in the areas that really matter.

The whole experience of working here has been utterly captivating, enormously hard work, deeply scary at times, but never ever dull. Christopher's collection is a vivid reminder of why Millfield is different from other schools and why it has been such a joy to have been at the helm for the last eight years.

Peter Johnson
Millfield 1998 –

EDITOR'S ACKNOWLEDGEMENTS

I want to offer my warmest thanks to all those who have kindly contributed to this collection; to John Davies and Kate in the Old Millfieldian office for their help and encouragement; to Dick Shilton, the current Archevist, for locating many of the photographs and to Roger Myddelton for his photo of Boss, to Roger Parsons for his contributions from Edgarley, to Barry Hobson for allowing me to quote from his comprehensive history of the school and for his introductions to each chapter; to Michael Goater for allowing me to quote from his biography of Boss; and especially to Adrian White, Chairman of Governors, for supporting this project from the outset.

And finally to all of you who have bought a copy, for in doing so you have helped in a modest way to build the Millfield Foundation whose objective is to sustain the "Millfield Mix", helping to fund future generations of pupils who will, in their turn, benefit from the opportunities which you yourselves have enjoyed.

C.S.M

Truly, Millfield Schools must be among the best in the world for added value, whatever the ability of the child. I should know, having had five average ability children not only shine in their individual ways, but become the well grounded graduates and adults that they are today.

Adrian E White CBE. DL
Chairman of Governors

THE
MEYER YEARS
1935 – 1970

Jack Meyer, OBE (picture by Roger Myddelton).

BOSS

The agreement, reached between the Maharaja of Dhrangadhra and Jack Meyer in 1935, established the setting up of a "Home from Home" in England for the Maharaja's three young sons, and for three of their princely cousins. The aim was to introduce the boys to the English Independent School system when Jack Meyer considered them fit to do so, educationally and socially.

The Meyers arrived, site unseen, in Street on 6th June1935, with six young princes, ages between 8 and 15, and one 17 year old commoner, the son of the Maharaja's Chief Minister. As it was the summer, everybody set about preparing a cricket pitch, while the four older boys were given riding lessons by a retired cavalry officer and were allowed to practise the rudiments of polo.

At the end of October, the Maharaja announced that he would not afford to support the project longer and was withdrawing three boys. The presence of those remaining made it difficult to close Millfield, which was naturally Jack's first reaction but he was persuaded to advertise for pupils requiring tutoring for entry to schools and universities. He offered country holidays for adults and even advice to parents of recalcitrant children.

Success came in the summer of 1936 with a Public School Scholarship, Common Entrance Exams and an entrance to Cambridge by a boy who had previously failed miserably. In the Autumn he had 12 resident pupils and six "Tutors", (the term is still used) and their successes led to a steady increase in numbers. Many who had found the life of a Preparatory or Public School irksome, flourished under Jack's *laisser faire* system and broadcast their findings to friends. At the outbreak of war in 1939 there were 40 pupils, but Jack expected the numbers to fall disastrously and even offered his own services to the Royal Air Force, whose recruiters wisely told him to go home and teach.

Thus throughout the pre-war years, Millfield's future hung by a thread. Even Jack at that time could never have envisaged his school's subsequent successes.

"You know, you've never lived properly if you've never tried to be first class at something. It doesn't matter what it is, cricket, physics, or tiddlywinks, because in getting there you will have learnt something about self-discipline, dedication and achievement. What better training for life could there be than that? It's not the silver cups and the rosettes which are important. It's the "trying" which makes the person, and we will certainly help you to keep on trying. We'll give you the time, the facilities and the coaching, and you'll get a hot shower and a good dinner afterwards."

Jack Meyer

1935. The first pupils prepare to leave for UK.

Barry Hobson "A History of Millfield"

Thus it was that Jack Meyer, who had rejected offers of teaching posts at Eton and Harrow in 1926, began his career in education three years later, first at Limbdi, then at Porbandur, and in 1932 as Headmaster of the Palace School at Dhrangadhra.

"I found myself teaching some 20 or so boys and girls with an age range of 22 down to three and an IQ range of 80 to 140. Half of them knew no English and I knew no Gujerati. A method of graded small group tuition had to be devised to meet the situation and it was perhaps here that the Millfield method was born."

On 6th June 1935, the physical birth of Millfield took place

9

when Jack and Joyce Meyer, with their small daughters, arrived at Street in Somerset accompanying the three sons of the Maharajah of Dhrangadhra, three other Indian Princes and one commoner, the mission being to act as tutor-guardians and to provide a home from home for the boys throughout their time in England.

The following summer the Maharajah himself paid the school a visit. There he was greeted without reservation by the whole party, as befitted the founder of this happy little community. His guns, his case of cigarettes and his case of cigars had preceded him through police and customs scrutiny and he was therefore able to assume the role of a country gentleman in some comfort. Wearing tweed, and consuming lavish amounts of well prepared food, he was able to keep the damp and the cold of a late English summer at bay. His attendant servants upset the Meyers by their indecorous attitude to personal hygiene, the least unpleasant being their wearing their boots in bed.

MICHAEL GOATER "JACK MEYER OF MILLFIELD"

Some parents were initially uncertain about Millfield's classless society, and among these was a noble Duke whose son had failed for Eton and who sought Jack's help.

"Meyer, do you mean to tell me that my son, heir to the line, might meet and get interested in someone like your butcher's daughter?"

"Well, you needn't worry, because the butcher isn't a snob and if his very intelligent daughter got interested in a rather puddingy boy like your son, I think you should be rather pleased."

The Duke went purple, and Jack was about to phone for a doctor when the Duchess indicated that he was coming round. The boy came to Millfield.

Impossibly confrontational parents wrote today asking me to admit their long-suffering son as a boarder next term. This far he has been a day boy and while his teachers admire his efforts, we have all found it hard to cope with the steady stream of criticism and invective visited on us by his parents. I replied that I should need some sort of guarantee of their general support before wishing them on any Houseparents. A furious fax from them then lands on my desk. "We demand an immediate meeting...you will explain your defamatory comments." I will probably end up offering the poor chap a place on compassionate grounds, if only to spare him from his parents.

Jack made a point of trying to back worthwhile but penniless pupils by seeking financial support for them from better-off parents, and in this he could often be disarmingly frank.

"Your son is not one of the brightest and has little inclination to work. If he comes here he will be occupying much of the time of highly qualified, well-paid staff, and even then it is unlikely that he will distinguish himself. However, I have a dossier here of a girl from a dockyard family in Bristol. She's 15, probably going to leave school in a year and thinks she wants to be a hairdresser. And do you know, she must have an IQ of around 180. Now I am sure you will agree that the country needs people like her."

Jack occasionally taught religious studies. In the course of his studies a number of moral issues inevitably surfaced.

"Sir, I certainly do believe in God now."

"Really Harry. Why now?"

"Because He saved me when I got lost on a school outing without any money, and I prayed for help. An old lady dropped a pound from her handbag and didn't notice. That pound got me home and I have believed in God ever since."

"Harry, sit down and let's talk."

NATHAN PENNEY (1936 – 1939)

At a reunion dinner not long ago the Headmaster jovially proclaimed: "Penney married a girl from Street and not a street girl." Some time ago, while in Somerset to attend our earliest family reunion, we had made a point of calling on Boss. At the time, he was in his study. We were greeted warmly, and as we shook hands he smiled at my wife and said: "It was Penney who married our local lovely."

Molire Molendo. The first school photograph.

FENTON RUTTER (1939 – 1940)

I went to Millfield for one term, which was enough for me to be taught sufficient Latin to gain entry to Cambridge. During that term, I used to play chess with Boss in the evenings and in return I taught him to play the trumpet. I used to play in the Glastonbury Band and he allowed me time off to go up to Bristol to broadcast in the BBC studios there. Boss also coached me in, and fired my enthusiasm for many games. We never thought we were particularly good at any of them while at school, but at Cambridge I found myself representing the College in five different sports and won the mile race against Oxford. Later I came back to play squash regularly against the school, and later still enjoyed bridge under the expert tutelage of Gordon McBride. So my experience of games at Millfield has spanned over 60 years, all of which has added enormously to the pleasures of life.

STEPHEN ELLIOTT (1941)

I was 17 and in the Army class at King's Taunton. I had passed the Matric but nobody seemed to think I had a chance of passing the Army exam, which existed at the time, so I arranged to go to Millfield, the local crammer, for the Easter holidays. The school seemed to operate all the time then, without regard to holidays. I had sent a postcard to R.J.O. Meyer telling him of my plan, an arrangement with which he seemed happy. The only snag was that he required a cheque for £80 as a down payment. This made me slightly apprehensive as I had not informed my father of my plan. However, he reluctantly agreed and I duly joined Millfield.

I recall that four of us slept in one room with a girls' room above. They could only reach their room via a spiral staircase in the corner of ours, a situation which could not have been entirely satisfactory at the time but about which no one seemed to complain. My colleagues there were Johnny Threllfel, Alec de Saumarez and Martin Atlee, the first two heading like me for the Army exam and Martin for the Merchant Navy. One other boy joined at the same time and brought four horses, grooms and a butler. I never somehow got to know him.

We were taught, if that is the right word, by an elderly parson who had been a teacher at Lancing where he was apparently known as Lucky Lucas. All we ever did was go through past exam questions. In the event, I was only able to achieve the minimum pass mark for the exam; 390 out of 900! Nevertheless, Millfield was a very happy experience for me. I told my father afterwards that there was no point in working harder than was strictly necessary and I think he was almost inclined to agree with me.

JASPER EVANS (1942)

Ernie, Peter and I bicycled off one fine evening in search of rabbits. A long way from home, going down a hill at some speed, Ernie cut across my bow tipping my front wheel. I crashed off onto the tarmac breaking the handle bar and buckling the front wheel and of course getting a bad graze on the knee. How were we to get home? Coming from Kenya, our motto was, "I will contrive!"

We contrived therefore to remove the front wheel and axle which enabled the forks to fit nicely onto the rear axle of Ernie's bicycle, thus converting his two-wheeler into a three wheel tandem. We had a long, hard ride back, and did not arrive until well after dark. Climbing the drain pipe and then over the roof to the attic dorm in Millfield house was rather painful. The very nice painting of Millfield by Steven Webb shows the drain pipe clearly on the right of the front door. The next morning, Boss, with a raised eyebrow, did not press his enquiry too closely.

The buckled wheel was fairly easily straightened but the broken handlebar had to be replaced with a wooden tiller lashed to the lamp bracket. With some vertical movement and a wire to the front brake it sufficed, however, but rather slowed down manoeuvre. This nearly led to my arrest. One dark night, having climbed the wall into the town swimming pool for a swim, I was pedalling back as best I could down Street high street with no lights, weaving erratically from side to side as I tried to control my hybrid cycle. Suddenly a Policeman leaped off the pavement at me, bent on capture. Luckily he missed his tackle and I made good my escape!

JOHN MISKIN (1941 – 1946)

"He seems to think that the world revolves around himself." This was the start of the Headmaster's report at the end of my first term at Millfield. Further comments included commendation for perseverance in those subjects which had caught my imagination and reprimands in those which had not. It sounds like the normal stuff of reports, but I was puzzled by this idea of myself as being somehow in the middle of a revolving globe. "What does he mean?" I asked. "He means that you are a very self-centred little boy with an exaggerated sense of your own importance", replied my Uncle Lance, in whose care my father had left me when he returned to Hong Kong in 1939.

Because of having athetoid cerebral palsy and being deaf, I was considered backward. I suppose too that the somewhat itinerant nature of my schooling until then must have added to the impression that I was behind others of the same age. I was also lazy. Millfield was to give me the chance to break out of the mould of frustration and boredom which had characterised things that far. And boarding was to be a particularly rude awakening.

Although I didn't realise it until many years later, the painful experience of boarding was to be my emancipation from such contradictions – the sheltering versus the encouragement – by my acceptance of paradox. I was torn between the desire to be as I perceived others, just ordinary, and the will to be, as I saw it, independent and in control, which meant overcoming apparently insuperable odds.

As is well documented, our Headmaster, whom we called Boss, never Sir, would accept pupils who had been rejected or expelled by other schools. Thanks to this extraordinary man there are many who, like me, were given a chance to break out of the hopeless cycle of social or intellectual rejection that might otherwise have been their lot.

Miss Rix, the Matron, was a diminutive hunch-backed woman with white hair drawn back tightly into a bun. "For Christ's sake stop snivelling", she snapped at me my first evening, but even then I saw the humorous twinkle in her eye. She made no allowance for disability or any other excuse, but at heart she understood what I always wanted; to be considered first as a human being, with "disability" or "handicap" merely incidental, and for this I was profoundly grateful.

Elnith Sankey was a marvellous teacher. She it was who kindled in us "dopes" an aspiration to learn, a desire to explore beyond the confines of our disabilities. She had that rare quality of inspiring a sense of wonder and poetry, helping us to an awareness of the way all things hang together. Her lessons, history of art, drawing and painting, English literature and grammar, together with her Scripture sessions, revealed to us the interconnectedness of the universe. For her, art was not an isolated discipline: it involved history, science, maths, psychology, literature and religion. I, for one, will never forget the debt I owe her for opening up my mind.

John Grimshaw of Sustrans gives a compelling talk to the sixth form on cycle power. He is an impressive missionary for cycle paths and associated sculpture. I show him our new cast iron sculpture in the quad and he is impressed. A 3rd former trots past on some mission and I ask him to join us and to let us know his opinion of the sculpture. "It's nice," he says non-committally. "Nice," says John. "How can this be just nice?" The small boy, who had plainly hardly noticed the piece before, having other preoccupations as small boys often do, studied us both warily and then gave the sculpture a really long, hard look. After a long silence, he declared with complete conviction, "It's tremendous."

I also have affectionate memories of 'Quack', Miss Drake, a grey-haired bespectacled lady who taught maths, and who good-humouredly walked around the premises followed by a string of cheeky pupils going "quack-quack – quack-quack!" Although she soon realised that my chances of passing exams in maths were absolutely zero, because of my physical difficulties, she never doubted my intelligence. Though she advised me against following the normal maths syllabus, she continued to allow me to attend geometry lessons, because I loved the logic made visible by reasoned analysis of the relationship between lines, angles, shapes and spaces.

The memory of the teasing I got is very painful. I was taunted in the freezing winter mornings when, because washing and making the bed was slower for me than for others, I had to rise ten minutes before everyone else to the accompaniment of the dormitory's chant of "gloat, gloat, gloat – lovely warm bed!". I realise now that I often over-reacted, rendering myself all the more absurd and asking for further ridicule. That I was oversensitive and insufferably truculent I have no doubt. Moreover, I disliked intensely authority, sometimes feeling, perhaps unwarrantably, that I was being picked upon. But it's not surprising that to this day I still tend to suspect authority as a licence to abuse, dominate and control. I remember being irked by orders which made little sense to me, like being forced to stand and cheer the cricket team when there was a match. As a non-participant, I never could rouse much enthusiasm for a game there was no way I could play. I recollect an occasion when I dug my heels in and refused to go to support the Millfield 1st IX v. Downside in a home match, and took a beating from The Boss for my 'gross insubordination'. By taking these stands I undoubtedly made community life more difficult for myself. And it would be dishonest if I failed to recall an occasion or two when I was shamefully guilty of taunting small boys even lower down the pecking order in an attempt to ingratiate myself with the normal boys.

Reminiscing from the vantage point of 2005, I see that it was inevitable that the Millfield experiences were harrowing for the likes of me. It was a shock to be cast away for twelve weeks at a time in the company of my peers, young boys, mostly as raw and unused to community life as I was myself. Some of them were decidedly unfriendly, teasing, bullying and taking advantage of the situation to claim dominance over anyone they perceived as weaker than themselves. But even if I had been offered special favour or protection, I would not have wanted it. Indeed, I wanted to be part of the group, to join in all that was possible, to move up the school's social hierarchy like everyone who was normal. I even tried to play cricket!

In a single day, four cases of children's distress are reported to me. First there's an anorexic girl who has gone from 11 to 7 stone in weight since the summer. Her mother refuses to acknowledge that there is a problem and has now disappeared to Tokyo. Another girl has been self-harming. Her mother died when she was young and her father has now wisely decided to remove her to have her close to him as a day pupil. As if this was not all bad enough, a boy still in his first year, whose grandfather admits to beating him with a horse whip on the family estate in Ireland, has just stolen a purse, the culmination of a long list of other offences. I cannot suspend him, for he will be attacked again at home, so we must all try to elicit understanding for him among his peers who are losing patience with him. And finally I learn of the plight of a girl whose father slashed her mother's throat, and who was recently released from prison. He has tried to make contact with the girl, leaving messages for her at her House. The CID are in touch, anxious both for the girl and for her mother, who has police protection. The local police have been

*informed but all this places an enormous burden of care
on her Houseparents. What an emotional roller coaster
of a day this has been!*

Another amongst these short-lived encounters, whom I still think of
as friends, was a tall, extremely handsome Ethiopian named
Endelkatchau Makkonen, known to us as 'George'. I understood he
was a distant relation of the Emperor Haile Salassie, and therefore
a high ranking aristocrat, but he gave himself no airs and graces. It
was refreshing and reassuring to be treated as an equal by this
highly intelligent and articulate 17 year-old African. Many years
later, in the 1970s, I read an account of the overthrow of Hailie
Sellassie, and his corrupt and nepotistic regime, before the Marxist
coup d'état in the '60s, and was saddened to learn from it of my
gentle and noble friend's torture and violent death by a revolution-
ary firing squad.

> *Later that evening in Hanoi, a family came to see me;
> three generations of Vietnamese, whose respective sec-
> ond languages reflect the various layers of colonial
> attachments to their country like a sort of linguistic
> archaeology. But sitting round late at night talking
> French to the grandfather, unsteady Russian to the
> father and English to the son, I sensed in them no feel-
> ing of resentment or bitterness that their country had
> been singled out for such international banditry. Cuong
> is a very bright chap and we will give him a top schol-
> arship. (Subsequently, Balliol did the same thing to
> enable him to read Mathematics there.) Two pretty girls
> will also join us next year. One turns out to be 21; her
> boyfriend will run her small restaurant here in her
> absence at Millfield as she studies for her A levels. She
> looks about 14 so I don't suppose anyone will object,
> and she certainly is not likely to play contact sports
> below her age-weight ratio, being light enough to pick
> up with one hand. Not that I tried.*

At the beginning of the Autumn Term 1945 after the end of the war
with Japan, to my surprise and delight I had been promoted to the

Senior Common Room, a very comfortable almost London club-like room, furnished with deep leather armchairs and sofas, its walls lined with bookshelves filled mainly with encyclopaedias and works of reference. The SCR's club atmosphere was further enhanced by its heavy veil of tobacco-smoke. Seniors, all over 17, were permitted to smoke provided they did so only in the Common Room. No more furtive gaspers behind the bushes at the back of the chalet or in the disused boathouse by the open-air swimming pool. Smoking was, for my generation and class, almost a cultural necessity. It was normal. It was fashionable. In short, I started smoking at 15 because I wanted to be like others, accepted in my peer group, normal.

During the winter and summer terms of 1946 our class studied English Literature with Joe Lalley in one of the Nissen huts. We dissected and analysed Coleridge's 'Ancient Mariner' which enthralled me with its poetic evocation of the lone survivor enduring the death of his companions – "...the many men so beautiful and they all dead do lie / and a thousand thousand slimy things lived on, and so did I" – and famine and thirst adrift in the midst of the ocean - "...alone, alone, alone all – all alone in the wide wide sea / and never a saint took pity on my soul in agony". I loved listening to Joe, a rather unimpressive-looking bald man who appeared half asleep and always wore a crumpled blue suit. He certainly made a lasting impression on me, reciting these passages in a deep resonant voice as we all huddled around the wood-burning stove in the centre of the hut.

> *Simon Armitage, with others including Christopher Booker and Gillian Clarke, spoke at our 6th form Literature Conference. He read his poetry and explained that once, when at school, his Headmaster had summoned him to remonstrate with him over something he had written in the school magazine. "In our school," he apparently argued, "We don't like poetry that has language in it."*

Without the specified qualifying subjects I was barred from the Oxford and Cambridge entrance examination, but Bristol and other provincial universities had less stringent entrance requirements. Discussing the possibilities with Boss, he advised me to wait for my father's imminent return from Hong Kong and internment before coming to a decision. In any case, in view of the fact that I had collapsed during my previous exams, I was reluctant to submit myself to such physical and mental strains again. Thus when my father arrived in England in early October, 1945, looking a little like Mahatma Gandhi after one of his 'fastings unto death', so thin and emaciated was he as a result of four years' incarceration, I persuaded him against his better judgement to let me skip exams and leave Millfield at the end of the summer term. I told him I hoped to find an opening in writing as a career.

I had longed to leave my school days behind me, for school had always felt a bit like a concentration camp. But when I came to say goodbye it was with a lump in my throat and, though I tried desperately to hold them back, a flood of tears. I like to think I managed to restrain them until I had shaken Boss's hand and walked away. This must be another example of my reluctance to leave the safety of the familiar for the uncertainty of the unknown, a fearful anticipation that new and strange experiences would prove more terrifying than those already encountered. In later life, I realised that these timid feelings holding me back from embarking on fresh ventures were similar to St Paul's 'kicking against the pricks', refusing to accept the inevitable, to recognise and to overcome.

BARRY HOBSON "A HISTORY OF MILLFIELD"

"In reply to a letter from a parent, Mrs Zvegintozov, in which she had suggested that he was less than cordial at their last meeting, RJOM replied;

"I shall certainly have to examine my features in the looking glass, for, in the absence of all else, I had thought that I was by nature inclined to bonhomie amounting at times to what the critics among my relatives call heartiness. However, when we next meet I must try to banish all thoughts of the plumber, the builder, the timetables, the absent cook, the next meeting, the prefects' discussion group, the damaged paint-work, the broken window, the unoiled cricket bats, the unrolled hockey fields, the leaky radiator, the sick gardener's wife, the multiple insurance policies, leases, contracts, wage-scales, salary lists, the missing library books, the unsolved coal problem, my children's education, my appointments with parents – in short, all the odds and ends which require concentrated thought in the centre of hussle, tapping typewriters, yelling children and buzzing telephones."

Who would be Headmaster of a small school in wartime?"

I had supper with the new staff at Edgarley. How young they look! But then so did our newcomers the next day when I welcomed them for their induction day. There were 19 of them; a new Chaplain, Heads of Maths and History, both women, and 11 people under the age of 25. This shifts the average age of the Common Room quite a bit and their total age has now subsided since last term by 400 years. The newcomers seem full of beans and apprehension in equal measure, which is pretty much how I feel too, as always at the start of a new term. I promised them that it never gets less exciting but perhaps they saw that as a warning. That evening, watching some of them finding their feet among the 250 people who came to the staff dinner, I sensed how lucky they were. The buzz was happening again, the feeling of barely controlled exhilaration was upon us all. Or upon most of us anyway. A newcomer could not help but feel he'd landed the right way up. Unlike my new computer which has just arrived and which I think I've installed upside down.

JOHN MULLER (1942 – 1947)

When I arrived, the school was divided into three groups; the Junior, Middle and Senior Common Rooms. Interaction between these was frowned upon. The Senior Common Room was where the prefects frequently wielded a bamboo cane on any misbehavers. We were mostly boys but with a few teenage girls thrown in, quite a volatile mix, you might think.

At the tender age of 12 it was the Junior Common Room for me. There were ten of us, but a couple of boys were way out of our age group in their late teens or even twenties – a very strange group. Towards the end of my time I was made head prefect, and I had the pleasure of caning the junior misbehavers. I kept the well worn cane, bound with electrical tape to minimize splitting, as a souvenir to show my children. The cane had certainly straightened me out in the earlier days.

One incident left me with a strong feeling of unfairness. I had taken a piece of string from another boy's open locker to tie an ice skate on my boot. Somehow or other it got to Boss's attention and I was called into his study immediately. He said that taking something from someone else without their permission was stealing, and reaching behind the mantelpiece, where he always kept the cane, he told me to bend over. Only one stroke this time.

Another caning incident worked out better for me, however. I was up before Boss on some trivial charge, but when he reached behind the mantelpiece for the rod as usual, it slid down behind the woodwork and was irretrievably lost. He said I was fortunate because, like the condemned man at the gallows, who was released because the trap door would not open, I also would be let off.

Many of my vivid earlier memories revolved around punishment for transgression. One in particular, the ultimate humiliation, was the custom of dunking a more senior boy who had failed to adhere to the rules of decency and honour. The culprit was dragged or carried, fully clothed, down to the duck pond at the bottom of the estate and was flung in by two of the heftier prefects. It was shallow and muddy so he climbed out in a real mess and then had to walk all the way back up to the school building, on his own, with everyone watching. This was probably the ultimate punishment for anyone and was only carried out rarely.

The main drive was quite long and lined principally with horse chestnut and walnut trees. Collecting and preparing the horse chestnuts for "Conkers" was a popular pastime, of course. We also gathered the walnuts and tried, more in hope than in expectation, to dry them for a few weeks in the drawers where our clothes should have been, although often it was so damp in these drawers that we just ended up with an inedible, mouldy mess.

We never had more than about eight people in a class which meant we got close attention from the teachers. This greatly benefited backward students, such as I was. We called our class Paranoia One because we had a very strange teacher who would regularly drop his chalk in the middle of writing something and rush out of the door. He would disappear for several minutes, and then come back and carry on as if nothing had happened. The rumour was that he was looking for someone who was after him. We never knew why but, on reflection, I'm sure he must have had a persecution complex. We used to be merciless in playing tricks on him, putting match heads in the chalk, carbide in the ink wells and so on.

On Public Works Days, we all left our books and were obliged to devote the afternoon to cleaning up the area, grooming horses, feeding the animals, pulling weeds and the like. This was an ongoing lesson in the need to get one's hands dirty. No task was too menial for any of us. There were quite a few animals around, principally geese and horses and one or two goats. The goats would eat anything, so we used to feed them our cigarette butts to dispose of the evidence after a clandestine smoke.

There were a number of American troops billeted in a field adjoining the drive. We used to talk to them over the fence, cadging cigarettes, tobacco and gum. The favourite expression when we confronted them was, "Got any gum, chum?" We thought they were great and we rarely came away without any spoils, such as Lucky Strike cigarettes, Half and Half tobacco and those long sticks of gum – things that were unobtainable in the shops even if we had the money.

People have started smoking in the dining room loos again, so we close them for a while. I am now worried that the trickle of pupils going down to the woods in break are not going there for a smoke but for a pee.

A group of about five of us had heard that there was a farm, near Priddy on the edge of the Mendips, where for a few "bob" you could get to see some very exciting caves. We set off on our bicycles and finally found the farmer. He charged us sixpence each to visit the cave and provided us with the key. We were told to go to the foot of an old oak tree, in a field, where we would find a padlocked iron grating over the cave entrance. This grating was incredibly small – no more than 30 inches in diameter. Into the hole we went.

Inside, it opened up into a maze with several directions and we decided to split up. Our equipment consisted of a few candles and a long piece of string, In some places we were crawling on our bellies with steep drops to one side and the possibility of getting stuck between floor and ceiling was very real.

However, we carried on for some time, relying on the long piece of string to guide us back. At some point, however, we lost the string and decided we must try to retrace our steps without it. The loss of the string was a major set back, but we thought we were making good progress until a draught of wind blew out our candles. Where were the matches? We had overlooked this detail and as we sat in the pitch dark the seriousness of our situation began to sink in. Gripped with fear we crouched on the rock surface in a blue funk, realising that in the dark you cannot possibly find your way out of a tortuous maze.

This was the most terrifying experience of my life. To cut a long story short, after what seemed a very long time, but may have only been a few minutes, the other three boys appeared from nowhere and we followed them out of the caves. To this day I am amazed that any adult would have allowed a few young boys, obviously inadequately prepared, to enter caves such as these.

One boy, Michael, was a particularly nasty bully, and as with all bullies, he had a few cronies doing his bidding. They were often employed to hold you down while he aimed punches. He was the terror of the Middle Common Room and no one dared to oppose him. One day I bumped into him alone and, having lost my fear for a moment, I confronted him with a challenge to fight it out. We fought it out in the middle of a large cabbage patch. Of course, the greatest damage was to the cabbages, but I do believe I came out the victor. Michael never troubled me again.

Another really unpleasant letter from a father accusing the school of untold horrors particularly involving bullying, a long list of sins of commission and of omission. None of it rings true with any of the tutors closest to his son. We invite him to come and meet everyone himself, offering access to those whom he accuses so that he can discover how things really are for himself. But he still refuses to come. He has never once been to the school,

*let alone to the House, and has never met either his
son's roommates or his Housemaster.*

At one time there was a craze for daggers, possibly as a result of all
the publicity during the war about the commandos and their
exploits. I had a super black one which at one point I managed to
stick into my right wrist while fooling around. Immediately the
blood spurted out and I realised I had penetrated an artery.
Applying pressure with my left hand I walked to the small dispensary where Mrs. Meyer used to administer First Aid. I told her I had
punctured an artery. "I don't think so," was her reply, so to prove
it I removed my finger from the wound and the blood spurted
across the room. No further hesitation then, and the doctor was
called immediately to stitch me up.

Near the duck pond at the bottom of the estate was a somewhat dilapidated concrete swimming pool. In the winter, when it
was cold enough for it to freeze, we went skating on the ice. One
cold Sunday after church, we thought it would be a good time to
test the ice to see if it was strong enough to permit skating. I was
selected to do the testing and in my Sunday best suit I slowly
walked out onto the ice. Suddenly a shout went out that I had
better get back quickly as my friends could see the ice bending
ominously beneath me. I started back, but too late. Down I went,
flailing all the way back to the side like an ice breaker. My suit,
which I later left on a hook in the locker room to dry, came out
several sizes smaller and I was never able to wear it again.

We used to enjoy making explosives. We found out that by
mixing 880 ammonia with iodine crystals and then filtering this
solution, a highly unstable, very potent, explosive could be
produced. The filtrate was extracted, separated into small aliquots,
and allowed to dry. It was then so unstable that the slightest
movement would cause it to explode. It could be used for such
things as the exploding door knob trick where the wet paste was
wiped onto door knobs and allowed to dry. This would then
produce a mild and slightly painful explosion for the unsuspecting
person opening the door.

Eric Jones was being inspected in his Chemistry laboratory when the inspector drew his attention to smoke ris-

25

ing from the waste paper basket. Incinerating a class is not always the best way to endear oneself to an inspector, so after the class Eric sought out the inspector in the Staff Room to offer him coffee and make amends. Sadly, he poured water from the cold kettle, and did not realise this until later when he tasted his own coffee. "A flaming good lesson, though," he added bravely, when the temperature had subsided.

We have had an excellent Inspection report, which we have circulated in full to all our parents. It is couched in inspector-ese, however, where superlatives are treated with some suspicion. The best reaction to this came at the end of the week from a father who had picked up on this linguistic style. "It sort of misses the point, "he said. "It's rather like Queen Victoria watching Arsenal."

Fooling around in the dormitory was a common occurrence, bouncing on beds, pillow fights and so on, but it was all in good fun. One day we were messing around and Matron, a stern woman wearing full regalia, caught Martin Attlee and me in one bed at the same time. There was nothing sinister in this but she did not think so and we were reported to Boss. The two of us were hauled into his study, one at a time, and I recall being grilled about what we were up to. I heard nothing more of this incident but later, as I became more worldly, I realised that homosexuality had been suspected – a very serious matter at a boys school in those days.

Somewhere along the way I became interested in electronics and started tinkering with ancient battery operated receivers, which led to the construction of a crystal radio. This then led to my selling an old radio set that I had bought from one boy for a pound, to another boy for six pounds, a massive profit, to say the least. This came to the attention of Boss who investigated the possibility of my having ripped off the recipient but finally he concluded it was a legitimate transaction and it was allowed to stand. Who could guess that my lifelong career in technical sales had actually just begun!

BARRY HOBSON "A HISTORY OF MILLFIELD"

In 1945, a Junior school was formed at Edgarley Hall. As the Japanese were surrendering in August in the wake of the dropping of the Atomic bombs, Everel Sankey was painting the new school in anticipation of the arrival in September of a new occupying army, 45 strong. Though Jack Meyer did not relinquish his Headship of the Juniors, after all it was still part of the establishment he owned, the rather special relationship which existed between the very young and the very senior at Millfield could not continue in quite the same way. This relationship was explained in an article in "The Windmill" in 1947.

"The house was acquired by a man who was famous. He could send any small ball for incredible distances and of course, you know, that means a lot. Around him he gathered a circle of those-who-were-nearly-grown-up. These prefects enjoyed themselves hugely, and what is so unusual in any other school, they saw that nobody was frightened."

BILL BREWER, EDGARLEY, (1946 – 1948)

I vaguely remember meeting Boss in the sitting room at Millfield as he discussed my future with Father. Suddenly, as I stood completely tongue tied, without warning he threw an orange at me. I am the world's worst fielder but somehow, by fluke, I caught it. "Oh, we must have him," said Boss, and so it was.

When Father asked about fees, he was aghast at the figure mentioned by Boss. "I can't afford that", he said. "Well, what can you afford?" and they settled a figure. It was often said unkindly of Boss that he knew exactly how much a parent could afford and how little a teacher would accept, but he was always very kind to me and was one of the greatest men I have ever met.

MALCOLM KIRKE (1948)

During the Higher Certificate exams in 1948 – I think it was a French exam – someone had the brilliant idea of bringing a tray of sticky iced buns and milk into the exam room which was one of those Nissen huts. The invigilator, whoever it was, must have raised no objection as I can remember enjoying the snack immensely while writing out my exam. Boss was understandably angry when this came to his notice, and sadly it never happened again. Why not, I wonder?

> *A GCSE candidate is found in an exam with five words written on his hand. The exam board will be notified, but in case they are lenient, the boy is allowed to continue his exam once he has been taken out of the exam hall to have the offending words washed off. It is only later that we realise that the board's rubric for such cases states that "evidence of improper conduct must be submitted to the Board." It's lucky for the boy that we do not live in Iran.*

Maurice Slapak (1948)

I arrived at Millfield in February 1948 with the avowed purpose of passing the "Little Go" Latin examination in order to gain admission to Cambridge in October of that year. When I had been there all of two days, Boss told me I was to be head of Pitt House in Glastonbury. One of my duties in this unexpected new role was to see that the boys in the house were all in bed at the regulation times. Two days later, I found myself having to tell a very well-built 17 year old Greek student called Antony that he had to be in bed by 9.30 p.m. and would he head in that direction right away please. I later discovered that Antony had been a guerrilla during the recently ended conflict in Greece. On this occasion, he just stared me coldly in the eye for what seemed a rather long time and muttered, "I keel you."

We later became friends.

> *Two weeks into the term and Alexei has now developed an unhealthily high profile already. When reprimanded by a teacher, he said darkly, "In Russia, people are shot for talking to me like that." The next day, he was found laying heavy bets during a PE lesson on whether someone could do 10 press*

ups. All this on top of his invitations during the House song for sexual favours to the girls standing next to him in rehearsal suggests he is not long for our world. Indeed he is filling my In-tray. Quads are arriving in profusion every day now. "He had a headache in class so I sent him to the medical centre. They sent him back, but instead of returning to class, he phoned his mother in Moscow. When I remonstrated, he said he had a right to phone home if he was dying. I find him utterly exasperating."

LOGAN HUNTER (1945 – 1949)

I arrived at Millfield just after the war, and started in the main house. Later I went to live at Kingweston, when it was first opened.

The food was just awful. We had to have lunch in a place in Street called a 'British Restaurant.' We had to walk there and back, of course. This kept us fit, which we needed to be, for if we missed the bus to Kingweston, it was either a very long walk or, if we were lucky, a cycle ride. Lessons were held in the notorious Nissen huts with concrete floors, which were in theory heated by coke stoves, though these seldom worked. The 'smarter' part of the school was housed in wooden huts.

Careers Advice was plain and rudimentary. When the Boss told me that I had passed my School Certificate with good grades, he asked me what I wanted to do with my life. I, of course, hadn't got the faintest idea, so the Boss said, 'You will join the Army class.' This I duly did, and spent the next 37 years in the Army!

ROBIN OSBORNE (1944 – 1950)

On D-Day, 5 June 1944, the school was directly under the flight path of planes, mostly bombers and others towing gliders, on the way to Normandy and the invasion of France. They all had the black and white identifying stripes on their fuselages. The whole thing started in the morning and went on right through the night and the following day. Nobody got any sleep, so Boss cancelled all classes next day and we had a free day off. One of the planes crash landed near Kingweston, and many boys raced off there and got quite a few souvenirs from the plane before the Home Guard arrived to cordon it off. My brother, Ivor, got a gyroscope. I wasn't so quick off the mark.

Again, somewhere around 1944, we had our maths lessons in one of the Nissen Huts. Our tutor was one Mr. Dixon, who was a marvellous tutor, to whom I owe a considerable debt. However, he had split from his wife and it had made him slightly eccentric, to the point that at any time and at intervals of a few minutes he would decide his wife was outside looking for him, and he would, without warning, rush outside, race round the Nissen hut, and come back in as if nothing had happened. It was all very strange, particularly for the uninitiated, but Boss tolerated it because he was such a good teacher. Finally, however, I believe Boss had to let him go.

JILL CLEAVE (1948 – 1949)

While I was at school we lived at Abbot's Leigh in Magdalene Street and Boss persuaded my mother to offer accommodation to some of my fellow students. Two interesting boys were Abdullah and Mohammed Kuatley whose father at the time was President of Syria, a friend of President Nasser of Egypt with whom he negotiated the UAR. The brothers also used to come and stay with us during the half term holidays in Bristol but I was never quite sure how they responded to the delights of that city after the exotic life they had led at home. Unfortunately their father was deposed and subsequently assassinated, and despite many enquiries we never knew what became of the two boys.

> *Christa, our Romanian scholar this year, has been paying £200 a term towards the cost of her food – the only charge we are making. In the same post as a request from her mother that her food be provided free of cost comes a letter from HRH Prince Paul of Romania, who wants to contact the Class of '68, with whom he was here as a boy. His timing could hardly be better and I have put him in touch with Christa's mother.*

Dr N. W. Glendinning (1949 – 1950)

I came as a refugee from my previous school to take my entrance exam into medical school, no one at my last school, Sedburgh, having ever succeeded in passing it at that time. There I had learnt all about rugby, running and survival!

On my first day at Millfield, at the tender age of 16, I was told to report to Kingweston house. I knocked on the prefects' door and a deep voice bellowed, "Come in". I opened the door and saw a man who looked about 40 to me, with his feet on the table, wearing a monocle and reading "Men Only". "My name's Glendinning, sir", I said. "No need to call me sir", he replied. "Are you a new boy as well?" He had just finished his Army service in the Guards and had come to Millfield to do his Cambridge entrance exam.

There were a lot of ex-service men there at the time doing university entrance and those of us who were younger learnt a lot from them

John Luke (1948 – 1950)

For me, the best thing was the curriculum. I sat on Boss' sofa and he asked me what I wanted to learn. I said I wanted to be a lawyer. To be exempt from the Law Society preliminary exam, I needed credits in at least Latin, English and one other subject at School Certificate.

"Well," he said, "You'd better join the Modern History set", and we proceeded to invent a weekly timetable with periods in all the required subjects. I also chose woodwork, which I still do to this day.

In other words, my whole week was tailor made to my needs. I loved it. What's more, there were about 20 girls then in the girls' house and several were in my class. They were horribly bright and we all worked like stink so as not to be outsmarted by them.

Boss was not always available in his study but his bedroom was up a vertical steel ladder leading to a trap door. To get permission for this or that out of office hours, one climbed the ladder, tapped on the trap door and stuck one's head through to communicate with him. In this posture, with one's head at floor level, one was imbued with a strong sense of inferiority. Thus any positive answer to one's query, unexpected as this was, came as manna from Heaven.

Those two years changed my life from a nervous wreck at Charterhouse, where I was bullied to hell, to someone who could believe in himself.

From 34 degrees in Bombay visiting OMs to -10 degrees at Heathrow. Snow cornices by the road on the way back. I got to school at 5.0 p.m. in time to accept an HMI oral report on their inspection. They were completely won over by the pupils. One said it was the best atmosphere in any school she had visited. Music in my ears. They have understood that Millfield has something unique. We all know it, but it is tantalisingly difficult to isolate the contributory factors. Later, as jet lag started to bite, I accepted a call from the Yeovil Conservative Women's Association. They wanted me to talk at one of their meetings. "We'll give a donation to any charity you like to name," added their secretary. "The Lib. Dems.?", I suggested helpfully. Luckily, she laughed.

IVOR OSBORNE (1943 – 1950)

In 1942 or 43 Boss was having one of his parent days. A parent approached him and said he thought his son should have extra tuition in Latin. Boss said that was not necessary because the son would easily get a credit in School Certificate. A few minutes later, the parent spoke to Boss again, and reiterated the idea of extra tuition in Latin. Boss repeated that this was quite unnecessary and the son was doing very well in the subject. Five minutes later, back came the same parent and said he would be happy to pay an additional £100 for extra tuition. Boss said he would be pleased to accept the £100 but would spend it on another boy who actually needed it.

At about the same time, Boss told a group of boys to go down to the swimming pool for a lesson in swimming. (He did this sort of thing at odd times.) I was one of them. However, he gave strict instructions that we were not to go in the water until the new tutor arrived. We duly got there and waited...and waited...and waited. Some 3 hours later we went back to the school and told Boss nobody had arrived. At this point the new tutor arrived full of apologies and said he had overslept. He was invited into Boss's Office. We hung around to see what would transpire, and shortly after, the tutor emerged, white as a sheet! Boss had sacked him on the spot.

JOHN TREVOR (1948 – 1950)

I went to Holmcroft on my return from the US at the tender age of 16 – a difficult stage at which to transfer. Nevertheless, I rose to the dizzy heights of House Prefect, and in this capacity one of my duties was to take prep. Being poor at maths, I was prepared to look for help from almost any source, and found it in a much younger and cleverer new boy. The deal we struck was that he would help me with my maths and in return I would turn a blind eye to him reading the Hornblower books hidden behind his text book during prep.

That young man would almost certainly have enjoyed a very successful career in the Royal Navy, if he had not been soaked while lining the route for the Coronation Parade, resulting in his being invalided out of the service. However he became a Chartered Accountant and later joined the Civil Service in a senior capacity with responsibilities which included coordinating the Budget. So my shrewd choice of maths assistant was somewhat vindicated. Who was this paragon? It was Sir Peter Kemp, until recently a Governor of the school.

BRIAN JENKINS (1951)

My parents removed me after just one term for I contracted chronic bronchitis and life in Holmcroft was rather Spartan back then. Evidently then, at the end of our first week as new boys, we were assessed as to our progress and aptitude, and the resulting reports were delivered personally to Boss. My diary for that first week reads;

Monday 15th January

Had french and art; saw Meyer – made me feel much better; had to have lot of medicine; had baked beans for din.

Tuesday 16th

Had satis. for divinity, good for history, good for metal-work and v. good for geography. Took it to Boss. He said hot stuff. Had rabbit for lunch.

Wednesday 17th

Did normal work in morning. Went to Gym to watch in afternoon. Wrote home.

Thursday 18th

Had lunch, did maths then P.T. but only read comics. Came back to Holmcroft and wrote letters and things.

CYRIL WILLIAMS (1950 – 1951)

The Nissen huts, of which there may have been as many as twenty covering the area to the north west of Millfield House, were used because there was insufficient permanent accommodation for the increasing numbers of pupils. Under moderate weather conditions, they were quite functional, but on a hot summer's day they were stifling and most teachers would move everyone and everything outside to teach. In winter irrespective as to whether the day was wet or frosty the huts were uncomfortable first thing in the morning and it was thus the duty of whoever arrived first to light one of the hut's two wood burning stoves.

A class's comfort depended a lot on the skill and experience of the firelighter. The Botanists and Zoologists seem to be lucky, in that they numbered many ex Scouts, Guides and other assorted backwoodsmen in their ranks, so our form rooms were invariably comfortable within ten minutes of the stove being fired up. Other huts were less well organised and the occupants were sometimes to be seen sitting through a whole lesson wearing gloves and overcoats, or else even standing partly kippered outside, having been driven out by a persistently smoky fire that had failed to catch and burn properly.

The Nissen huts: a worm's eye view.

One morning Mr Syd Hill was trying to explain to us about an energy- and food-generating group of cells called stomata found in the leaves of all plants. Possibly being aware of the fact that I had an appreciative twinkle in my eye for the members of the Young Ladies Club, Mr Hill turned to me and said in his beautiful Welsh intonation, "Now Cyril, remember this please. The stomata are starchy at night but sweet during the day. And that, Cyril boyyo, is as you may well know exactly opposite to young ladies!"

The rest of the form clapped and roared their approval while this small but important fact was registered indelibly in my brain and is still remembered to this very day, nearly sixty years later.

John Humble (1948 – 1952)

The eleven boys at Middle Leigh were presided over by Colonel and Mrs R A Heard whose kitchen had a hard stone floor. One day a stock of new glass tumblers arrived which were claimed to be unbreakable. The colonel proudly demonstrated this property to several of us and we duly admired the tumbler actually bouncing off the hard floor. Then Mrs Heard appeared and the demonstration was repeated. By then the tumbler had had enough, and instead of bouncing it just shattered into a thousand pieces. There was a short silence while we all tried to work out where to look and what to say. We slunk away as quickly as possible.

The tuition, by and large, was excellent. I particularly valued the English expression classes given by Mr Cunningham which have served me very well over the years. His careful insistence on parsing sentences (most Australian students today don't know the meaning of the word), his use of accurate punctuation and frequent precis exercises have left me a lasting legacy. I often wish that he could be available to tutor some of my research students today.

Dr. Michael St. George Wilson (1951 – 1952)

I came to Millfield when I returned from schooling in South Africa. I was in Restholme in Glastonbury – later changed to Chindit, as it was not thought to be good for the boys to be living in a "Rest Home"!

My first day I remember the Boss standing over me in his study with Miss Sankey in the corner, asking me what I wanted to do? I didn't have a clue, but as my father was a Doctor, I said, "I would like to be a Doctor". The school worked hard for me and eventually got me into Cambridge and I duly became a Doctor. But I soon found that the quality of the teaching at Cambridge was greatly inferior to Millfield's.

Richard Constable (1953)

Most of us in the 1950's did our National Service. I volunteered for entirely the wrong reasons to go to Korea. I had heard that peace talks were taking place and visualised long, romantic days, surrounded by oriental beauties in a country well known for its mountains, rivers, exotic flowers and wildlife. This vision was perhaps the less likely for the fact that I had grown up on Dartmoor and as a child had bred butterflies, moths and snakes.

Things were, of course very different in reality and after 15 months in the Canadian and British armies fighting the Chinese and the North Koreans, I arrived back in the UK in December 1952, an older and much wiser man.

On the very day I was due to be demobbed, I travelled down to Millfield to be interviewed for a place as a pupil by Boss. Those were the days when it was necessary to have passed School Certificate Latin in order to be accepted at any University, and this was a qualification I was determined to get. "What can you do for us?" Boss asked. I told him what skills I thought I possessed. We haggled for half an hour and I ended up with a place for £52 a term.

"Daddy" Fisher, Mr Cunningham, Robert Bolt and Emma Sawtell were my teachers, either in the Nissen huts or in the Chicken Runs. Selma Hedges taught Art in the greenhouse. The teacher-pupil ratio was one to seven, but I often ended up being taught by myself. It was not all that easy to adapt from living in a trench in winter in Korea to sitting in a classroom with Miss Sawtell in Somerset just five weeks later.

Two terms later I was a Prefect in Millfield House. One day it was discovered that someone had left some cigarettes in the Common Room. At lunch, Boss stood up and asked who ever was responsible to make himself known. No one moved. "I will give you until this time tomorrow for the boy responsible to own up," he said. "Otherwise the whole house will be beaten by the Prefects." Twenty four hours later still no one had owned up and so three of us Prefects were delegated to beat every boy in the house. Despite my military experience, it was generally thought that I would be less likely than the other two to hurt anyone, and since the boys were allowed to choose who beat them, I ended up with a very long queue of customers.

I left that term to go to Cambridge University. There was an added bonus for me to life at Millfield, for I married the Head Girl and we had four children.

SIR ROGER GIBBS (1952 – 1953)

As is well known, children grow up at different speeds and at different stages. Until I was 17, I did neither. In my defence, on my 17th Birthday, I was 5 feet 5? inches – and, on my 19th, 6 feet 3?. However, I always felt I was likely to become relatively normal, partly due to the brilliant child specialist Dr Gardiner-Hill's recommended course of hormone injections – and my size eleven feet!

I had three and a half very happy years at Eton, but achieved little. However, I did have one good idea. I firmly believed that boys either liked sweets more than money, or money more than sweets – and there was not a "don't know" in sight. Here was an irresistible opportunity. With the help of my great friend, Colin Ingleby-Mackenzie, we developed a sweet coupon market, and a very successful venture it was. We had a year of active trading until, totally from out of the blue, the Government decided to abolish sweet rationing – leaving Mackenzie and me with no cash and a tin full of useless sweet coupons.

At that point, Eton decided they could do nothing more for me, leaving my parents frantically trying to find another school – not an easy task in the early 1950s – and I was an exceptionally difficult pupil to place. Millfield drew the short straw.

I arrived at Kingweston for the Summer term of 1952 feeling distinctly apprehensive. However, within minutes, I bumped into a good friend of mine, John Leon (later the distinguished actor John Standing). He, too, had been eased out of Eton – a year ahead of me – he for repeated insubordination, and me for a total lack of academic attainment. John said, "This place is wonderful if you are a House Prefect – otherwise, it's pretty good hell. I seem to have some influence over our congenial German Housemaster, Alfie Neuman – a kindly soul. Would you like me to see if I can get you promoted to House Prefect? You simply can't stay in the Green dormitory with nine others – you'd hate that."

Minutes later, Alfie Neuman sent for me. "Gibbs, I am glad you already have a good friend here – it will help you settle in quickly. Leon tells me you have strong, but somewhat hidden, leadership qualities. He feels you would make an admirable House Prefect. I have decided to take Leon's advice." Just two years ago, my wife found my old Millfield reports. My first term's ended, "Roger has settled in well but, so far, he has been a disappointment as a House Prefect."

Boss, our dynamic Headmaster, tried to make life at Millfield as interesting as possible. There was always something going on. He even turned The Derby into a school event. He encouraged all of us to put half a crown (12?p) on the horse of our choice – bets which we had to place with him – at slightly cramped odds! 1953 was a particularly important race because it was possible that Gordon Richards would win his first ever Derby on the favourite Pinza. I was the self appointed school bookmaker with a substantial clientele. I was convinced Pinza would win and, therefore, offered the boys slightly inflated prices on all the other runners. Pinza duly sailed home. Boss, somewhat bewildered, attracted very few bets compared with the previous year – and almost all of them were on Pinza! He soon realised that he had a very junior bookmaking competitor but sportingly decided to do nothing about it – maybe because, as a rabid punter on the horses himself, he had a sneaking admiration for someone with similar inclinations.

If you are a late developer and a schoolboy struggler like me, you obviously need all the support you can muster. My parents, my four brothers and my sister, were all towers of strength as far as I was concerned but in addition, I was incredibly lucky at Millfield. I was taught by two quite exceptional and most understanding people – John Paxton, later a Director of Macmillan's, the publishers, and by Robert Bolt, author of *A Man for All Seasons*.

Robert Bolt was the most engaging person and an inspirational teacher. He certainly taught the eight of us, in our stark Nissen Hut, how to express ourselves and thus gave us considerable confidence – something never previously present in my make up. One morning, he came into our class in a state of great excitement. "Boys, before we get down to work, I have news for you. I have written a play which I have called *The Flowering Cherry*. Just for fun I sent it to the BBC. In today's post, I received a letter from them telling me that they would like to broadcast it this Autumn – and they would pay me £1 a minute. It runs for 90 minutes. They added that it is likely that they will want to repeat it next Spring – another £1 a minute!" (*The Flowering Cherry* later became Robert Bolt's first West End play.)

In 1965, I wrecked my knee in an accident on the Cresta Run and one morning, while undergoing intensive physiotherapy in London, I couldn't fail to recognise the distinctive voice in the next cubicle. I poked my head round the curtain. "Mr Bolt, you won't remember me..." Before I could go further, Robert Bolt interjected with his open genial smile, "I do. You were a nice enough schoolboy, but not, I believe, of above average intelligence!" I reminded him about *The Flowering Cherry* and the £1 a minute, and I couldn't resist asking him what terms he had achieved for writing the screenplays of *Lawrence of Arabia* and *Dr Zhivago*. Bolt replied, "I never thought about the terms until I was in a taxi on the way to sign up. I said to myself, the right fee for Lawrence is probably £5,000, but, being totally naïve about finance, I was determined not to be taken for a ride – so I multiplied it by eight and boldly suggested £40,000. The response was, "In all the circumstances, Mr Bolt, that seems a reasonable figure. Please sign here." I did. Three years later it was *Dr Zhivago* and a repeat performance. This time I went bald headed for £60,000. Exactly the same phraseology was produced – so I signed again! Since those days, I have learnt the real meaning of a share of the equity and a slice of the action – but too late!" I pointed out that he had won a few Oscars, to which Bolt, always as modest as they come, replied, "Yes, but they were mostly due to the efforts of others." In 1969 came the film version of *A Man for All Seasons*. I gather, on this occasion, he struck rather better terms.

I had a truly wonderful year at Millfield, even though, as at Eton, I achieved little. I was only allowed to take six O Levels – and not until I was 18. I failed three of them, including German, which obviously reflected very badly on me, but even less well on my likeable German House Master. I look back on my time at Millfield with considerable affection, but meeting Robert Bolt was all important. It is, in no small measure, due to him that I have muddled through in adult life – so far!

MICHAEL SELL (1952 – 1953)

I am sure that dear LEW Smith, who taught me English, would have something to say about my prose style, but all I can say is that he really did try hard with me and I thank him for all that he did for me all those years ago. I think the other major influence for me was Col. Barter who, more than anyone else, taught me how to learn – the most valuable asset I have ever acquired, and still invaluable to me, even at my advanced age! Harry Smith taught me how to strive on the athletics track, and Jock Riley gave me confidence with numbers. I was not a scholar at school, or even at university as I am much too practical for most academics – but I get things done!

HENRY TIMMS (1949 – 1953)

In the early 50's, the Combined Cadet force was commanded by Lt Col R A Heard. We were fallen in twice weekly, marching up and down Millfield's drive and eventually parading in front of the main house by the ha-ha. There the Colonel would stand on a special rostrum to drill us mere novices, as no doubt in earlier days he had drilled real soldiers in the Enniskillen Dragoon Guards.

One day he was addressing us, his troops, from his rostrum as usual at the top of his not inconsiderable voice. He brought us all to attention finally by shouting "Parade", at which point his false teeth flew from his mouth and landed at the bottom of the ha-ha. It was the best parade we had and the only one I can actually remember.

> As always I am as nervous as a kitten at the start of term. Four Assemblies to the various year groups really take it out of me, and no doubt out of my long suffering audiences as well. I quote at one point GBS; "My education was only interrupted by my time at school." Afterwards, I hear one L6th boy, talking to a pal as he left, say with a hint of exasperation, "Now he tells us."

LADY CASSIDI (1954 – 1955)

The three things that spring most vividly to mind are Boss lending me Proust and firmly putting my name on a postcard on the bookshelf from which the book came; Robert Bolt reading from the "Song of Solomon" and our savouring the beauty of the English language with him, and the sight of swathes of fritillaries under the trees.

DICK CHAMPION, ESQ, (EDGARLEY)

In those days the bicycle allowed us to do certain things which we wouldn't be able to do very easily otherwise. There was a large field outside Glastonbury on the way to Meare, that had flooded, then frozen in the very cold winter of 1955, I think it was. This field was considerably bigger than a football pitch and of course the water couldn't have been more than a foot deep, probably only 6 inches, and it was the most wonderful skating rink. We couldn't play any games at school because the fields were all frozen, so every Wednesday and Saturday afternoon I used to take the children out there, the whole school, anyone who wanted to come, and we'd slide and skate and ride bicycles on the ice. Only about 10 boys had skates and I had some of course, so we used to organize relay races, the cyclists against the skaters. The skaters, who of course had to take their shoes off, would make four piles of shoes in a large rectangle and the races would be round this rectangle. The cyclists could go much faster on the straight, but of course when they got to the corners they couldn't take them very quickly, and the skaters, who were a bit like the tortoise, would come up behind, and nip round the corners. I remember that when the cyclists won we'd make the rectangle a little smaller, and when the skaters won we'd make it a little bigger and so eventually it was really touch and go as to who would win. It was great fun. A few years later in 1963, a very cold winter indeed, I actually took boys skating on the Brue!

BILL GORDON-THOMPSON (1955)

My Latin was weak and I was given individual tuition by a personal tutor in order to lift my standard to that required by the Oxford college examiners. It worried me that I appeared to know more Latin that he did and eventually he got disheartened and stopped coming to give me these lessons. For the first couple of days I enjoyed loafing about when I should have been studying for University entrance exams, but then decided that I had better enquire of the Boss what was going on. He had forgotten to tell me that my tutor wouldn't be coming back because he had been arrested for bigamy!

The incident which caused the most trouble and a dressing down by the Boss was when a group of us at an end of season rugby party decided that it would be fun to hide a master's car. The car selected belonged to Mr Bromfield, then housemaster of "Chindit" in Glastonbury. It was a ridiculously simple matter, really. All we had to do was push it off the driveway onto the lawn and around the corner of the house. It all took just a few seconds, but the aftermath lasted much longer. We were eventually bussed back to our digs and were unaware of the consternation back at the party venue when the car was found to be missing. The police were involved, and even later on some of the local councillors, but the car was not located that night. When in daylight it was found only a few yards from its original parking spot, everybody in authority looked a bit foolish. The owner was not amused and demanded heavy punishment, to which the Boss replied, "You've got the car back, haven't you?"

Tea with four local councillors in sombre mood, contemplating the light pollution threatened by our plans for a double astro hockey complex. In other circumstances I would have sided with them over this, but I bend my instincts in favour of the school's long term interests, as I must. Their visit recalled for me the occasion recently at the Pre-Prep school when the Headmistress, Maggie Greenhalgh, was awaiting an important visit from two town councillors to discuss a planning application. On arrival, they were intercepted by a four year old girl who invited them immediately to have tea with her. Assuming that this was all part of the official reception committee, and clearly entranced by the warmth of the welcome, the councillors manfully accepted her invitation and soon found themselves bent double, squeezing into the Wendy house behind their diminutive hostess. Once they were all squashed in, she poured three imaginary cups of tea and struck up a conversation with them. Some minutes later they were all discovered in this cramped space by the Head, who had been alerted to the fact that the Councillors were on site and had been frantically searching for them for some time.

KEN CARTER (1955-1956)

My father and I were asked by Miss Sankey (Boss's Personal Assistant) to attend an interview so that the idea of a Sports Scholarship could be explored. The evening before the interview, I was given "scatter gun" type questions by my father to ensure that I would respond in an intelligent and quick thinking manner. So, on entering Boss's study, I was absolutely amazed to be thrown a cricket ball at high velocity. Fortunately, my reflexes were quick then and I duly caught the ball and felt very pleased with myself. Boss announced with an air of delight that he would take me on and give me a scholarship. We did have a chat for about 10 minutes about my other interests and he finished the "interview" by asking Miss Sankey to fix me up with a speech therapist so as to improve my enunciation. You can't win them all, but it is ironic that I have spent my life helping others with deafness and special needs with their speech, language and communication.

Having your English and Economics classes taught in the two different halves of a wartime Nissen hut was an experience not to be missed at Millfield! One half of the hut belonged to our English Tutor, Robert Bolt and the other half to Dr. Paxton who tried to teach us Economics. Mr. Bolt was a fervent socialist but you got the feeling that, like D.H. Lawrence, he didn't much care for teaching. I suspect we got in the way of his writing, for at the time he was working on "A Man for all Seasons" and was understandably far more interested in Sir Thomas More than in us.

If on occasion we felt unwanted in classes, we did however enjoy the breaks between them. It was then that Messrs. Bolt and Paxton would argue about socialism and capitalism in a fiercely aggressive way. It really was a heavyweight contest with far more than ten rounds at stake. There was intellectual blood all over the floor and we crowded around the two pugilists, trying to follow the arguments and inevitably looking for weaknesses in the contestants. One rumour circulating at the time was that Dr. Paxton was a bankrupt and had been struck off the Companies House Register. But in that case, we wondered, why was he still a capitalist? Also, why was Mr. Bolt teaching at a public school when he was such an ardent supporter of state education and deeply sympathetic to the communist party? These questions were never answered as we were not expected in the 1950's to challenge our teachers' personal beliefs.

As I had been given a Sports Scholarship to Millfield, mainly thanks to the Headteacher of the Street Board School, my father knew my passion for all sports but was concerned that this wouldn't ensure a financially rewarding and prestigious career. Scanning the comments in Boss's report, he suddenly blurted out, "When he gets to Cambridge, Kenneth will get a "blue"". What the hell does this mean?" He was totally confused with the words "Cambridge" and "blue". My father was astute enough to know my academic performance was not up to the Cambridge requirements. So what was this barmy Millfield Headteacher saying? The word "blue" was mystifying to say the least to him, so I deliberately played dumb so that he could focus on the word "Cambridge" instead. This conjured up for him an excellent education, class, power and success. For the next week or so I basked in the thought that Boss wanted me to go to Cambridge to get that "blue" for representing "his" University against Oxford at rugby.

> *Reports are finished. I must have written 20,000 words. Will any of them help anyone in their studies or their wider development? The level of interest in and knowledge of the young is high among nearly all tutors, and for the main part their reports illustrate this again and again, yet some persist in writing cliches which could apply to almost anyone, young or old. My acid test as a teacher is to read each class's reports through when I've written them, without looking at the names. If I cannot attribute a report to the right pupil, then it needs to be done again. But as Head there is no chance of this, except perhaps in the senior year.*

If, on average, every report contains 12 report slips, and given that they are written in triplicate, there are some 45,000 report slips to be handled twice a year, a massive logistical operation, managed impeccably by the whole office staff in unison. I only recall so far one error being drawn to our attention. This involved two boys in the 4th year with the same first and last names, though with different middle initials. One report was misattributed, and resulted, understandably I suppose, in a letter of censure from the parent concerned.

This term my favourite reports are:

"Orally, he has found his feet."

"He has worked steadily, though his work is erratic."

"His powers of concentration are not quite up to keeping all his balls in the air at once."

In 1956, the Seven-a-Side Rugby team, comprising John Norman, Farouk Mulla, John Waelchi, Derek Needham, Jack Melan, Richard Cooper-Driver and me, made great strides into this relatively new lung draining game. We won the Oxford and Clifton sevens and were semi finalists at the Rosslyn Park Public Schools' tournament. Behind the scenes, a great deal of speed training was required even though Derek Needham and Jack Melan were UK Sprint Champions. To make our training sessions more interesting, Jack Melan, Walter Gluck and a reluctant "Brom" introduced a young and very attractive woman athlete to be part of our preparations. She could run faster than most of us, tackle like a demon and pass a rugby ball with spin and – an attribute not normally associated with rugby players - beautifully swivelling hips. She clearly enjoyed the competitiveness and boisterous play with the rest of us and indeed seemed more at home, at that time, in our company than with the other girls. Her name was Mary and given her appetite for athletic success, and the fact that she was not intimidated by anyone, she went on to become an Olympic champion and the Golden Girl of athletics. She later married two Olympic champions – though not at the same time – and remains in my mind a beacon of gender equality. Thank goodness Millfield has never discriminated on grounds of gender.

An epic game of cricket between the newly formed sen-
ior girls team and the Foals C team, some of which I am
lucky enough to see. The boys posted their highest score
of the season – 80 all out on the last ball of their allot-
ted overs. The girls clearly scented victory but in the
event their game plan foundered on dodgy preparation.
They admitted that they had "done" bowling and field-
ing but had unfortunately omitted to "do" batting. Thus
they were all out for 30, despite some impressive chival-
ry from the little boys, who offered tactful advice on
how to avoid being lbw and judiciously dropped a num-
ber of gifted catches in the slips. Perhaps they feared
that the senior girls might issue detentions for over-zeal-
ous fielding. It was touching to see these mature young
women bending down to shake hands with their oppo-
nents at the end of the game.

TONY HESKETH-GARDENER (1954 – 1956)

A cricket match between RJO Meyer's XI and the Oxford University Authentics was due to take place the day before my A level exams began. Boss's team included several county players, but the Authentics boasted the fastest bowler in England at the time. In the middle of our class just after break, the door was thrown open and Boss strode in. "Come on, Anthony, you are opening the batting in 20 minutes." "But my kit's at Sharpham, sir, and my exams start tomorrow." "It's in my car," he replied impatiently. "And if you don't know your subject by now, you never will. Now come on."

We were 32 for 5 when Boss joined me at the crease. We were still there some time later when Joyce walked up to the boundary flourishing a portable radio, and waving. One of their bowlers was in full stride, tearing up to the wicket, when Boss, who was facing, suddenly stood away from the stumps and called, "I declare. The Derby's starting." With that he trotted off to join Joyce, followed by everyone else, and we all gathered round the radio to follow the race.

That night he wrote to my parents, saying, "I have no doubt that Anthony will pass his exams. You should see him stand up to fast bowling."

Mike Brearley comes for the week-end. He lectures to the 6th form and is brilliant at fielding questions, which rattle around bewilderingly between cricket, leadership and psychology. These seem to come at him almost antiphonally. "Do you go along with Freud's view on hedonism?" "What do you think of Atherton as a captain?" "Is Utilitarianism a sensible code for life?" "How did you manage to get the best out of Boycott?" In the evening, we take him to "Expressive Edge", two hours of dance involving our 70 dancers, technicians, sound and light people and a battery of drummers. It is superbly invigorating, slick, packed with energy, well rehearsed, snappy.

QUENTIN SEYMOUR SMITH
(EDGARLEY, 1952 – 1956)

When I left home for the first time to join Edgarley, my mother gave me a tin full of cottons, safety pins and needles. These were quickly put to use when we made an apple pie bed for a friend and he put his feet right through the sheet. It took six of us – three on each side of the bed – to do a stitch repair job. The tin was more or less on permanent loan in our dormitory and by the end of each term when it was returned to me it had a fairly full complement of reels and even occasionally with new colours added.

We used to spend a lot of time cycling off round the lanes in the evenings. We had to tell the duty master roughly – very roughly – where we were going and who would be with us but otherwise we were free as air to explore as we wished. I suppose there was a time by which we had to be back but I can't remember when that was.

Funnily enough, while no-one seemed fussed about the dangers of cycling, the thought that we might have cycled off to buy sweets caused a good deal of adult anxiety. Sweets were very strictly controlled and consumption was only allowed in moderation, and it was Matron's idea of what constituted moderation that counted. My granny used to send me bars of Cadbury's chocolate which were taken away immediately and put under lock and key in the sweet cupboard before even moderate consumption could take place. Each day after lunch we would form a disorderly queue while Matron solemnly unlocked the cupboard and allowed us to take a moderate amount of sweets. To my delight, I found that my granny would slip a half crown piece into each chocolate bar as an added bonus.

Clare, our Counsellor, has had a major operation and we are all hugely relieved to know that it has gone well. After a week on a drip, she is now eating again. Apparently her granddaughter Sophie, aged four, tried to call her at the hospital. She got through to the front desk and said, "May I speak to my granny please?" The receptionist naturally needed a little more to work on and asked, "Which granny is that?" to which Sophie apparently replied with asperity, "I've only got one granny."

I played in the 1st XV for three years, during which time I believe we were unbeaten. We had one boy who could convert from the half way line, and some very quick three-quarters. I played in two matches where boys actually died, though I'm sure this was nothing to do with the competitive nature of the game. In one game against All Hallows, the game started and ended in perfect sunshine but in the middle the fog came down so thickly that you could barely see your hand in front of your face. During this period I scored, or thought I had scored, one of my very few tries for the school. I dashed over the line with their referee right on my shoulder in a perfect position to award the try, which, to my amazement and delight, he did. Sadly, just as I was picking myself up, the touch judge emerged through the fog and pointed out that I had scored my "try" not over the try line but over the touch line. This was where I learnt that referees do sometimes change their minds.

I went back to Edgarley the term that Mr Champion retired. I found him in the building in the old vegetable garden writing reports. He said, "Do you mind taking a seat? I'll be with you in just a minute," and sure enough he was. He said, "You were here as a boy, weren't you?" I said yes. He said, "You played rugby, didn't you?" I said yes. He said, "You're Seymour Smith, aren't you?" It was wonderful to be recognised like that after all that time.

I learnt today of Dick Champion's favourite report that he read as Deputy Head at Edgarley. It was from the woodwork teacher, who had apparently written, "James has taken all term to produce a good stool."

DR. LOUIS ADHIHETTY (1956 – 1957)

I thank God for Millfield, which made a way for me, where there seemed to be no way! Today, I am what I am because of the School.

Way back in 1954, I tried to pass the examination in Sri Lanka to qualify for entry to the University of Sri Lanka. But I failed. So I asked my mother to send me to England because my knowledge of Sinhalese, (the new medium of instruction in Sri Lanka), was inadequate. She said, "Find a school in England and we will do our best to support you." I confidently accepted the challenge and promptly made inquiries. Soon I came across a reference to Millfield. I became convinced that this was the best place for me because sports were given an important place in the curriculum and the school was multi-cultural. In 1956 at least 36 countries were represented.

Being somewhat big headed, having played in the First team for seven games at my old school in Sri Lanka, I reckoned that I had an excellent chance of winning a Sports Scholarship and since there is nothing lost in trying, I wrote a personal letter to the Headmaster. After about four weeks, I received a reply informing me that although the fees were £ 550 per annum, Millfield was prepared to offer me a Sports Scholarship of £200. This reduced sum was still a big sum of money for a Sri Lankan Government Servant, my father being Superintendent of Prisons. He was just flabbergasted because his annual income was less than £1,000 a year, but all the same he sent the registration fee and I was on my way.

In April 1956, I left Sri Lanka with the cheapest ticket – twin-deck cabin class, £80 from Colombo to London – on a French boat bound for Marseille. From there, I travelled overland by train to London, and then on to Street. On my arrival at school, I was taken to see Boss, who was stern but quite friendly. I felt very content and comfortable. After a few days, my Tutor discovered that my qualifications were inadequate to enter any British University. So the tutorial staff worked out a timetable which was just right for me and in keeping with my background. Despite playing Cricket and Hockey for the 1st teams, I passed my A Levels. Boss was very pleased because he had invested a lot of time and money in me. One afternoon, I was summoned by him and was asked to apply for a place at either Cambridge or Oxford University. I obediently did so. I applied to four Cambridge Colleges and three Oxford Colleges. I was invited to at least five interviews but achieved nothing, until one morning I received a telegram from Christ's College, Cambridge offering me a place in 1958.

I thank God for the opportunities I was afforded by Millfield; the excellent co-educational atmosphere among students from numerous countries, the exceptional teaching by a very competent staff and the fantastic coaching in sports by ex-British Olympic players, Cambridge "Blues" and previous Somerset County Cricketers. I am also truly grateful to Mrs. Joyce Meyer, Boss's dear wife, who was a "mother" to us foreigners, and to Boss himself for all the encouragement and moral support we all received. Long live Millfield.

I went to visit Joyce Meyer again on what was to be her last night based in Somerset since she returned from India in 1935 with Jack. To my great sadness she had deteriorated significantly in the last two weeks and her daughter had now arranged for her to be looked after closer to her home in Surrey. I gave her John Rae's book, in which Jack is featured, and read her some extracts from it, but I think it was all a bit too much for her. It was a very moving parting and turned out to be the last time I saw her alive.

ROBERT APPLESON (1955 – 1957)

I went to Millfield in the autumn of 1955. I was supposed to have a test for a cricket scholarship during the summer holiday as I was quite handy, but my mother confused the day of the test. The night before, at around 9.00, Boss rang up to enquire why I was not at the school for the test the following day. We lived in Leeds. My father offered to drive me down to Street there and then but Boss said that I would be in no fit condition to play. The result was that I was not awarded a scholarship and my parents had to pay the full fee for a year at the school.

One late November afternoon after hockey I was standing outside Boss' office reading the notice board still in my hockey gear when his door opened and he looked down on me from his great height and said, "Ah, Appleson, you play tennis don't you?" I said I did indeed play at which he told me to go to the tennis courts and play with the boy who was waiting there.

I told him that I had neither a racquet nor any other suitable kit but he refused to accept this feeble excuse. He dug around in a large chest that stood in the hall, found me an old racquet and a pair of plimsolls and told me to take 30 points in every game as the other fellow was pretty useful.

I wandered down to the courts and saw a boy just practising his serve into a howling gale. I told him what the Boss had said but that I would take upwind and he could play into the wind. I was promptly beaten 6-1. I suggested that we switch ends and that I would start. Still no joy. It turned out that I was playing Jimmy Tattersall who went on to win junior Wimbledon twice and who, sadly, passed away very young.

NIGEL GODFREY (1956 – 1957)

As a Canadian teenager newly arrived in the British Isles in 1953, my adjustment to the British public school system was laden with confusion and frustration. I was out of synch with the education system and playing academic catch up. By 1956, my parents made the decision that a change was needed so off I went to Street.

The late '50s at Millfield offered unforgettable times. For me, it was a huge relief to leave the confines of a British public school and finish my pre-university education at co-educational Millfield. 'Boss' offered a learning environment at the time that was breaking the traditional schooling mould in the UK. Millfield was second to none where students could flourish in an opportunity environment, receiving top-notch teaching in the classroom and coaching in sports.

One weekend afternoon, "Boss' called me to his office and told me that I should play a game of squash with a newly arrived student. I was to meet the young lad at the squash courts. When I got there, I was greeted by the student, all 4 foot 11 inches of him! A walk-over, I thought. Three quarters of an hour later, dripping in perspiration and three games down, I left the court a chastened chap. I later learned that the 'student' was none other than one of the Khan brothers; later still I learned that he became the World Champion of Squash! Millfield taught me many valuable lessons, not the least being humility.

BARRY HOBSON "A HISTORY OF MILLFIELD"

In 1958, Boss appointed a young History graduate with a First from Cambridge, Anthony Kerr.

He was rather short and sported a long, droopy moustache, even at a time when a military appearance was still in vogue. He was distinctly eccentric and added to the picture by riding a huge, high-powered motor-cycle.

At that time, one of the most popular game shows on television was "Double Your Money", in which an ultimate prize of £1000 was offered, about a year's salary for a young teacher. All you had to do was sit in a sound proof box with ear-phones on and answer correctly a few questions on a subject of your own choice.

Anthony applied to take part and was interviewed on History in September 1959. Apparently his "posh" accent occasioned much laughter among the studio audience. When asked by the question master, Hughie Green, how he pronounced his surname, he replied, "Care, car or cur, whichever you like." This was greeted with a roar of approval. He got all the answers right, caught the public's attention and inevitably also the attention of the press.

Boss was immediately inundated with calls requesting to hear his views on his junior colleague's success. Putting his response as succinctly as possible, he said that he believed it was wrong for professional people to prostitute their calling for mere gain and the entertainment of the masses, that it might be alright if the recipient gave the winnings to charity, but that if he did not, he need not expect to keep his job.

This made headlines in the tabloids. Millfield was just another hotbed of snobbery, however much it attempted to show it was different, and the Headmaster was a dictator with no trace of benevolence. Hughie Green became the defender of "the little man", ITV improved its viewing figures and the show's advertisers sold more of their products. But Boss came across to the Middle

An early view of Millfield House.

Classes – his bread and butter – as someone determined to fight for the maintenance of the highest standards of behaviour in professional circles. This did Millfield no harm at all.

PENROSE HALSON (1957 – 1958)

My first kiss! Aged 17, I'd always been to girls' schools, and thus kept eyes firmly on the ground at Millfield, where there were only about 25 of us girls, and was therefore overwhelmed by the attentions of Issam El-Said, grandson of the ex-prime minister of Iraq. He took me to Wells, where, in an out-of-bounds hotel, we solemnly drank Babycham. I thought the world would explode. Back at school in the gloaming came the kiss. I don't think he ever kissed me again – I was patently totally ignorant and Issam patently was not.

There were a number of teachers who couldn't look girls in the face, one of whom was an elderly scholar who taught Latin and who addressed us in the third person: "If Miss Colyer would care to complete the exercise on page 39, would she then hand her endeavours to me by next Wednesday". Mr Bunbury, a teacher of French, resorted through embarrassment rather than egalitarianism to addressing girls just as he did boys: by surname only.

Colonel Barter had acquired smatterings of many languages, more and less obscure, during his military career, and boasted that he was able to teach several at one and the same time. But before any new pupil was privileged to receive his instruction, he or she had to read the manuscripts of his two great but alas unpublished works: Babel Re-labelled and The Classics Re-classified.

Robert Bolt, a gain to drama but a loss to teaching, inspired both a powerful love of language and startling, blush-making new thoughts in our small classes of three or four who, huddled round the great stove in his Nissen hut, listened to him declaiming Andrew Marvell, John Donne et al while striding up and down the gloomy tunnel.

Mr (Bud) and Mrs Atkinson ran the girls' house Wraxleigh with a sharp eye to the profit and loss account. Girls were allowed one or two baths per week, the bath water being shared between two, but there was no great anxiety to be in first and get the clean water – that was just the way it was. The food was mostly huge, thick slabs of bread which we toasted and ate with lashings of butter – otherwise there was not much else at all. Mrs At once made a fabulous fruit cake, a slab of which was for eating at the time, but a much bigger chunk was for storing away for Christmas. When she opened the sellotaped tin, however, she found half of it gone, her trusty head and deputy head of house having sneaked down on various hungry nights and carved off just a little bit each time. The head and deputy head left in the summer.

There was a great scandal when Mary Bignal (Rand) was exposed by the Daily Mail for doing something heinous and exciting. Reporters came down to the school from miles around and tried to buy corroborating saucy details from her schoolmates. Nobody talked, however, probably because none of us knew anything about it. Boss rewarded his self-righteous pupils with a day off.

The Daily Mail has published today a full page article vilifying the school. No one had taken the trouble to check any of the information with us in advance, so it turns out to be a tissue of fanciful innuendo and invention based on the ageing imagination of someone claiming to have been here as a pupil. In this capacity he suggests he has the up-to-date, inside story on the school. We delve into the records and find that he was indeed a boy here. In fact, he had spent an entire term at Millfield in 1977. He has located five assorted "scoundrels" who had been at Millfield over the last 25 years. They included the Big Issue chap, Princess Diana's military lover, a lay clerk at Wells Cathedral about whom some salacious story had appeared in the news recently, and the formidable "Madam Millfield", whoever she may have been, who is said to run a whore house in Los Angeles. We know nothing of the latter, though she sounds much the most interesting of the bunch.

I talk about the issues raised by such a publication in my four assemblies during the day and find the pupils as outraged by it as I am. In between times, we manage

to track down the managing director of the Mail on a
snow slope at Verbier on a mobile phone. Hopefully, he
is embarrassed by the news of this latest example of his
impoverished journalism, but I would not bet on it.

GRAHAM MCGOWAN (1958)

I wonder how many people know that back in 1958 – perhaps it is still done since it makes enormous sense – Boss insisted on us having our IQ's measured before he would interview us, let alone admit us. He had this novel idea, correct, I suppose, that it took a minimum IQ to get into and then stay at a university. This may have been an inverse function of how much our parents were going to pay!

Our great pride was that we were the only co-educational boarding school in England. I don't know if this was true or not, but we thought so. I think the ratio was one girl to ten boys, which made it all rather competitive. The ordeal of having to ask Boss for permission to take one of the girls out is something no 16-18 year-old male should do without. Some of us tried to do this most weekends, with greater or lesser degrees of success. Naturally our intentions were not always exactly those that we had put to Boss by way of justification for the proposed outing.

> *A delightful sixth form girl came to see me after just a*
> *week of the new term and said that, regrettably, she was*
> *going to have to return to her home in Cardiff. "But*
> *why?" I asked, wracked with guilt that already things*
> *had not worked out for her as we would have hoped.*
> *"Well, you see," she said, "It's just that my boy friend*
> *lives with my mother and I don't trust her with him."*

I was very fortunate to have been taught by John Paxton and Bob Bolt who had adjoining huts, both great characters. Sometimes Bob Bolt would conduct his classes at the pub. Dr. Paxton who should really have been at the University of Chicago but seemed to have wound up at Millfield by mistake, was the founder of what I believe is now the defunct Millfield Exploring Society. Our exploring really only consisted of skiing at Grindelwald during the Christmas holidays and our coat of arms was crossed beer bottles held together by a climbing rope on a background closely resembling the colour of pale ale. Somebody, at some point, actually had some ties made up with this.

However, before you get the idea that we only explored Grindelwald's ski slopes, I should point out that we also made a good job of exploring its nightclubs as well. One of the more exotic members of the Society at that time was Abbas Hilmi. I am reminded of the ruse we used to employ, exploiting his status and background, to get a table at a Swiss nightclub where we had not made reservations. One of us, usually the best dressed, would walk in and request a table for "His Royal Highness and friends" from the Maître d'. Being a good Swiss, if he did not have a table immediately to hand, he would soon produce one, whereupon a mob, including HRH, who may or may not have known about the use of his name and title, would descend on the unsuspecting Maître d' and enjoy an undeserved good evening.

LIN TATERSALL (NEE HAYES) 1956 – 1958

At my interview for an athletics scholarship, Boss asked my dad how much he could afford to pay for my schooling. Dad said about £100 a year. Boss was happy with that and said he had someone else coming for interview that afternoon whose contribution would be enough for a new tennis court and would offset my fees at the same time. So it was that in September 1956 I cycled the five miles from Somerton to start my studies at Millfield. Little did I know that the two years I would spend there would give me far more than mere academic qualifications.

I soon began to realise that girls were very much in the minority and that a date with a boy was pretty well assured. However, Boss had a rule. If a boy wanted to take a girl out, he had to ask permission. I became aware of a tennis player, Jim Tattersall, who was there on a tennis scholarship. On Fridays after school the boys' CCF paraded on the tennis court next to the court where we girls played. Jim was a cadet and to attract his attention I used to lob tennis balls over onto the parade area and then go coyly in my short tennis outfit to ask Colonel Barter if I could retrieve them.

It must have worked, for Jim went to ask Boss if he could take me to the cinema in Street. I was to discover that the cinema had double seats in the back row and there was always a scramble for them. This date was the first of many but the only one that Jim ever asked Boss to sanction. At break times Jim and I would meet by the bicycle sheds and Mr Brom would stroll by saying, "I see you're kicking up the leaves again".

My two years at Millfield meant that I got the exams that qualified me to become a physical education and games teacher. It allowed me to meet Jim, the man I was to marry. We were together for 31 years raising 3 daughters before his untimely death in 1997. Somewhere in the grounds of Millfield I have been told there is a bench seat to mark Jim's tennis achievements, and one day I hope to return with my family to try and find it.

IAN BALDING (1957 – 1959)

I arrived in 1957 just before my 19th birthday, and in the next two years I would be attempting to get the necessary A Levels to ensure my place on the Cambridge University veterinary course. Boss was well aware that I had been riding in races as an amateur at the time, and told me that I could continue to do so during the winter terms providing that I sought his permission first.

I did not realise at the time just how interested he was in racing and no-one was more surprised than I when my elder brother Toby, who was a prominent National Hunt trainer, told me that he had just sold my Headmaster a jumper! The horse in question was a smashing little grey gelding called Milk Shake, and although not a super-star, he was one of the best jumpers of a steeplechase fence that I had ever ridden.

One Thursday afternoon in the Spring Term of my second year, Milk Shake was entered in a 2 mile 5 furlong handicap chase at Wincanton and Toby rang me with the good news that I would be his jockey. I was Boss's senior prefect at the time and for this rather special occasion the Headmaster actually allowed a coach load of Millfield pupils to attend Wincanton races.

I think it was quite a poignant moment for Boss when I entered the paddock in his own racing colours – a mixture of red, green, black and white of course. He insisted on giving me the riding instructions himself – normally the trainer's prerogative – before hurrying off to have a bet on his horse.

Happily all went well and Milk Shake, who must have known it was an important event, put his best foot forward. We won comfortably and the scene in the winner's enclosure afterwards as Boss greeted his senior prefect on his own horse in those famous Millfield colours was as joyful a moment as I can remember during my time at the school. Boss himself looked as proud and happy as I had ever seen him.

> *A cheering letter from a parent on a Gary Larson card. "I am in a bit of a panic. I realise I have just put some of Sophie's fees for next term on a horse." From the tenor of the rest of the letter, it appeared that the horse had not only failed to win, but had had a hard time coming in last, and this would entail some delay in clearing their account, and would I kindly smile nicely at the Bursar for her? Irresistible.*

GUSTAV HAGEMANN (1958 – 1959) EDGARLEY

When I started at Edgarley I did not speak a word of English. When you are very young you learn very quickly and so did I. I had a great time and got a lot of nice friends.

One evening I was doing my homework. This was very strict and we were not allowed to do anything else but homework. I had smuggled in a Swedish book – "Fem böckerna" - and this was much more fun than doing homework. Soon the headmaster found out what I was doing. The next day I was to come to his office. I had to take down my trousers and then I was hit by a hairbrush made of metal needles! I screamed and my backside got 1000 small red dots. But that was not the worst - I could now not sit down for a long time! I never again read a Swedish book during time for homework.

I had a wonderful time at Edgarley Hall and I missed the school very much when I was sent to school at Sigtunaskolan outside Stockholm.

COLIN SIDNEY-WILMOT (1953 – 1960)

I was sent up to Boss because I had been caught smoking. I was ushered into his study expecting a caning. I feared a severe one, one that would make it difficult to sit down for several days, because at my interview he had asked if I liked cricket and I had told him I loathed the game. I was worried he might lay it on hard to get his own back.

I walked from the study door to his desk where he was bent forward writing with concentration. I stood silently waiting for him to finish and get up and tell me to bend over. Boss finished writing, pushed the paper to one side, looked up at me and smiled. " Well don't just stand there, get one of those chairs and come and sit down." I hastily obeyed and sat tensely in front of him, with the desk between us. He reached across the desk, picked up a large cigar box, opened it and very pleasantly offered me one. Hesitantly I selected a cigar. He took one himself, cut the ends of our cigars with a cigar cutter and then lit his cigar, before handing me the matchbox. He told me to hold the cigar tip above the flame, not in it and to rotate the cigar while drawing on it.

Bemused at this unexpected turn of events but beginning to relax, I lent back in my chair and we smoked in companionable silence for several minutes. Boss broke the silence saying. " Anything you do is worth doing properly. Now tell me about school in Australia and Singapore." I talked of how much I had liked and missed Singapore until we had finished our cigars. Just before I left his study he told me that in future I would have to obey the eleventh commandment, which was not to be found out. If I were caught smoking again he would be obliged to punish me severely. It may be this was the first time I heard that rules are for the guidance of the wise and the obedience of fools, but now I am not so sure.

JOHN BELL (1958 – 1961)

On arriving at Hill Home, whose weathered gate amusingly bore the letters HILI HOMF, I found that I was to share a small dormitory with three boys, the remaining two occupying a tiny

1961. The Nissen huts: an aerial view.

spare room across the landing. Mr. and Mrs. Dickens had a couple of kids of their own, so it was to be a tight squeeze! Accustomed as I had been to having a bedroom to myself, I was disturbed at first by the loss of privacy resulting from being obliged to share one. But I soon got used to that, as well as to the regimented way in which life at a boarding school is organized, however progressive it may purport to be. In any case, these abridgments of freedom paled into insignificance alongside the homesickness – now so remote! – that dogged me throughout my first year at Millfield. Beneath my every waking hour ran an undercurrent of melancholy which would sometimes erupt in a flood of tears. Astonishing as it now seems to me, this could occur at the drop of a hat. I recall, for instance, suddenly beginning to blubber uncontrollably in the middle of a mathematics class. It was indicative of the essential benignity of the regime at the school that the master – in this case the estimable Captain Clarkson (R.N. ret.) – interrupted his instruction, took me outside, gave me a few words of comfort in his bluff way, and advised me to take the rest of the day off.

Certain details of life at Hili Homf still stand out in my recollection. Table polishing, for instance. In this bizarre ritual one of the boys was grabbed by the others and stretched out on the common-room table. His hands and feet firmly held, he would then be swung violently back and forth across the table until he begged for mercy. It seems surprising in retrospect that none of the victims sustained serious injury.

Mr. Dickens occasionally gave some of us a lift to school in his Morris Minor. He took great pride in this vehicle, describing it with proprietary satisfaction as "the ideal family car in many ways." This struck us boys as risible and so we naturally began to use the phrase, *mutatis mutandis*, whenever possible. Thus the Dickens's television set became "the ideal family television in many ways," their cat "the ideal family cat in many ways," and, inevitably, the Dickens household itself "the ideal family in many ways."

On alternate weekends the strange ritual known as "Corps" took place, in which the boys of the whole school would don military uniform and earnestly march about in a kind of caricature of regular army manoeuvres. When I first arrived at Millfield I feared that I, too, might have to engage in this nonsense, but fortunately I noticed the clause in my passport asserting that "it is not valid for travel to or in any foreign state for the purpose of entering or serving in the armed forces of such a state." I reasoned that if the school governors really took their cadet force (or farce) seriously, they would regard it as being genuinely part of the British armed forces, in which case they would acknowledge that by joining it I would be violating the conditions laid down by the American consular authorities. This line of reasoning must have been substantially correct, because I was spared all squarebashing at Millfield.

My history teacher, Miss Emma Maud Sawtell, had a cultivated mind and was, in fact, a considerable scholar in her own right, as I learned when I took a course in general civilization with her in my last term at Millfield. I shall always remain grateful to her for introducing me to Tolstoy's *War and Peace*, which I read in the Penguin translation by Rosemary Edmonds, and which instilled in me a lifelong fascination with Russian literature. Although I cannot recall any of Miss Sawtell's actual utterances, in my mind's eye I can still see her striding stiffly into class, her face reddened by the cold of a winter morning. Dressed in an enveloping skirt of dense brown wool, grey jumper and sensible shoes, she appears every inch the archetypal English schoolmistress. Sitting down at her desk, she summons the class to attention with an awkward gesture. She essays a witticism, correctly anticipating the class's lack of response by appending a chortle of her own.

I received instruction in chemistry from Mr. Bromfield. Known to all as "Brom", he was a flamboyant red-haired man sporting an RAF-issue handlebar moustache. He brought to his teaching a panache which made classes with him great fun. His chemical demonstrations were accompanied by a gaudy patter which ran something like the following: "First one triturates the jolly old crystals in ye olde mortar and pestle, then one bungs them into yon beaker, adds a spot – a *soupçon,* as the dear old French would say – of this liquid of roseate hue, stirs gently, stands back, and awaits developments." What appeal chemistry had for me lay in these developments, which, under optimum conditions, took the form of arresting bangs and stinks. O-level chemistry practicals were in fact far more interesting than their counterparts in physics. These consisted chiefly of stultifying experiments involving antique Wheatstone bridges and rudimentary thermal expansion devices. But in respect of theory I saw the relationship as the exact reverse: physics was theoretically deep, while as far as I could see chemistry had no theory to speak of.

Still, I enjoyed heating test tubes to near incandescence over Bunsen burners, plunging lit spills into merrily bubbling flasks, and watching strips of litmus paper change colour as they were removed, dripping, from nameless fluids, which latter could then be induced, by suitable stimulation, to deposit flocculent precipitates. The acme of my experience as a juvenile chemist was attained the afternoon that I and my fellow delinquents dumped a number of large copper penny coins into beakers of nitric acid, causing the emission of clouds of brown nitric oxide of such copiousness as to necessitate the evacuation of the entire lab.

Games did not come naturally to me. Rugger was a matter of sliding about in a sea of mud, and Hockey was, if anything, worse since the ordeal was conducted in the depths of winter when one's whole body was numbed with cold. On the other hand I did enjoy basketball. My one moment of glory on the basketball court occurred during a home match and was the result, in truth, of frustration. Prevented by members of the opposing team from getting closer than ten yards or so to their basket, in desperation I flung the ball in its general direction. Having not the slightest expectation of the shot's being successful, I immediately turned away without following the ball's trajectory. A few seconds later I was surprised to hear the spectators clapping and cheering, for the ball had, as if guided by an unseen hand, passed straight into the basket. I fancy that the feat must have seemed doubly impressive because of my apparent nonchalance in turning away, as if a successful outcome was a *fait accompli*.

Now and then the Boss would summon me to Millfield House for an audience. I would wait until the ingenious set of miniature traffic lights mounted alongside the baize-covered door of his study changed to green, indicating that it was permissible to enter the inner sanctum. There Boss could usually be seen sitting in his shabby old armchair, a telephone in his lap, surrounded by teetering piles of books and papers. On one such occasion I recall him saying to me "I'm taking a few chaps up to Cambridge [or Oxford] next week to meet some people, and I want you to join us," or words to that effect. Then he got up – very tall and thin, it was as if he unfolded himself from his chair – went over to one of the piles, extracted a book from it, and handed it to me. "I think you'll find this interesting." (The book was, I recall, O. R. Frisch's *Handbook of Nuclear Physics*.) Indicating that the interview was at an end – he was a very busy man – he said he hoped that on the Cambridge (or Oxford) trip "I would be on my best behaviour."

The Boss encouraged my teenage "prodigism" in other ways as well, for example, by entering me for 'O'- levels at 13 and 'A'-levels at 14. He even suggested that I give lectures to some of the other boys on my interests in physics and mathematics. So on

Boss in his study.

Saturday afternoons I found myself in front of a blackboard in one of the makeshift classrooms (known as chicken runs) expatiating on the expanding universe to a tiny captive audience of my contemporaries – capital preparation for my future career as a dispenser of soporifics to bored students in the lecture theatre! I was acquainted with the steady-state theory of the cosmos and had had the brainstorm – which I also recall presenting in the form of an article in the school magazine – that the edge of our expanding universe at which objects are receding at near-luminal velocity actually marks the boundary of another expanding universe whose corresponding edge marks the boundary of yet another expanding universe, and so on *ad infinitum*. So much for precocity!

In early 1961 the Boss sent me (along with P.D. Norton) to Oxford to sit the scholarship examination. Just before we left, he told us – using one of the racing metaphors of which he was so fond – that we should regard our efforts there as a mere "preliminary canter". I have only the haziest recollection of my interview at Exeter

College, but it must have gone well, for following my return to Millfield a letter arrived from the college authorities informing me of the award of an Open Scholarship in Physics. The fact that I was 15 at the time of the award resulted in a blaze of publicity, with newspaper reports and interviews, which the Boss must surely have felt could do the school's reputation no harm. But even this, unquestionably my finest hour, was tinged with sadness, for I could not help thinking how proud my mother would have been of me had she been alive.

MALCOLM ROBERTS (1958 – 1961)

My friend Graham Burgess was batting in a house match one day. He was going well when I managed to get an outside edge and he was caught behind by the wicket keeper. There was a loud, confident appeal all around the ground, but to our bemusement Mr Baker, the umpire, announced, "NOT OUT". Now this shot was a big swipe at a ball going through at about shoulder height accompanied by a very loud snick. "Didn't you hear the snick, sir?" I retaliated. " "Yes," replied Mr Baker. "But there was no deviation of the ball ". With this, Graham collapsed at the crease with laughter. He then hit my next delivery for four, but, perfect sportsman that he was, he surrendered his wicket to me the very next ball and left the field with tears of laughter pouring down his face.

I was visiting Kevin Cheney at his prep school at Cranmore and remarked on the beautiful setting and condition of his cricket pitch. "Ah, that's Norman," said Kevin. It was several seconds, as I wrestled in my mind with a distant doubt that cricket after all might have been French before it became English, before I realised he was talking about his groundsman.

JEAN PIKE
(TEACHER AT EDGARLEY AND AT MILLFIELD,)

The incident I recall with most pleasure from my earliest days of the staff occurred one May 4th in the late 1950s. In those days, the whole school, both staff and I.S.P. (*in statu pupillari* as the pupils were then described) formed up to parade into Street to celebrate Empire Day. Everyone dressed in their smartest clothes – the OTC in full uniform – and we processed in some semblance of a crocodile fashion down to the shabby, one horse cinema in Leigh Road, with the OTC unsure whether to march in step and swing their arms vigorously or whether just to shamble along with the rest of us.

There we were invariably treated to a lecture by some aspiring politician chosen by Boss, not for any talent he might have for engaging the attention and interest of the young, or even of the old for that matter, but merely because he was a Tory.

This particular year he was a particularly boring speaker. Boss introduced him briefly and then settled himself in a comfortable chair placed on the stage specially for him. The speaker droned on and on and after a while my charges, who being the youngest were seated in the front row, became understandably restless and started fidgeting and whispering noisily. I was finding it hard to keep some semblance of control, when suddenly we all became aware of a new noise which seemed to be coming from the stage. Slowly it dawned on us what was happening and my charges fell silent, transfixed at first with amazement and soon with glee. Gradually a ripple of laughter ran through the whole cinema. Boss was fast asleep and gently snoring.

It says a lot for the good manners of pupils in those far-off days that the laughter was quickly stifled. It says a lot for Boss, too, that when the polite applause at the end of this uninspired speech woke him up with a start, he rose to his feet and confidently delivered suitable if not exactly sincere words of thanks to the speaker. It was a classic example of the *sangfroid* and *savoir faire* of a typical English gentleman, though of course Boss could not really be said to have been typical of anything.

JOHN SERGEANT (1957 – 1962)

Jack Meyer's philosophy was very simple: children of the very rich were accepted however dim and they paid full fees, while the rest of us would have to prove our usefulness to the school. The sons of millionaires were usually not at all bright. At our first evening meal I was surprised to find that I was the only person on our table who was capable of cutting slices from a loaf of bread. But then I was sitting between a boy worth a million pounds in his own right and another worth half a million pounds more. They were amazingly rich and had been pampered at home. I had thirty shillings, or £1.50, to spend each term and my mother was far too busy to cut slices of bread whenever we were hungry.

I once managed to win my house colours, the right to wear a special tie, because I tackled the largest boy in the school. A great roar went up from the crowd because my team won as a result. But, I may as well admit, I was trying to move away from him at the time and we collided. After the age of sixteen we were allowed to choose whether we played games. I chose golf and chess. My games report said, "Sergeant is sometimes seen leaning on a borrowed club in the vicinity of the golf course." But I did manage to become captain of chess.

We lived a life set apart from the normal world and I thought of Millfield as a prisoner of war camp. We had, as far as I could tell, done nothing wrong but we were prisoners and it was difficult to escape. Boss, however, was a charmer and a showman and he appeared genuinely excited about the possibility of dramatically extending pupils' horizons. On one occasion he assembled all of Millfield's top golfers to spend the morning trying to get a hole in one. His theory was that British golfers were too modest in their approach; they merely tried to get the ball onto the green, so a hole in one was an accident. He wanted them to try for the seemingly impossible. He also made sure that the *Sunday Times* was on hand to record the event.

One of his other theories was that people only learn properly if they are allowed to find their own level. This was not possible in large classes so at Millfield the average class size was about eight or ten. It made for intensive lessons but required able teachers, whose personalities became of crucial importance. I was fortunate in being taught English by Robert Bolt, who was about to become one of the foremost playwrights in the country and later found fame as the script writer of *Lawrence of Arabia* and *Dr Zhivago*. My first piece of work for him was a précis. I was describing how "the war clouds of Europe were gathering" and, being thirteen at the time, thought that the phrase had a certain ring to it. Not for Robert Bolt; it was a cliché and had to be struck out. When he was recovering from a stroke many years later, I wrote to commiserate and mentioned this incident. "Perhaps," he replied, "I was a little harsh." He turned into one of my heroes because of the way he triumphed from these modest beginnings in Somerset.

RITA HUTCHISON (NEÉ STONE) (1959 – 1962)

The YLC (Young Ladies Club) had but 42 young ladies in 1959, so we all had rather inflated ideas about ourselves, with nearly 400 male students in sight and on site!

There was a well established system for finding boy friends. A YLC member simply let her fancy be known and this got passed along in some mysterious way to the boy in question. In due course, and through the same devious channels, the answer came back as to whether or not he was likewise interested in going out with the YLC member. I am thankful that my husband turned me down then, that first time, because those relationships seem rarely to have lasted. At a Leavers Party, for which I returned in 1963, we began our relationship afresh, and now 37 years later we are still very happily married.

JOHN KNEE (1957 – 1963, EDGARLEY)

I started at Edgarley in September 1957. In those days the academic side of the school was largely geared to Common Entrance, and as soon as one reached the "B" Block the exam. papers for each of the three terms consisted of the Common Entrance papers for that term. Consequently it was quite normal to take these sets of papers six times. The end of term reports for all groups were also written with C.E. in mind. At the end of my first term, when I was aged only six, my English teacher Joan Phillpotts wrote, "He did not appear to know any grammar at the beginning of term." I was a little hurt, but my mother found this extremely funny.

ELLIOT B.LEWIS (1959-1962)

I had to spend my first year at an old Abbey in Glastonbury as they did not have room for me in the main school. It reminded me of Colditz – a huge building, of large bricks and cold rooms. Glastonbury Tor had a blossom tree near a spring at the main entrance, from which Jesus was supposed to have drunk. People came from far and wide to drink from the Spring. There was also a large swimming pool, built by the Romans, and I recall our filling it, and jumping into this freezing water, trying to imagine if it was used by Roman soldiers or monks.

Later at Shapwick, Walter Gluck and his American born wife were our Houseparents. He was a highly respected Housemaster. He loved sports, and enjoyed our company. It was a terrible shock, when one evening, driving home, his car swerved into a water-filled ditch that ran alongside the road. The car fell on its side, and he and his friend both drowned.

Barry and Rosemary Hobson were introduced to us all, as the new Housemaster and his wife. I recall that Rosemary made the most wonderful toast and marshmallows in the evening. I think we were charged a penny for these special nourishments.

Going round Shapwick last night, John in the U6th told us he had just been accepted for a course in Mechanical Engineering and Japanese, perhaps the least predictable combination I have yet encountered. We were talking later that evening with a group of 3rd formers, when I thought I saw a girl slipping into one of the rooms arm in arm with a boy. My suspicions were immediately red hot and I had already begun to remonstrate mildly with them before I realised that she was in fact his mother, making an unscheduled visit. My mistake was not, I think, entirely unwelcome to her and she promised not to keep her embarrassed son from his prep for too long.

A friend of mine, William Pitt, who now lives in Australia (great, great, great grandson of William Pitt the Younger),decided one day to visit his Aunt in Bath. To do so, we had to take our bikes.

A long way, but we felt we'd manage. Little did I know that there were many hills on the way, and my old Hercules bike was too heavy for such a trip. So we decided that we would tie our bikes together on a long piece of rope and William would pull me along. Everything was fine, until we started down a very steep hill and our speed started to increase. As William reached the corner he swerved to the other side of the road, not seeing an oncoming car. He braked, and was thrown through the air like 'Superman'. My bike turned over and over on the road. When I came to, William was totally white and out cold. I thought he had died! Ten minutes later he started to move and I told passing cars that we were fine. Our bikes were totalled, so we dumped them and started to walk painfully back to Shapwick. To our astonishment, our own house bus passed by and the driver asked what we were doing. We said, "Just hiking", and he agreed to drive us back. What good fortune.

Saturdays were the days when everything happened that was not supposed to happen. I recall one Saturday afternoon, when boys who had left the previous term, came back to take me and a friend out to Bath, in their car. I had no idea that we were going to spend the evening drinking vodka, and by the time we arrived in Bath, it was dark, and we found ourselves driving up the main street on the wrong side of the road. I kept asking why all the headlights seemed to be parting as they approached our car. We finally all agreed that this was not the correct side of the street to be on, and headed back to Shapwick. I was pleased to find on our return that at least our bathrooms were where they should be.

> *Three naughty girls are gated for drinking. Their respective parents' reactions to the news are instructive. One parent calls me to threaten legal action against the school for "allowing" her daughter to drink and for not examining his incontinent, foul-mouthed off-spring on admission to the medical centre. Another arrives late and unannounced at her daughter's house, terrifies her room-mates and others by screaming at her that she "will be working in a factory at 9.0 tomorrow" before dragging the horrified girl away, only to ring the next day to say she will be returning her daughter at lunchtime. And the third calls me to apologise for his daughter and to thank us for tak-*

ing action to impress the seriousness of her offence upon her. Three good young girls who have all made the same mistake, generating a considered disciplinary response here, but eliciting three staggeringly different responses from their parents.

I was very fortunate to have some very good teachers at Millfield, Mr Sargeant taught me Divinity. He spoke ten languages fluently. One teacher loved photography and whilst taking photographs of elderly, wrinkled people, would ask them if they were members of the working class. When they said "Yes", he asked why they were not working. I was glad I wasn't there to hear their response.

My days at Millfield were a magical period for me. I was taught to respect and to get along with other people from all countries and all walks of life. That becomes part of you for ever.

MICHAEL PALIN (1963)

In the days before UCCA, the only way to get to Oxbridge if one missed the entrance exam was to apply for a scholarship, but my previous school had no interest in teaching beyond A level. So my father, who was an eye surgeon, talked with Meyer – a man who loved his ducks, which waddled around all over the drive. It emerged during the conversation that one of them had a cataract, so Meyer said "OK, I'll operate on your lame duck if you'll operate on mine!" In the event I needed another A level, and the result, courtesy of Dr. John Paxton, was an A grade in Economics, learnt and taken in just ten weeks flat. This was a great tribute to his teaching me just enough to understand how to answer the questions, but not so much that I became confused by too much knowledge. I may say this has stood me in good stead throughout life.

ROGER PATENALL (1961 – 1963)

A particular weekend comes to mind. A significant weekend, which marked the time when I started to grow up.

It must have been June, 1962. The Millfield Athletic team were attending a meet near Taunton on a beautiful Saturday afternoon. Our party included current and former pupils, together with a few, loyal, non-competing supporters. My friend – everyone's friend – Simon Pruin came with us, and we passed the time between events in a Millfield 'camp' under the trees. I remember it well because it was the first occasion that I met Mary Rand, supporting and competing with the Millfield team in spite of her, by then, exalted status.

During the early afternoon, I remember Simon seeking me out to say he did not feel well. Being a doctor's son, I was obviously seen as the right person to take him over to the First Aid tent.

The meeting went on late into the evening. The euphoria of setting a new county record (as most of the team probably did!) meant that I went home knowing only that Simon had been taken to hospital.

The news on Monday that Simon had died of peritonitis stunned me, along with everyone else. It was, I think, the first time that I had experienced a close death. How had I left on Saturday evening so full of my day that I had never even asked after him?

I suppose that this is how one learns lessons.

CHRIS BLOOR (1962-1964)

We played a rugby match against Cardiff High School, and won 6-3 in the mud. When we got back to the coach at the designated time, Syd Hill, our rugby master, thrust a whole cooked chicken into my hands. For once it was he rather than we who was rather the worse for alcohol!

Rugby training involved running from the school to the top of Glastonbury Tor and back, crossing, jumping, perhaps swimming – I can't quite remember – the various rhines that criss-cross the Levels between Street and Glastonbury. And our classes were all conducted in the Nissen huts, where we huddled in winter round a pot boiler stove.

But my over riding memory is that of being part of a great family team whose every achievement contributed to the winning ethos which ' Boss' clearly wished to foster.

STEPHEN COOPER (1960 - 1964)

We were in class in the chemistry labs which at that time were just by the main road to Somerton. Suddenly, there was an almighty bang outside which shook the entire building. We rushed to the windows as the noise seemed to have come from below us on the road. There was a lorry stopped in the middle of the road and the driver was walking round it looking at the tyres, scratching his head. We assumed one of his tyres had burst and thought no more about it until the end of class. When we trooped outside, however, we discovered the real cause of the noise.

Those of us fortunate enough to have been taught chemistry will know that one of the first things you learn is never, NEVER to mix water with sodium. The reason for this is that quite a violent reaction takes place, even with small amounts. On this occasion the head of the chemistry department, Mr. Taylor, had decided he wanted to reduce the stock of sodium because some of it "looked a bit dodgy". He had duly put the dodgy stuff into a galvanised bucket outside, retreated about five yards and squirted water from a distilled water bottle onto it. The resulting explosion had blown Mr. Taylor off his feet, destroyed the bucket and caused a passing lorry driver to think he had had a blow out. The poor lorry driver could not have guessed the cause of the blast, and we were certainly not going to tell him.

TONY LAING (1961 – 1964)

I was at one time the senior Warrant Officer in the CCF – a rank of dizzying importance which allowed me to shout at everyone loudly once a week. Even school prefects were under my command for those two alarmingly powerful hours. It was therefore particularly galling one afternoon, to be brought down to earth with a bump. Some friends and I were rehearsing our group in one of the Nissen Huts. I was playing the drums, the others were all on electric guitars and we were singing the only song we knew, 'She was just seventeen.' We were in full flow, when I noticed the head of school appear at the window. We dried up immediately, knowing that we were breaking sound barriers in all directions and that the people in Glastonbury, let alone Street, were probably being deafened by us. "Far too loud," he shouted. "You are all on report." We were chastened, but I got my own back on him later in the week on the parade ground.

TIM RANDALL (1961 – 1964)

I suppose it all started during the dreaded hockey term. Somehow the subject of cricket had come up in the middle of all that is grim and cold at that time of the year and somehow the idea was born. It was a surprisingly simple idea, really. It just involved hijacking the fourth cricket eleven and turning it into a side to play the local villages. We even had a name: the Millfield Nomads. I mean, who would want to play the 4th Xl?

So later that term I stood outside Boss's door, heart thumping, and finally mustered the courage to enter and blurt out my idea. The answer was quick and affirmative: "Anything that sees more cricket played is good: do it."

Unfortunately my Housemaster clearly did not approve of the what I had done, for I was now the only boy who had his own cricket team, a team which, needless to say, required the participation of other essential players, including vice captain John Wiseman, also from my house. We had a master nominally in charge of us, however, and luckily he was generous to a fault. The Nomads immediately became a popular side to play for, more perhaps for the après cricket than for the cricket itself, for cricket in Somerset villages is invariably followed by deep and often protracted match analysis in the pub afterwards.

When our exams were over, we started playing 18 over evening matches. Team selection for such matches was much sought after, and soon we had a galaxy of talented players on our books, not only players from the 4th but also from the 3rd and even from the star-studded 2nd X1. These heroic figures were prepared to lower their high cricketing standards to play on pitches on many of which it was possible to lose the ball completely, even inside the boundary. They had their own reasons for this compromise, of course, but we never bothered to ask them what they were. Perhaps we didn't need to.

In our second year, the Nomads had as big a fixture list as the 1st X1. One of the lowlights of that summer was losing to Chilton

Cantello, even though this was considered an absolute walk over. Our spin bowler, Colin Vandervell, always took to the field wearing sunglasses. In the sixties in Somerset villages, a cricketer wearing sunglasses was something of an oddity, so when he came on to bowl, he would hand his glasses to the umpire. Sadly this often meant that his vision was affected, not necessarily for the better. Some of us were not even sure that he could actually see the batsman to whom he was bowling!

However, we more than made up for this humiliation by beating Shapwick in a Sunday match at Kingweston. Shapwick had been unbeaten all season but Sheriff Kahn, whom we had recruited from the firsts and who was an even better squash player, made 80 match winning runs. This match received massive publicity in the Street papers. Shapwick had finally been beaten! Boss even acknowledged our success with an encouraging grunt as we practiced in the nets.

The 4th *XV have decided to call themselves the Neanderthals this year and seem to be surprised that other schools' opposition, clearly awed by what they must see in prospect as more than just a sporting challenge, appear to be cancelling matches with them. To help drum up some fixtures for them, I suggested helpfully that they should call themselves the Fairies instead, but they turned down my idea.*

CHARLES WHEATMAN (1964)

B rom was of course a keen athlete, but had very little sympathy for cricket. On this particular afternoon, the heats for the House athletics finals coincided most unfortunately with a practice for those of us who played cricket in the 1st XI. Brom would never take no for an answer or indeed brook any excuse for non-attendance in athletics heats, and thus I was made to run the 400 yards heat in full cricket kit, boots, pads, the lot. I did not make the finals.

Jo Edwards, a good marathon runner and even better mathematician, and I are watching Barney Stephenson win the Mendip Open cross-country race with his char-

acteristic grit. She remarks how foolish the Cambridge dons were to have missed him this year. Without really thinking, I observe that they missed me too, to which Jo replies equally absentmindedly but with conviction, "That's more understandable."

MICHAEL BULL (1961 – 1965)

Although I loved sport, I never enjoyed my time at school. I am one of those awkward people who do not take kindly to orders. I was in Kingweston, and needless to say life there became pretty intolerable. Then one day I heard that you could apply to Boss to transfer between houses. All you had to do was enter your name in a book outside his study and he would then summon you to discuss your concerns with him. At the first opportunity, therefore, I located the book and was about to put my name down when I saw to my horror that there were almost no other names there at all. I had to decide whether to sign, knowing that if Boss turned down my request, the Housemaster and prefects at Kingweston would not be very happy with me for such disloyalty. I signed my name in the book.

I then waited for a fortnight – the longest two weeks of my life – until Boss summoned me. He was in every way polite, but I was terrified. He asked me about my problems at Kingweston. I knew he knew that I was lying but I refused to make any complaints about anyone. Boss was persuasive but I stuck to my story. He then produced a bunch of my past reports and said that in one respect they did not make very happy reading – namely, that I was always up against authority. I think "bolshy" was the word he used. He asked me how I thought a school could function if the pupils did not relinquish some of their independence. He then asked me what I wanted to do with my life and I said that I wanted to be a "tax accountant".

There was a deathly hush for what seemed to me to be five minutes. I had no idea what was going through his mind, but I was a complete bag of nerves. Finally he looked up and said that he thought that I was well qualified to be a "tax accountant" because a good "tax accountant" is up against authority all the time. The only problem he could see was what he was going to do with me for the next two years. He dismissed the possibility of joining another house, and finally suggested that I might like to go into "digs" in Glastonbury.

I jumped at the chance. Leaving his study, I could not believe that Boss, the Headmaster of Millfield, not only believed in me but trusted me sufficiently to allow me to live alone in digs. This moment changed my life. Boss was the man who enabled me to believe in myself.

Dan came to see me. He is quite a demanding boy, not surprisingly perhaps, given that both his parents are dead, poor fellow, and he has been drifting for some time with dire results in his GCSEs. I have allowed him back on compassionate grounds but the term has not started well. He's a tough guy, a good rugby player, and so what he had to say really shook me. "I spoke with my mother last night. I often have conversations with her when I need help. She's told me what to do. It's the best advice I've ever had. I'm going to take three A levels and become a really positive pupil. You'll see." The conversation, he told me, was held through a medium. He seemed so sure that he can make it work this time, so obviously I gave him a final chance.

ROBERT CLARK (1960 – 1965)

In 1963 the South African Nuffield Schools Cricket team toured England. This was essentially the equivalent of the South African under 19 team of today. Their fixture list did not include any fixtures against schools but Boss managed to secure a fixture for R.J.O.Meyer's XI. This team consisted of nine members of the school first XI strengthened by Harold Gimblett of Somerset and England who captained the team and Roy Gilchrist, the West Indian fast bowler.

About a week before the match, Boss posted the team on his notice board. I was delighted to see that I had been selected but immediately realised that I was supposed to be taking Religious Knowledge 'O' level on the day of the match. I immediately rang the bell on his study door and the traffic light system that he operated indicated that I should go in. I explained about the clash between the match and the exam. He immediately said, "Oh never mind. Play in the match it will do you far more good."

R.J.O.M's XI batted first and I opened the batting with Harold Gimblett. I was foolish enough to get out before lunch, only to find Boss waiting on the boundary as I walked off. "That was careless Robert. Now you can go and sit your exam and if necessary the twelfth man can field until you get back."

In Boss's day if you wanted to take one of the girls to the Maxim cinema it was necessary to secure Boss's permission first. This entailed going to see him at break time usually on Thursday or Friday.

On one occasion when I went to ask for permission, he said that it would be OK but would I mind coming back and asking him again in about twenty minutes. Apparently he had some prospective parents coming to see him and he wanted to show them how things were done at Millfield in order to reassure them that their daughter would be OK.

After kicking my heels for twenty minutes I returned to his study to find that he was interviewing the parents. 'Yes Robert, what can I do for you?' Please can I have permission to take Miss X to the cinema on Saturday?' 'Of course you can'. He gave me a knowing smile and started to explain what was happening to the rather surprised parents.

TIMOTHY FOK (1960 – 1965)

I had just entered adolescence when I crossed the threshold at Millfield, then reported to be among the most expensive private academies, and saw the Old Rectory which looked as if the vicar had left it just a few days before – which, in fact, he had. For some reason, this did not seem to augur well for my time there. My housemaster was a fierce "Bonnie" Scot, partial to kilt and to the skirl of fifes and bagpipes as well as to iron discipline of the highlander persuasion. He was perhaps convinced that lowlanders like us were irredeemably soft and therefore had to be whipped into a semblance of shape. His spartan rigour certainly helped us, not so much in toning our bodies and toughening our minds as in deepening our appreciation of the periodic breaks from this treadmill.

The most dreaded and excruciating of our weekend pursuits was the eight-mile each way bicycle ride over the wind-scraped levels which was our version of the Tour de France. Its objective was the Black Cat cafe. Part of this grind was uphill which tested lungs and will power to the full. With the monotony of school momentarily broken, we narrowed the divide between town and gown while tasting a bit of the life outside school which our headmaster had turned into a barracks. On reflection, even the desolation of the landscape seems now a bit romantic, but then when one is young, hardships have a certain mystical appeal that one can always explain away later as a process of growing up.

Back then, when rock and roll was forbidden and thus delectable, a Chinese lad like myself did not travel very much. The journey from Hong Kong to England was an odyssey. To be plunged into another milieu, another culture, was traumatic. My home city just seemed so far away. Having been wrested from my family, I had to find a replacement for it and thus Millfield became its substitute. I had great expectations, some of which were eventually dashed against the cliff face of conformity to life in a group. If anyone of us had been pampered in his previous life, such pampering did not last long. The gates of school slammed shut on the privileges into which most of us had been born.

Millfield was already renowned then for its sports, which seemed appropriate, as it started as a finishing school for Indian princes. Ours was the only school in the country to boast a polo team and we employed a fearsome former cavalry Captain, as the master in charge. This sport appeared to me to be cloaked in palatial splendour juxtaposed with the mossy grimness and decay of the stables, but images and first impressions can be deceptive.

Polo turned out to be less glamourous and rather more time consuming than I had expected for we were put to use as ostlers in the "Tack Room". In other words, we were there as servants to the horses, whose interests were certainly closer to the Captain's heart than ours were. Our master was merciless but that too was explained away as a part of our education which seemed primarily to comprise a series of degradations. Perhaps, though, my labours in the stables were not entirely in vain, for since then Hong Kong has been awarded the staging of the 2008 Olympics and Paralympics equestrian events, thus tapping a bit into my "expertise" as a groom. I am even tempted to get back into the saddle again myself, for as my friends never stop telling me, one never forgets how to ride a bike or a horse.

Am I a better man for having endured Millfield, of which I cherish fond memories if only because it was an integral aspect of my life? The only answer I can muster is what Chou En-lai is supposed to have said to a reporter when asked his verdict on the value of the French Revolution: "After only 200 years, it is surely far too early to judge."

JOHN DAVIES ESQ

I will never forget my interview for a teaching position at the school. Having met several tutors, all of whom had delivered their reports to the Headmaster, I waited for quite some time outside his office. When the door finally opened, it was not to admit me. Boss greeted me warmly and then, without a word of explanation, led me over to his Hillman estate car. This was parked in the garage in the yard opposite Millfield House, and it was while we made our way round there that my interview began. Boss interviewed me en route to his bank in Street. There I waited outside in the car for 10 minutes while he withdrew money. He interviewed me as we drove round to the betting shop, outside which I waited in the car for 20 more minutes while he placed his bets. We then returned to his office to complete the interview. It was unconventional to say the least. But I was lucky enough to be offered the job, a moment which changed my life for ever.

I worked at Millfield throughout the Atkinson years and I got to know him well. Colin often said, "I'm not always right...but I'm never wrong," and indeed, he had this message framed on his desk. This absolutely categorises his positive leadership and the confidence he had in himself. It was the rock from which he directed Millfield for 20 years.

Nothing illustrates his gritty approach to life better than an incident in August 1969, near Valons Pont D'Arc in the warm, clear waters of the Ardeche in Southern France, when he and I joined one of Tony Chadburn's large C.C.F. canoeing expeditions. Other tutors on that trip included Bill Marshall, Peter Mabey, Syd Hill and Mike

Cole. As part of his routine, every evening Colin read most conscientiously in his tent "Teach Yourself Accountancy", for he wanted to learn enough to understand the school's finances. However, in general, he mixed well with everyone, helping to soften his rather fierce public persona.

Colin and I were new to canoeing and, truth be told, we were not terribly good at it. We were instructed that, if, or in all probability *when* we capsized, we were to extricate ourselves from our canoes which were to be towed to the bank to be emptied before resuming our descent. During the initial training phase, Colin managed to fall out in calm, limpid water that should not have caused him any difficulty at all. He was deeply embarrassed and, because we were some way from the bank, he decided to clamber back into the canoe in mid-stream, a most difficult operation even for veteran canoists. Half a dozen of our other canoes quickly surrounded him, everyone enjoying the spectacle of the Headmaster, literally and metaphorically out of his depth, in what became an epic man-versus-canoe encounter. He must have tried 15 or 20 times to get back into that canoe, never quite succeeding but succeeding in scraping himself badly, swallowing a lot of water and, ultimately, because of his strenuous efforts, gasping for air. He may have been about to surrender when fortunately perhaps, the canoe broke clean in half and that was the end of it. Colin declared it a 50/50 result. He never liked to lose. At anything.

SULTAN GHALIB AL QU'AITI (1962 – 1966)

I was taken for my interview at Millfield by Mrs Swingler, the wife of my prep school's Headmaster and an old acquaintance of the Boss. No sooner had I entered the study than Boss, after a quick look to size me up, while speaking to his old friend, fired his first question at me. "Does your father like the British?" I was to discover later on that this question may have had a lot to do with the fate of an OM parent, Nuri Pasha of Iraq, a few years earlier.
He then decided to take Mrs. Swingler and me for a walk around the grounds. He asked me if I liked any games. I answered that I enjoyed cricket and football, so I was rather surprised when he called over the tennis instructor and told him to find out if I was any good at tennis,

while he walked around exchanging conversation with Mrs Swingler. I am sure that if it had not been for Mrs Swingler's intimate relations with Boss, I would not have been given a place.

Unfortunately, I did not blossom as a tennis player at all.

I was cheered to hear today that the Wally of Swot, in Pakistan, had been in touch about his dyslexic son's possible entry. There is unseemly speculation in the Admissions office as to what the son of a Wally could be called, especially one from Swot. This was only interrupted by the arrival of the next British Ambassador to a Middle Eastern fiefdom, who, it turned out, had only yesterday kissed hands with the Queen on his appointment. She had asked him what he thought of the Arab peoples with whom he has previously worked. His reply was no doubt diplomatic, but he had apparently added that he thought that they were often prone to make quick, unexpected decisions. "Just like my daughters-in-law! Those two!" she had replied with conviction.

DAVID DUGGAN (1963 – 1966)

I first met Boss in the summer of 1963 as a ten year old school boy, accompanied by my mother, sitting in his study hoping to be accepted into Edgarley House. We hoped to get a sports scholarship as I was seriously dyslexic and virtually illiterate. In the middle of our chat, without warning, Boss suddenly flicked an orange across the room at me. Fortunately, by some reflex action, I caught it left handed. Boss offered my mother a place for me on the spot.

PETER KINNISTON (1962 – 1966)

The annual Sports Day saw me and a few other boys allocated to the side show attractions that were set up every year to entertain the boys and parents alike. I was working on the one which involves putting your head through the cut out faces of those large photo boards you get at seaside resorts with people in old fashioned bathing suits. The idea was for punters to pay for 3 sponges which they then soaked in buckets of water before taking aim at us.

I had been enjoying a good, dry session with very few good shots among boys or parents. Then to my surprise I saw Stanley Baker, whose son was a friend, pay his money and line up his sponges. It was just after the release of Zulu so I was quite honoured that he was willing to have a go. I should have guessed he would be a fair shot so it was no surprise that on his second throw I received a direct hit in the face which soaked me thoroughly. Sports Days were always good fun....

Mencap Day, surely the best day of the year. We have over a thousand visitors this year from Gateway clubs all over the South West. They have so much to teach us when it comes to tenacity, determination and sheer good humour. When I asked one of our boys what he had appreciated most about the day, he was moved to tears. Some of the girls found themselves the objects of unusually overt affection from our guests, but they seemed to handle this with extraordinary tact and restraint. I was immensely proud of them all. Others were overwhelmed by the gratitude they received. The best thing, as always, is watching our average see-how-cool-I-am 4th Formers demonstrating endless patience and affectionate care for the visitors in their charge. One came rushing up on the pitch-and-put with more enthusiasm than I think I'd ever seen in him; "My man Bill's just got a hole in one." Inside every young person there is a streak of pure gold..

PETER EISNER (1960 – 1967)

By the time I was 10 years of age my parents must have been in a desperate state about my lack of educational development, as I could neither read nor write. Even with this problem in mind, somehow my parents persuaded Jack Meyer to meet me. I was in a pretty sad way, because my failure was extremely humiliating and confusing for me. So you can imagine the state of naked fear that overwhelmed me when I was told that I was to be interviewed by the great Headmaster of Millfield.

The scene that greeted us as we entered Boss' study will be no surprise to those who knew him. He served us tea in a very relaxed way amongst the towers of magazines everywhere and I think that we were all electrified by his commanding manner. I knew immediately that this was a different kind of adult, one that wasn't going to scream at me for not understanding things that others found simple but which I found hard. Nevertheless, it was with great trepidation that I remained alone with him for my interview when my parents were asked to leave.

He talked to me in a way that made me feel respected and I quickly warmed to the way he probed my problems over issues like fractions and spelling which had become dreaded topics for me. Somehow or other, in a matter of minutes he taught me all I needed to know about both. In other words, in less than half an hour he had advanced my educational standard, on a narrow front from that of a seven year old to that of a normal ten year old. We then went on to more fun things like bouncing a ball around and he quickly discovered that I was pretty uncoordinated in my movements. Unknown to me, he had determined that it was from my general lack of coordination and smooth movement that all my problems sprang. The school psychologist later concluded that I was dyslexic.

My parents were called back in. He announced that he had the necessary material to work with and that provided I could (a) get into my prep school's 1st Rugby team, (b) bounce a ball off the wall 50 times with each hand and catch it with the other and (c) do 50 skips, he would accept me into his school. I was a pretty ecstatic child going home from that interview, as a vale of never ending depression and defeatism had been lifted from me. I can honestly say that I have always been proud and grateful to have been part of Millfield. I just loved Boss' stimulating, eccentric and exceptionally intelligent approach to leadership and education. Who else would have the courage to set such bizarre tests for a candidate as those that he set for me? The world is a much poorer place without him.

JUDY NORMAN (1967)

I spent five miserable years at a well known girls' school. I didn't know who I was or what was going on. I was bottom of every class. I had no self confidence at all.

In desperation my parents sent me to Millfield for O level retakes.

'What do you like doing?' they asked. "Music and theatre," I replied.

So they put me on the stage.

I passed my O levels, and am still a professional working actress.

Millfield changed my life. Brilliant.

The French play is "Un ami imprévu" which turns out to be a version of the Mousetrap. At the curtain call an enthusiastic audience reserves its biggest round of applause for Ed Finlay, killed in his wheelchair early on before being required to utter a single word.

CHRISTOPHER RAPHAEL (1965 – 1967)

I was once told that 'School is the best time of your life'. To this day, this remains absolutely true for me. I was at Kingweston with Tom Wilkinson as my Housemaster – he was the greatest. My friends there were really such a terrific mix of people from every intellectual and social background you can imagine. On one occasion, my father had a horse running at Sandown and I went to Boss to try to get permission to attend the race. We could always tell when he was in a good mood; when the previous person came out of his study holding an apple we could be pretty sure that our request would be approved. Sure enough Boss not only gave me four days off but also asked me to place a bet on my father's horse.

Boss, Joyce and their daughters at his investiture.

BARRY HOBSON "A HISTORY OF MILLFIELD"

The Millfield Project Appeal, which resulted in 1966 and 1967 in the building of A and B Blocks, was an immensely ambitious venture. Earl Attlee, K.G., P.C., O.M endorsed the Appeal in the following words; "I have marvelled for some time at the way in which you have created a public school at Millfield and at your numerous successes. I send you my best wishes for what seems to me to be an educational development of great importance." For a fairly recently retired Labour Party Prime Minister to support the ambitious plans of a lifelong Conservative Party member must have been manna indeed.

There were many events designed to try to raise the funds required, among them a Gala Opening in London of the film "The Charge of the Light Brigade". There were high hopes that the Duchess of Gloucester might be persuaded to attend, but when this fell through it was suggested that the next best substitutes would be Elizabeth Taylor and Richard Burton. They agreed to be the Guests of Honour, as her two sons, Michael and Christopher Wilding, were enjoying, or possibly enduring, life at Kingweston and Edgarley respectively.

Unfortunately, once it became clear that there was to be no Royal presence, Boss seems to have lost interest in this event, which took place in April 1968 at the Odeon Leicester Square. Burton's first enquiry on arriving at the cinema was to know where the Headmaster was. He was nowhere to be found. Joyce calmed things down somewhat, but then there was a disastrous mix-up over the seating, for Elizabeth and Richard had been placed some distance apart. Thus as the film began, they walked out.

In the ensuing twelve months there was no direct communication between the Burtons and the school, even though the elder boy's tutors were constantly complaining about his lack of effort, and so it was no great surprise to Boss when it was announced in the press that Michael and Christopher were being withdrawn.

There is a vituperative letter from Mrs. X. following my insistence that fees in lieu of notice will be charged, in the wake of her inexplicable withdrawal of her son without reference to any one here at all. She immediately threatens legal action. Her son's Housemaster, Peter Mills, a man of great experience and sagacity, not easily stirred to anger and whose sense of humour almost never deserts him, writes to me at the end of an exasperated letter reporting on the withdrawal, "If Lady Macbeth has sons, send them all to me, but please, no more sons from Mrs. X."

JARRAR AQHA-JAFFAR (1964 – 1968)

Before 1965, boys were only allowed to wear lace-up shoes, but in that year, as I remember, this rule was changed in a characteristically pragmatic way. For a while, there had been considerable pressure to revise the dress code to allow us to wear 'Chelsea Boots' or slip-ons – those things with elasticated sides. This had been resisted by Boss on the spurious grounds that they could easily be dislodged from the feet of the wearer.

Ultimately, the Head Boy managed to convince Boss that if it could be proved that these boots would stay on in any circumstances that Boss could devise, we would be allowed to wear them. Now the question was to agree a 'scientific' experiment that would provide such incontrovertible evidence.

So it was that one games afternoon, in late winter, the whole school – all 800 of us -assembled by a muddy field next to the main buildings, to witness Boss' experiment.

The challenge was that if the Head Boy could run across the field and back without the boots being sucked off by the cloying mud, Boss would amend the dress code. So the Head Boy pulled on a pair of these Chelsea Boots and, cheered on by the rest of us, staggered across the field and back. The boots stayed on, the dress code was revised and we were all wearing them in no time.

If only rules could always be changed so simply!

MICHAEL CHARLTON-WEEDY, (1963-1968)

I had been practising chipping onto the green located in front of the main house, and was walking round towards the drive, when I encountered Boss with two prospective parents. Pleased that I had been practising hard, and having extolled the virtues of what was then a formidable golf team, Boss invited me to demonstrate my skills. However, in order to show how Millfield prepared its pupils for the rigours of competition and real life, I was required not only to chip off the tarmac (rather than grass) on to the circular patch of lawn at the rear of the house, but also to place a sequence of three shots within two feet of the half crown Boss had placed some 20 feet away in order to win it as a prize. One ball finished a couple of inches outside the distance. He rightly kept the half crown.

All my many memories of those five years are unreservedly happy.

Two Thai brothers have given up golf already. Why? "Because it's too tiring, sir." "But you've played plenty of golf before." "Yes sir, but only with a buggy or a caddy. Here you have to walk and carry your clubs at the same time all by yourself."

ROGER WHYTE ESQ

One day in the late 1960's when I was head of the Engineering Drawing department, I arranged a sixth form visit to the Bristol Aeroplane Company Technical College at Filton, where a friend was principal lecturer. As part of the day's outing we were to tour the iconic Concorde airliner.

As we were about to board the minibus, I was approached by a pupil – not one of my class – who was very eager to join our party. As he appeared to have the necessary permissions from his group tutor, I accepted him and off we set. He was a Saudi, name of Binladen, by the way.

At one point during the day my friend mentioned to me that one lad was showing a special interest in some BA-111 executive jets standing on the tarmac. Apparently he'd said that he wanted to buy one. "Take no notice," I said. "Just puerile mickey-taking." The trip passed off well and I assumed that was the end of the matter.

But no, not quite. My friend called me a week or two later. "You know that lad who was talking about buying a BA-111 jet? Well, he wasn't joking. He's just ordered one. And paid for it." It turned out that his father was the boss of Saudi Airlines and thus parental approval had been no problem. Unfortunately Salim Mohammed Binladen was killed a few years later in a flying accident in America.

A couple from India came to see me to register their gratitude for the successful conclusion of their son's

first week with us. They are delightful people who own
an airline, "the only private one flying out of Delhi",
hospitals, schools and commercial outlets and whose
base is a town bearing their name. They educate 3000
children free of charge. Karam, who is in Orchards
house, has told them with some pride that he has just
made himself a cheese sandwich and poured himself a
Coke – the first things he has ever had to do for himself.
There are, it appears, 30 servants at home. There are
none, of course, in Orchards

Every year the various sections of the CCF were required to under-take "training" and this particular year the Naval Section found itself aboard a 45 ton Motor Fishing Vessel moored at Tarbert, a pleasant fishing village on the Mull of Kintyre. The MFV was loaned to us by the Royal Fleet Auxiliary. There were a dozen Millfield pupils aboard, along with a crew comprising a skipper and an engineer, who kept their heads well down. My instructions, as officer-in-charge, were to go anywhere we liked as long as we did not go beyond Ailsa Craig, and to radio in at 0800 each morning to say where we were.

One morning we were on passage for Campbelltown, a cadet at the wheel, and others plotting courses, taking bearings and so forth, whilst the watch below was preparing lunch under the direction of the senior boy, John Grace. This happy and industrious scene was sudden-ly disturbed by a shrill call on the radio from the office of the Commander-in-Chief Clyde. "Lieutenant Whyte required urgently to make for the nearest landfall and to contact Millfield school."

Lochranza is a tiny hamlet on the north-east corner of the Isle of Arran, a delightful spot offering an anchorage, but with no pier alongside which we could have moored. So we had to anchor off and it took much hauling and lifting to get the rowing boat launched so that I could get ashore. Somewhat anxiously I rowed across to the little jetty, made fast and sought out the lonely tele-phone box to make the vital call.

Ruth Hillard used to run the school's telephone exchange and with the world at her fingertips she could never resist a challenge. She knew I was somewhere away with the Royal Naval section, so who better to contact than the Admiralty in Whitehall. There, officers of various ranks entered into the spirit of the search, culminating eventually at the Clyde Naval HQ at Gourock and the relay of the vital message. This read, "Mr Hammond (Housemaster of Kernick) wants Roger Whyte to find out from John Grace if he has permission to escort Miss X (one of his charges) to the end of term dance."

The thought that the entire North Atlantic fleet may for some time have been anxious about the outcome of this disturbs me somewhat, but I imagine the Admiral i/c Clyde and all those nuclear submarines will have been pleased by the efficiency of their communications systems.

ANDREW FIELDING (1963 – 1968)

Like any one else of our age, we enjoyed the fashions of the day while we were at school, and so the draconian rules, which applied to the way in which we wore our clothes, were generally respected. For example, our pockets were sewn up if we were seen with both hands in them. Our trouser bottoms were measured to be exactly 16 inches wide and we had a hair cut every fortnight.

When I became a prefect, I had to hand out sticky buns in break armed with a large wooden spoon to whack anyone who tried to grab one out of turn. Mrs Meyer was always behind us in the kitchen window watching to make sure that the rules were properly observed.

WILLIAM FLYNN (1964 – 1969)

I attended an interview with Boss when my parents applied for entry. My mother asked him if he would like to see a report on me from my previous Headmaster. Boss replied with some asperity, "No. I would rather see a report on his previous Headmaster."

Discipline was quite harsh in the early '60s. One evening, we were busy in our Common Room watching our television using a metal coat hanger as an arial! The head boy and his deputy walked in. Turning the lights on, they discovered a Junior smoking a cigarette behind the couch. We had all been too engaged in smoking the latest in aromatic pipe tobaccos, which way back then we were permitted to do, to have noticed the smell of a cigarette, so we had no idea that he was bending the rules. Swift retribution followed, and in my last term at Millfield I, as Head of the Common Room, was forbidden to attend the Leavers dance. I was heart broken at the time, and come to think about it I'm still fairly browned off now. Ah well, Oh for the old days, eh!

Amanda flouts our dress code persistently and has started to remonstrate with tutors who patiently, or nowadays not so patiently, try to correct her. Her defiance means that she really cannot now return to the sixth form next year. When I put this to her, reminding her of the long string of examples of tiresome and uncooperative behaviour which have brought us to this point, she is outraged and accuses me bitterly of being petty minded. Perhaps she is right, but her refusal to meet us even half way, and her current defiance of colleagues leave me no alternative. But I am sorry she will be going all the same.

BRYANT FELL ESQ

Mike Mumford was one of the best swimmers in the school, and one day, on a whim, I suggested that he might like to take up the Tetrathlon. This event comprises not just swimming, of course, but also running, shooting and riding. Mike was enthusiastic but pointed out that he had never been on a horse before. Indeed, he said he could only distinguish one end of a horse from the other with difficulty. I managed to get him some ad hoc riding lessons and later that year, he won the inter-schools championships.

This fired us both up to the point where I thought he needed a new challenge. The British Junior Pentathlon championships were coming up shortly, so I entered him for these. But then of course he had to become a fencer as well. Being Millfield, it was not too difficult to fix him up with some fencing lessons in the Salle and in due course we sent him off to do battle, more in hope than in expectation. In truth, I just hoped he'd get some good experience and enjoy himself.

The night of the championships, the phone rang. It was Mike. "Well, how did you get on?" "Sir, I won it. I was really lucky. I drew a very good horse and all I had to do was hang on to him and not fall off."

Ten years later, Mike took part in the Los Angeles Olympics.

A bitterly estranged couple came in, not to talk about their poor daughter, but about her horse. Father says we must resist any move by his ex-wife to remove the horse. Mother, who is hell-bent on doing exactly that, takes an altogether more dramatic line and says the father "has trained our daughter to beat me up, which she did last week." I'm inclined to adopt a Solomon-like stance over this and offer two equine legs each – split the difference and be done.

SIMON LUXMORE (1966 – 1969)

The interview process in my case was unusual. Like Boss, I was the son of a clergyman. When I went for interview, the condition set for me attending was that my dear late father should preach a sermon at the annual 'Parade Service', which of course he duly did at the church in Glastonbury! On the same note, the deal with Boss was that I could retain my scholarship if I maintained my place in the Ist XV. I did so for three years.

The status of the 1st XV was only equalled by the 'Heads of House' in those days. Only they could walk on the main drive – not even school prefects were allowed this honour and had to take the long muddy route via the old Riding school. School prefects used to ride on bikes round the Nissen huts 'tolling' bells to signify the end of lessons.

At Millfield House, during mid morning break, currant buns were collected individually. A school prefect marshalled events armed with a large wooden spoon. The skilled ran the gauntlet and took two before suffering a fractured finger, or achieved the same without risk if you were favoured. The bad boys had a fractured finger even before they could touch the first bun!

I remember Boss's favourite duck being impaled with an arrow through its head on the front lawn. I also remember two years of French with Dick Snelling, never attending a lesson, and still receiving an end of term report on all six occasions.

Millfield to me was the most wonderful place imaginable. It was however not for the faint hearted. You had to stand on your own two feet. You mixed with Brunei students who used to pay their inflated fees in cash, Princes, the offspring of the stars, and the wonderful kids of 'ordinary' folk as well. I find going back very hard indeed because of the memories it evokes. But I loved it.

Today saw the immensely saddening business of having to say goodbye to a poor, bereft sixth former, new to us this term, who does not enjoy life here. He had been compelled to return after the half term holiday by his father, whose chauffeur had forced him physically into the car, locked the doors, driven him to Street and man-handled him into his house. The boy has been trauma-tised by this ghastly experience and refuses now to lie in his bed, insisting he will not sleep until he is sent home. This is the reverse of the case last year when an Indian boy climbed into his bed on the first day and refused to leave it until collected by his long-suffering mother, her-self the headmistress of a very well respected school near Delhi. How I bled for her then, but now, in this new case, my sympathies are entirely with the boy.

A little 13 year old boy refuses to join his house, Orchards. To convince his father of the depth of his conviction on this issue, he lies down in front of his father's car outside the house and refuses to budge. Wisely his father decides to take him home again and try a different persuasive tack with him. I think he had taken the hint that his son meant business when earlier in the day at home the boy had let down the car tyres.

DR HANNAH MORTIMER
(NEE ROBINSON; 1967 –1969)

Pam Warner, who was Head of Girls, saw me one break and told me to take a slip of paper to Boss and to wait while he read it.

In I went, peering around the piles of paper to see where Boss actually was. He read the slip of paper. "Oh, so you are Hannah Robinson. Right. I want you to be my Head of YLC. Will you accept?" He had not even known me.

This meant that the next year was a very busy one for me. At meal times, I sat between Mrs M. and the Crown Prince of Thailand, while Boss held court at the other end of the long table. It was the fashion at the time to wear wigs and I had one with very long hair. Boss insisted on calling me "Heather" when I had it on and "Hannah" when I didn't. I often wondered at the time whether he knew, but of course he did!

Stuart Creed and I often had to escort him on special occasions. When it was our turn to show important visitors around the school, he would always reverse our status, telling the VIPs to remember *our* names very carefully, because one day *we* would be very famous.

He was kind to me during the exams and arranged for me to have the key to one of the huts where I could work at 5 am in order to be able to do all my other duties during the school day. He insisted I apply for Somerville ("all my head girls go there") so I stayed on for the Oxbridge term and was Colin Atkinson's first head girl, along with Mike Irving as head boy.

I have a card from Jo Beadsworth, a born communicator though not a particularly gifted linguist, who used to be in my German set a couple of years ago. "Dear Sir, you always said that if my German class was dropped into Germany by parachute, I'd be the one who would survive the longest. Well now I feel I have been dropped into Hungary, though my Hungarian is much worse than my German. The fencing here is much tougher than in the UK but I hope to surprise them before I leave. Lots of love from Jo. P.S. I hope you can use this much paprika." She was always a spicy girl, so I was not entirely surprised that she had enclosed enough paprika to last me a lifetime. She's now in the GB fencing squad, it seems.

SUE PATERSON (1968 – 1969)

I won a scholarship for cheek. As a fifteen year old school girl, I wrote to Boss saying that I wanted to go to Millfield, then the most expensive school in the country, but that my parents would not pay any more for me than they would at Sherborne School for Girls, so I would need a scholarship. He replied to my parents – "because that is the way these things are done" – and invited me to visit the school. At my interview, my mother said that I lived in a dream world. Boss said that he would make sure that I stayed there as long as I wanted, and offered me on the spot a scholarship, reducing the fees by over half, to exactly the same amount as they were paying at Sherborne.

Political correctness had not been invented in those days. Three glaring examples of this were the school's attitude towards girls, prefects, and the inclusion of Asian pupils. Girls were all considered members of the Young Ladies Club (YLC). We were always allowed to go straight to the front of queues, a move which hardly endeared us to the boys, though since we were such a small minority, this fortunately did not prove fatal to relationships which we enjoyed with boys individually! Girl prefects could give defaulters to boys, but not the other way round. Skirts had to be no shorter than 6" from the ground when kneeling. This height was carefully measured initially but quickly became observed much more in the breach as time went on.

Prefects were allowed to smoke cigarettes, and all boys over 16 – but not, in fact, girls – could smoke a pipe. Prefects could walk down the drive, while others for some quaint reason had to walk down the path alongside it. Prefects could not beat other boys (only Boss could do this) but did sometimes impose punishments like having to run around the field in underpants, for which the prefects themselves were disciplined. Boss often seemed to make prefects of boys who had been expelled from their previous schools. He must have believed in the art of making gamekeepers out of poachers, but he also had a soft spot for the rebel in us all.

But the wierdest memory I have is of the way in which, on arrival, Chinese pupils were "named". When they arrived without a European name, there was a "naming session" in the library where the wretched new boy or girl sat in the middle while other pupils called out suggestions for names until eventually one was chosen. It's absolutely unbelievable now! Some of them ended up with very odd names, like Norman.

> *Xiao Baoquiang, one of the three new Beijing scholars, was playing on the golf course today and struck a good shot. His Tutor, who was passing, congratulated him and suggested that he had obviously played before. "Yes, I have," said Xiao. "Yesterday." Bow, as the boys call him, confused his Tutor with his Housemaster in the house last night, and immediately apologised. "All you westerners look alike to me, I'm afraid."*
>
> *Huong-Joon, a Korean boy, joined us two years ago with almost no English. Only his determination, a fine sense of humour and the support of his teachers have seen him through, but that's a pretty powerful combination, of course. Yesterday, he suffered a torsion of the testicle and was taken to hospital by Dick Boustead, his Housemaster. A woman doctor examined him, to his intense embarrassment. "Does it always hang like this?" she asked him. Fixing the ceiling stoically, Huong -Joon replied, "Don't know. I never watch it."*
>
> *Rachel, who has just joined us from Taiwan, still has trouble with her genders and pronouns. Apparently she has told her Tutor group, "I'm not sleeping well. My roommate, he keep me awake all night."*

PHILIPPA FLYNN, (1968 – 1970) EDGARLEY

During my time at Edgarley, I lived in "Brants" Farmhouse, a mixed boarding house. Normally, the dividing door between the girls' and the boys' dormitories was kept locked but one evening we found it open. We immediately decided it would be amusing to raid the boys and thump them with our pillows.

Accordingly, when Mrs. Brant turned out our lights that night we all pretended to settle down and eagerly awaited the time when we assumed she would be asleep. When we judged the moment to be ripe, we gathered our pillows and prepared to invade. We were certain we were very quiet, but in fact we must have sounded like a herd of elephants. However, we reached the boys' dormitories undetected and were enthusiastically bashing them over the heads with our pillows when, to our amazement, Mrs. Brant suddenly appeared. Disaster!

Only four of us admitted to our misdemeanour and we were marched downstairs to receive our punishment. Mrs. Brant

1971 The Kitchen Gardens.

produced her cane, told us to bend over an armchair and we were given "three of the best" before being ordered back up to bed. It was amazing just how much warmth emanated from our backsides that night, and indeed I still have a warm glow when I recall the event.

Needless to say, we never found that door open again.

Four times a week, prospective parents visit me in small groups to grill me on Millfield and my views on everything from compulsory games to bulimia. Today, however, there was a variation on the theme, which I enjoyed. "Headmaster, what is your stance on sex?" In my reply, I hope I succeeded in giving satisfaction.

Just two days into the new term and already we have a new variant on sexual obsession. The parents of a 14 year old boy are concerned, with good reason, that the mother of one of his contemporaries has developed a thoroughly unhealthy infatuation for him, writing to him often twice a day in the most inappropriate terms. I am shown some of her letters by way of illustration of what is going on. I assure them that we will try to protect their son, and indeed later talk on the phone to the mother concerned, who of course expresses surprise at my anxiety. I cannot offer guarantees that he will never again receive expressions of her devotion. Only a court injunction can achieve that.

TRYPHEYNA McSHANE (1966 – 1970)

I was being interviewed to see if Boss would accept me. He said, "I can tell that you are wild, and I am going to tame you like a Tiger." Maybe I was wild, but Boss was always my greatest advocate during my time at Millfield. I have very fond memories of him. It meant a lot to me to know he considered me valuable, even though I didn't fit into a particular mould. Boss was the first person to understand that what I was struggling with was in fact dyslexia. I was given very effective training on how to deal with it. I remember sitting in class with Liz Taylor's son, Michael Wilding, who also struggled with academic learning due to dyslexia, and who became a friend. We had a great time together. Boss had managed to find a way to tame the tiger within us both without destroying our spirit , even though we were a little wild.

A girl is defaulted for being improperly dressed. She's very pretty, knows it and, as a fully signed up 15 year old, is not above trying to exploit her looks with anyone who might prove susceptible. This time, however, she resorts to a letter to her Housemaster which he finds on his desk at the end of break.

"Dear Mr Warne,
I went to the staff room and waited for ages but sadly – obviously – our paths did not cross. Anyway, I have to go to my lesson now. What I wanted to tell you was that my shirt was in my bag. It was there because a fourth year flicked poster paint at me in first period. As it is Janice's shirt, I had to try to wash it out immediately. I've even left the shirt for you here to see it's the truth, risking being defaulted by all the other teachers for being late, but I suppose I have no choice otherwise you may not believe me. Kate.
P.S. Mr Harper was there too so you could ask him.
P.P.S. As you can see it's unwearable."

In the genre of excuse concoction, this is clearly worth a Nobel Prize. It is so good that we have no difficulty in agreeing not to default her at all.

GEORGE STAMBOULIEH (1964 – 1970)

When I came to Millfield, I was a scrawny kid. When the Boss saw me, he told me that I would have to toughen up and get involved in sports. I remember that I hated sports back then. I chose to do archery, but he told me that I could not do that because I would not be able to pull a bow back, because my arms were so small. He suggested that if I chose archery, I would also have to do proper exercises to build up my strength. I reluctantly agreed, but my ego was sorely bruised. I decided to go all out to train to prove him wrong. I trained till I was blue in the face, hour after hour, day after day. Eventually I realized that Boss' challenge had really worked, for I went on to become the Captain of the Archery team, and the SW England junior champion. I have Boss to thank for this.

THE
ATKINSON YEARS
1970 – 1986

Colin Atkinson, CBE.

COLIN

As early as 1956 Boss had been casting his eye around for his own successor, but it was not until 1968 that Colin Atkinson became Deputy Head and was introduced by Boss at Open Day as his successor from 1971.

The early part of that year was an uneasy period for everyone, especially for the pupils, for many of whom Boss was their idol. Rumour was rife. Boss still occupied the Study, and eventually the Chalet was adapted to house him, as the Warden, and his Secretary, Amothe Sankey. Many Old Millfieldians found the position intolerable at this time and cut their ties with the school. School numbers faltered slightly, but, by 1973, were back to normal at 1250. Examination results continued to improve, as did those in all sorts of sports, while a greater emphasis, and larger percentage of the budget, was directed to improving art, music and drama.

Many changes came for the teaching staff, as Colin delegated authority as Boss never had. New appointments, such as Heads of Year, gave hope of advancement to tutors, and improved relationships with parents, who found it easier to discover exactly how hard their children were working. Colin also made changes to school life by banning the use of the cane, ending "fagging" and stopping all smoking of pipes and cigarettes. Naturally these moves were received in different ways by the pupils, but with great enthusiasm by their parents.

The physical appearance of the School changed dramatically over the next few years as the Nissen hut "Camp" disappeared and the Biology block, the AV Centre, Fencing Salle, Music Lodge, Jubilee Pitch, various boarding houses and most importantly the Dining Hall appeared.

In 1985 Colin was diagnosed as suffering from cancer of the colon. The operation was successful but the Governors decided that he should be relieved of some of his duties, created him Principal of Millfield School and promoted the Deputy, Brian Gaskell, as Headmaster in 1986.

ANDREW DAVEY (1961 – 1972)

My parents took over the Post Office in Butleigh and I went to the village school, where, at the age of seven I was taught in the morning, and in turn taught the younger children in the afternoon. Anyway, my parents thought it would be a good idea if I went to Millfield, so my father phoned the school and spoke to Boss, telling him he thought the school was right for me. Boss apparently liked my father's straight manner with him and said that he would meet us on the following Wednesday afternoon. My father replied, "We cannot make that, as our half day is on Saturday."

Boss told him that if he valued his shop more than his son's education, he would be in Butleigh – but if he valued his son's education more than his shop, he would be in Street. We ended up in Street.

My interview went roughly along these lines.

Boss. "I don't expect you to read the words on the mantlepiece, but what is the middle letter?" When I read it, he said, "Now hold up an imaginary telescope to your eye to see the ship". This I did. "Yes, you have a lazy eye, but we will soon cure that."

Just then Amothe Sankey, his personal assistant, appeared with the tea tray and dropped her handkerchief. I picked it up and returned it to her. I later discovered this was all part of the 'interview act'.

"Right", said Boss, "Let's go and feed the ducks." As my parents rose to come with us, he told them that he was interested in me, not them – their part was to pay the bill. Off we went, with a dustbin lid full of corn, feeding the birds as we went. When we returned, he told me to take two apples from the basket, and to sit in the car while he discussed money with my parents, but he assured me that although he would have the shirt off my father's back if he could, even if my parents could not afford a penny I would be given a music scholarship for Edgarley Hall and Millfield through to 'A' Levels. Why music, I never did discover, although in due course I did in fact learn the piano, organ and 'cello.

Boss later told me I had taken the place of a certain wealthy prince, who had arrived at the School in a helicopter a few days before, and whose father thought he could use the cricket pitch as a landing pad. His interview, it seemed, was somewhat short. Boss simply told him that if he did now know what a cricket square was for (and it was not for landing helicopters) he had no place for his son at Millfield.

I later learned from Boss of another interview with some extremely wealthy parents. Having agreed to take their daughter, the girl's father asked who would be in the same set as their progeny. The list was called for, and each name read out, together with the father's profession. They came to one boy, whose father was a local dustman. "Do you think it is right that my daughter should be educated in the same class as a dustman's son?" asked the father. Boss apparently picked up the telephone immediately, spoke to the boy's father, then handed the receiver to the girl's father, saying, "He doesn't seem to mind his son being in your daughter's class – perhaps you would like to have a word with him yourself."

The French mistress lived in Butleigh, and upon hearing I was to go to Edgarley, came into the Post Office, and told me that the last word I would ever hear from her in English was the word, 'More'. When questioned, she said simply, "Now you will have to learn French, and so I shall not speak to you in English any more." And from that moment onwards, she never did.

In those days, the Music Department was run by Peter F Fox. His daughter, Sarah, taught us music – sometimes, and sometimes other things, like how to cross our eyes at great speed – Millfield always had a knack of preparing you for any eventuality in life. The whole thing was housed in the Lodge. Some of us held our own keys for the front door, and it became more of a refuge than anything else, where we sat and drank coffee – mainly! I seem to recall PFF being hired to teach Geography, and when Boss discovered he could play the trumpet – among other instruments – he suggested he start a Music Department. That was where I discovered that clarinet players had to be able to smoke; it was a good way of testing for leaks in their instruments.

I take Stephanie Owen, Young Musician of the Year semi-finalist, Isla McRae, harpist, Kirsten Griffiths and Ali Oyston, violinists, to the Rib next to Wells Cathedral to play in Hilly Cansdale's hall in aid of Save the Children. They look dazzling in their evening dresses, play breathtakingly well and then charm the socks off everyone afterwards. I am quite unreasonably proud of them, having played no part in their triumph other than as their chauffeur. But I am aware that none of them has been practising for less than ten years. That is why they are so stunningly accomplished. That, plus raw talent, of course.

There was a nine hole chip and putt course in front of the House. On one occasion, I threw a ball down onto the first mat, took a very laid back swing – and got a hole in one! Boss immediately appeared, with a bottle of sherry in one hand and a bottle of whiskey in the other. "Davey," he said, "The sherry is yours – and if you can do it again, so is the whiskey." Not for one moment thinking I either could or would, I repeated the performance – exactly. As he gave me the scotch, he grinned and said, "And I'd like to be with you as you explain that away to your father."

A few months after I had left, I was invited to dinner with my girlfriend by Boss in the Chalet. We arrived at the appointed time, to find Boss about to leave. He said everything was about ready to be dished up, and would we please help ourselves. He apologised, saying that he had to go to Shepton Mallet prison to see an old boy who had been caught by the police for some crime or other, sentenced, sent down, escaped, and was now back inside. "I am sure he will enjoy your visit," said I. "No he won't," said Boss. "Getting caught once is one thing. Escaping is to be commended. But I am absolutely disgusted that a Millfield boy should get caught twice."

> *A new 14 year old has been caught drinking, and this on top of a smoking offence. I took him from another HMC school to give him a second chance. A second chance for what, I now ask myself. He is unrepentant, indeed, aggressive; real attitude. I take another close look at his reference. It is supportive but now I can spot an ambiguous sentence. "We have recommended Millfield because J. is more likely to prosper on the larger stage with you than in our much smaller school." When I call the Head to test out this comment, it translates as "He'd have been fired if he hadn't left. He was in trouble in and out of school. He had a very strong influence on others. I'm not surprised he's giving trouble." Thanks a lot! Now it's up to me to fire him, instead, but at a cost to teachers and pupils here that I much regret.*

CHRIS KING (1968 – 1972)

A couple of my friends, Chris Baillie and Nigel Clark, were passionate about the wild life they collected and stored in the Biology block. Amongst their collection were a python and two alligators. At one stage I was asked if I would mind taking them home for the holidays, but my unreasonable mother refused point blank. However, our wonderful Headmaster's wife, Joyce Meyer, was far more understanding. Whilst she was unable to help over this particular problem, she allowed us to use her fruit cage as a trap for live birds and voles, so at least the reptiles were well fed.

These same two also formed the core of a Long Distance Kayaking team which I was lucky enough to be invited to join to race in Spain. Unknown to most of the team, they caught a wide variety of wild life to bring home on the Minibus. Just as we were coming off the ferry and were about to confront British customs, they discovered that their snakes and lizards had escaped and were making a dash for freedom whilst hotly pursued by Chris and Nigel. As it turned out, the only bag examined by Customs was the one which had, until seconds earlier, contained the menagerie. Our leader, a Physics teacher by the name of Dave Owen, realising that the customs official was dangerously close to finding another package with yet more wild life, drew his attention to an overloaded vehicle alongside us, implying that it looked highly suspicious. The official obligingly headed off in hot pursuit, just as we spotted one heroic lizard leaping from our Minibus door. Nigel leapt after it with an attempted rugby tackle, landing painfully on the tarmac just out of sight of the retreating customs official, but alas in vain. The lizard or its descendants are hopefully now contented denizens of the Dover underworld.

A few of my friends were keen golfers and one day they gave me the opportunity to have a go on the nine hole course behind Millfield House. Never having played before, I was dressed in my usual day clothes. Unfortunately, Boss was showing some potential parents around when he stumbled across me and demanded to know why I was not correctly dressed for the game in hand. I offered a few feeble excuses but he interrupted and told me that if I were to get a hole in one, I need never bother to dress properly for the sport again. I teed up under the critical gaze of my small audience, probably closed my eyes and took a wild swipe. To my astonishment, the ball took off perfectly and landed on the green within six inches of the pin. As my best shot to date had landed in the middle of the Duck Pond, I was impressed. Sadly Boss did not share my delight. He remained impassive and glancing with barely disguised pity in my direction as he guided the parents away said, " Make sure you wear the appropriate clothing next time, King, and then you may at least maximise your potential."

SIMON MEREDITH (1967 – 1972)

I recollect the new boy experience of fagging. I forget the terminology but distinctly recollect the experience. I fagged for Chris Raleigh, a South African, and my job was to keep his rugby boots clean and on a daily basis, to shine his school shoes. Chris only had one pair of shoes, so I became very familiar with that pair of shoes as the year progressed. I didn't much mind the work. Chris was nice enough and I took heart that in due course I would be old enough to have my shoes shined by a new boy. As luck would have it, the practice was abolished the very next year.

I remember the packing list for our trunks; a specified number of each piece of clothing all to be stuffed in a little cubby hole in our new boy dorm; four bunk beds for eight boys with one window with a view of Glastonbury Tor and a crack that allowed the cold air to invade the room. Hot water for the showers was in short supply so a schedule for the 40 boys was posted. We were allowed two showers per week – one morning and one evening.

On Monday evenings we had the dreaded selection of those in need of a haircut. Those selected would suffer at the completely unskilled hands of Pete the Barber. One hoped to avoid Pete doing any more than a few snips because a full haircut would trigger a week of ridicule from the rest of the lads. Fortunately we quickly learned that for a few bob, Pete would leave you unscathed.

My 1st year Physics class on Monday afternoons was from 4-6 pm. We rode our bikes to school in those days from Glastonbury, and by the time we got done with Monday afternoon games, we were badly in need of a nap and Mr. Blythman's class provided the perfect venue. Although there were only four students in his Nissen hut lab, he seemed content to let us fade in and out of consciousness. He himself was very old and seemed permanently tired. Indeed, I think he died the following year. It did seem as though we had many really old teachers. We even had a teacher called Tolstoy, the grandson of the author of War and Peace, and his Great Dane seemed always to be bounding across the campus, putting herds of smaller students to flight.

I remember feeling very sorry for a lonely new boy, who walked by Mr Lawrence Hills' Economics class one morning. He always wore a cap to hide his bald head and it was only years later that I realised that the boy was Duncan Goodhew.

It is 7.20 a.m. by the pool. A sleepy Edgarley boy is sitting on the floor outside, fully clothed, staring vacantly into space. "Are you bored?" I ask inanely. "No, sir," he replies locking his brain into gear. "I'm a day boy."

JEAN PIKE, (EDGARLEY)

Manes Goldsmith was a real chip off the old block in 1972, bursting with charm, hopeless at spelling but a brilliant Mr.Fix-it. It was his –very popular- idea that the group's summer outing that year should be a tour of his father's sweet-factory in Bristol, his father later being Sir James of that ilk. He, Manes, would arrange it all. He did too, and we had a splendid time. We were received like royalty, dressed up in white overalls and hats and were guided round every colourful and fragrant production-line, at each of which we were offered tastings and laden with samples.

Miraculously we got back without anyone being sick, but soon afterwards Manes and I were somewhat peremptorily summoned to the Headmaster's study. Apparently Goldsmith Senior had just returned from abroad to discover that, without his knowledge or permission, his son had instructed his secretary to organize the whole trip to the factory – which she had done very efficiently, Manes very skillfully having managed to convey to both her and me that his father had blessed the enterprise.

His father was furious – but mercifully only with his son. The rest of us thanked our lucky stars that the misdemeanour was discovered too late to abort the treat, and consoled ourselves with our ill-gotten gains – which in my case was a huge box of Elizabeth Shaw chocolate mints. The young entrepreneur took his rebuke philosophically and bathed in the glory of being his grateful group's indubitable hero!

Nicola Wicksteed (1972)

In my day, the school had no uniform. Although attempts were made to restrict excesses, clothes worn at Millfield were at the heart of fashion. My older sister by seven years used to check with me on what was "in" according to what was being worn at Millfield. It didn't matter if you were not super-fashionable though. It certainly was not a time for labels which, far from being flaunted, tended to be hidden away. There were also some pretty lurid applications of make up, though seldom among the boys. Some girls enjoyed putting on the full war-paint even for classes, which would create flutters of alarm among the more conservative members of staff.

I always loved the way that we all seemed to fit so comfortably into the school. I attribute this to the sheer diversity of backgrounds. This prevented there being a particular Millfield "type", which would have created outcasts of those who did not conform to the pattern. There were those whose parents were fabulously rich, those whose parents could never have afforded the fees without large scholarships, those who came from umpteen different countries and those with wildly differing sets of expectations.

Mr. S. calls from Kansas, at 3.00 a.m. his time to defend his son who has had a positive drug test. Father owns and hires Boeing 747s, is fabulously wealthy and is used to getting his way. Later in the morning, Mrs B. comes to see me about her daughter. Her husband has left them to go and live in San Diego and they are practically destitute, on social security. Could any two parents illustrate more vividly the extraordinary range of financial backing available to youngsters here.

We took the children of famous or eminent people totally for granted. By contrast to our current cult of celebrity, we were then refreshingly un-star-struck. My mother, who taught at the school, took a Thai boy called Mahidol under her wing to help him find his niche within the school. She invited him to our home on Sundays and we took him on a number of expeditions. One Sunday we invited two other Thai boys along as well, but neither of them would say a word. It was all rather difficult and clearly our attempt to encourage companionship for Mahidol had failed that day. It was not until later that we realised that the others were simply too much in awe of their Crown Prince to speak in his company.

Dick Snelling was the most extraordinary teacher I encountered. He could teach around 20 languages; Swahili, Malay, Mandarin, Greek, – you name it. And on the side he offered expertise in Anthropology which may have been his real love.

> *Dick Snelling died yesterday aged 70. He taught some 20 languages here for over 30 years. I saw his timetable when I first arrived. Monday 1st period; classical Greek, Swahili, Mandarin and Portuguese, all at the same time, to individual pupils, moving between them in a personalised, systematic procedure that ensured everyone was working all the time. But he was really an anthropologist who was still teaching with undiminished gusto right to the end of his life. His pupils and colleagues are devastated. Perhaps the key to his unequalled success was that he was still so clearly learning all the time. He must be the last of the best of Jack Meyer's eccentric scholars. We are going to put a bench up for him on the cricket boundary where he used to like to be, and at his request it will bear the inscription, "There is some corner of an English field that is forever foreign."*

All our public exams were taken in the Marquee, set up on the pitch and put in front of Millfield House. I loved the reassuring summer sounds of the thwacking of tennis balls and the scent of new mown grass wafting through the side flaps. It was as well not to be squeamish about insects. I remember ants trooping up the chairs, spider webs strung between the table legs, and sometimes between our legs too, and the sudden arrival of a beetle on the exam script. Once the famous Millfield ducks came waddling in, checked that we were all hard at work and waddled out again. But perhaps the best moment was when, in addition to all the other manifestations of nature in the raw, a golf ball dribbled past our feet, hotly pursued by the Headmaster. The expression on his face lightened when the location of his ball was indicated to him. He scooped it up and left soundlessly, fortunately resisting the temptation to try a shot from inside the Marquee.

For all the sex and rock n' roll of the sixties, I think we were comparative innocents and in a way a lot less peer-pressured than is currently the case. The children of the sixties had structures in their society against which they could rebel. By dismantling them 20 years later, they seem to have denied this luxury to later generations.

DONALD BELL (1971 – 1973)

I lived in Chindit House during my first year, where I became very good friends with a chap from Nigeria, Alaba Shonibare. In those days, we used to congregate in the lounge for *Thought for the Day* which was broadcast on Radio 4 at 7:45am. Most of us had one eye open at that time of the morning and some of us could even see through both, but even at that hour there would be some half hearted competition for the most comfortable chairs, into which we would slump with that degree of lethargy normally associated with the end of the day, rather than with its beginning.

Thought for the Day usually comprised a positive moral message to get the brain stirred up for the challenges which were likely to confront us during the school day. Back then, boys of a certain age had permission to smoke a pipe, though no cigarettes were allowed. Most mornings as we listened to *Thought for the Day* my friend Alaba would light his pipe. It always amazed me how he could smoke so early in the morning. He lounged in the most comfortable chair he could find, clouds of smoke billowing above his head and eventually filling the room as he puffed away, inhaling (as the veteran cigarette smoker he was!) deeply more often than not. Well before the end of *Thought for the Day* he was somewhere else in a world of his own, his bulky frame slumped even further into the lounge chair, his eyes rolled back staring vacantly at the ceiling, hoping, perhaps, not to fall on the floor or pass out. I don't think he ever heard a word of those radio talks. That was his morning "buzz" to get the day started. It worked for him. The rest of us just listened passively to whatever uplifting message we got on the airwaves.

A 3rd form Tutor Group do an Assembly based on the hypothesis that I have lifted all bans on smoking, alcohol and drugs. This scenario appears very popular. They enjoy drunken classes, decline all physical activity and generally have a ball. Then, however, they start some serious coughing and finally the 1st XI loses to Butleigh Village 3rd team. At that point they vote to revert to the original rules. It was snappy, funny, not too heavy on the good sense and very encouraging to see them devising such original stuff so early in their time here.

Numbers in 1972 (from "70 Not Out".)

Peter Matthews (1969 – 1973)

I was in Joan's Kitchen with Syd Hill as our Housemaster. There were just ten of us and at 16 I was the youngest. We all knew that on Sundays we were expected to go to church, not a choice but an obligation. Unfortunately we all seemed to have better things to do and so it never happened. Syd, who was wonderfully laid back about this as about all things except rugby, certainly never encouraged us.

Somehow, Boss found out and went crazy. We were all summoned as a group, including Syd, to explain ourselves to him. As we stood in the hall outside his study, Syd quickly told us the score. He said it was not our fault but his, and that he would deal with it. We were not to say a word. Syd would sometimes get nervous. He would fidget, blink a lot and run his fingers through his hair. On this occasion, he had it really bad; he was worse than a schoolboy expecting a beating.

When we had been kept waiting long enough, Boss called us in. Syd opened the door, pushed us in and then, to our amazement, marched in like an army recruit right up to the desk where Boss was sitting, stamped his feet to attention and saluted. Boss appeared to ignore this and attacked us on all fronts; no discipline, no respect, bringing the school into disrepute, on and on. At even the slightest pause, Syd piped up "Yes sir" and saluted again. We were all beside ourselves with suppressed – carefully suppressed – laughter.

We left Millfield House a dejected, sorry group, in silence. But we had not gone ten yards when Syd chirped up, "Well, that wasn't so bad after all. Gather round boys. I have a plan", and he then laid out the way forward. There were ten of us and from then on three or four of us were to go to church each Sunday. There were about six churches in Street, he said, and plenty of others close by. We were to go to them all, though never to the same one on consecutive Sundays. That way no one would be able to keep track of us.

His plan worked well. We were getting away with it, only going to church every third week. We tried everything; Baptists, Methodists, Catholics, all very friendly and welcoming. We even tried the Friends meeting house of the Quakers, but this turned out to be a mistake. They were very serious and grim, and though we only went once, we realised that to return would have ruined everything. We felt they would go out of their way to redeem us, and this was never part of the plan.

This regime turned out well for us. We were given insight into the different churches to which we went, and indeed we went happily for we knew we were getting away with it and this meant that church attendance was no longer a chore.

On the other hand Syd, after all his "Yes sir's" and his saluting, never went once and was proud of it.

> *Father Aidan, an admirable Franciscan friar, talked in Chapel today about his three vows. Poverty; "I own nothing, not even my sandals or my underwear." Chastity; "A tough one, much to the girls' disappointment", and Obedience; "If anyone needs what I have more than I do, I must give it to him." The pupils are mesmerised. Some, I suspect, who are more victims than others of the post-Thatcherite mind-set, simply cannot believe him. Afterwards, with those who stayed behind to talk, he refers to his isolation for two years in the Australian desert, of his loneliness as a chaplain with Missions to Seamen and of his alcoholism. "I was on one and a half litres of whisky a day." The impact he undoubtedly has on the youngsters around him seems to stem from this magic mixture of his religious conviction and devotion on the one side, and of his flawed humanity, just like the rest of us, on the other. He is the sort of person you just don't forget.*

My fondest memories of Millfield seem to be the bus rides home to Kingweston. Although it was only a short drive home, about 10-15 minutes, it was always the best and most comforting time of the day. It was the moment you got to catch up with all that had happened to your friends during the day, and it was the time you made your plans for the evening.

Everything about it was reassuring. Getting into a warm bus after you had been waiting so long by the sports hall, the scenic route back home, the occasional sing-song and the conversations you had with all your juniors and seniors.

I can still visualize clearly the entire route back to the boarding house which is probably not surprising because we took it so many times. But if I were to concentrate hard enough, I could probably also remember each pothole and every individual sheep that crossed our way on those halcyon journeys.

CHRISTOPHER MAYES (1970 – 1973)

My recollections are dominated by my late Housemaster Mr Bromfield and his wife of the time, and by my former basketball and commerce teacher David Hemery. We also had a Weight Lifting instructor called George McHugh who appears to have done less to distinguish himself on leaving Millfield than we all expected, rather like so many of us students. Suffice to say, even if it was painful at the time, I recall all my days at the school with a rosy glow. What would I change? With the benefit of hindsight, not much!

GIANETTA RANDS (1971 – 1973)

When I arrived, I had just had the great trauma of becoming blind in one eye following a viral infection, and the experience of being treated with steroids - not good for a teenage girl's body image or confidence. There was also the uncertainly of not knowing whether or not this was the beginning of a neurodegenerative condition that would progress. So Millfield took quite a risk accepting me!

My sporting achievements were modest – my sports were shooting (lying down), archery (standing still), and chess (sitting down). However, I did eventually do the school some credit by getting into Oxford to read Experimental Psychology, and for this I have to thank Bev Dovey. He was the biology teacher who inspired me to think of myself as a biological scientist (which I still do). And Mr Taylor, head of Chemistry, enabled my greatest academic achievement to date – Chemistry A Level!

The Music department was a retreat for me. I remember Mr and Mrs Keating telling me that I should never stop singing and in some ways I wish I had followed their advice. I have started playing the piano again – Grade 6 this Easter – so maybe I'll be singing again by the time I retire.

SUE ROCHARD (1971 – 1973)

Our group tutor, Mr. Busby, would ask us during our weekly group tutorials if we had any problems with which he could help us. On one occasion I raised my hand and said I had a problem, and he very kindly gave me his full attention. I explained: "My problem is that my cheeks often ache and even get cramp because I am always smiling and laughing so much here". After much laughter, he suggested that I buy some cheek supports which, he said, were sold in various sizes in the school sports shop. I actually believed him! Then, upon reflection, he added: "Since they are quite expensive, I usually use my wife's cut-down bras." At this point the whole class exploded and everyone had the problem – not only of cheek ache but also stomach ache. Life was a lot of fun at Millfield.

ELIZABETH THEOKRITOFF, (NEE BRIERE) (1969 – 1973)

If I focus on Hugh Elder as a towering figure of my time at Millfield, it is not for lack of other memorable tutors. But because he taught Ancient Greek and Ancient History, and part time at that, he is likely to be, undeservedly, among the least remembered. As the only pure classicist ('A' levels in Latin, Greek and Ancient History) of my generation at Millfield, I had the inestimable privilege of spending several hours a week with this wise, humane and dedicated man in groups of two or three, and latterly one-to-one.

Mr Elder was a former headmaster (of Merchant Tailors' School), who in retirement had taken a position at Millfield purely out of love of teaching. He took education seriously, and could be exacting. There was the sunny morning when he appeared studiously impervious to the welcome message 'Tutor's discretion' – only to dismiss us with a gruff 'Off you go!' a few minutes later, having made his point. But his somewhat dour exterior concealed a dry sense of humour (it was he that introduced me to P.G. Wodehouse; as a special treat, we would read such tales as *Leave it to Psmith* round the Ancient History class on the last day of term), and a

119

readiness to take endless pains for his pupils.

His unlikely domain was in the Chicken Run – room 2, if I recall. The eponymous occupants had been displaced some time since; perches and nesting boxes had given place to lumpy lino and decrepit desks; and in compensation for the new residents' lack of feathers, there was a temperamental and distinctly niffy paraffin stove. Those details aside, however, the name gives a reasonable idea of the quality of the accommodation. And it must have been something about the state of the room that inspired a reminiscence ('I have a tendency to digress – a tendency that my pupils encourage') about a former colleague who had rashly used 'If the ceiling were to fall in' as an example of the unlikely condition in future time. Yet if truth be known, Chicken Run 2 was a time machine. For three years of my life, it was the anteroom to Homer's wine-dark sea and the epic carnage of Troy; to Antigone defying the tyrant in the name of a higher law; to Athenian marbles under the Attic sun, and the terrible stone quarries of Sicily.

Mr Elder's basic methods owed little to modern educational theory; we either read texts around the class, or wrote down his dictated notes. But of course, with such small classes, he was never bound by his own structure; and somehow the facts which had to be mastered were never allowed to eclipse the great tragi-comedy of human experience into which we were daily being initiated. A lesson could start with the number of triremes required to defeat Philip of Macedon and progress seamlessly to ultimate questions of the meaning of life, as ancient texts in dog-eared books unfolded to reveal timeless vignettes from the human drama. I especially recall Mr Elder expounding Pericles's funeral speech for the first casualties of the Peloponnesian War, one of Thucydides' masterpieces. 'You do not know this', he said at the end, 'but I have lost a child...'

Teaching, for Mr Elder – the teaching which he loved – was nothing other than the transmission of culture, in the broadest sense. The fabled digressions, both the serious and the light-hearted, were an integral part of his legacy. The formation of mind and character that he imparted so memorably was not readily separable from the common and comic trivia that bind people together. So it was that I not only laboured to commit to memory Socrates' majestic farewell discourse ('No

evil befalls a good man, either in his life or in his death...')
but also picked up along the way the more readily memorised
ditty, 'I eat my peas with honey/ I've done so all my life:/ it
makes the peas taste funny,/ but it keeps them on the knife'.
Not only was Mr Elder a man of culture, a teacher in the
fullest sense; he was also a man of true authority. 'Believe me,
I know how difficult it is to master Greek grammar', he would
repeat in his deliberate way, as I struggled grumpily with principle parts of verbs; 'but once you are able to read the literature, it *is* worth it'. I did believe him; it was a leap of faith
such as few others could have inspired. And it was one of the
defining choices of my life.

> *At a conference in London yesterday, I was immensely*
> *cheered to hear Anthea Millett, Chairman of the Teacher*
> *Training Agency, admit ruefully that she respected "the*
> *irritating success of wrong methods."*

CLIVE WARING-FLOOD (1969 – 1973)

Boss was renowned for his irreverent, anti-traditional,
anti-establishment, unorthodox behaviour, but it was exactly
this trait that commanded so much respect and loyalty from his
students and made him so successful. An interview with a headmaster can be a very intimidating experience for a thirteen year old,
even more so when that headmaster's reputation extended far and
wide where Millfield's sports prowess was discussed in awed
whispers at all the schools I had previously visited.

"Now Clive, be on your best behaviour, only speak when you
are spoken to, sit up, look forward and answer any questions
quickly and politely," urged my aunt, mother and grandmother, all
of whom for some reason had decided to attend this interview with
me. This was not to provide me with moral support, I later
gathered, but because they were just curious to meet this unusual
headmaster.

The study was littered with books, papers and a large wicker-
work basket full of bread and grain to feed sporadically to ducks
that would wander through or past the open window onto the

lawns. The interview was directed more to my aunt than to me. After sitting quietly for what seemed like eternity, I was suddenly asked by Boss what sport I enjoyed. I said swimming. "Right, let's see how fast you are."

We all followed him out of the French windows, onto the lawn and across to this transparent bubble which turned out to be a small swimming pool. As we arrived I stammered that I had no swimming trunks. "Then swim in your underpants," he replied. Having to undress in front of all the females in my family plumbed new depths of embarrassment for me, but I dutifully obeyed. Boss took out a stop watch and on the count of three I dived into the pool to swim a few lengths. On finishing he just said, "Good swim. I think we can use you at this school," and left me to my own devices whilst he walked back across the lawn chatting to my aunt.

After three months of training with the squad I decided that there was more to life than being a potential Olympian and asked Paddy Garrett to excuse me from three hours of training a day. I got involved in drama instead and started producing House and School plays, but the swimming has stayed with me, and I still swim my laps at the Olympic pool twice a week. Thank you, Boss, for providing me with the groundwork and opportunities for my adult life.

HENRY WODEHOUSE (1970 – 1973)

I was interviewed by Boss in the presence of my Parents. As I had just failed my Common Entrance to Eton, this was tough stuff. He asked me a mathematical question to which I had not the foggiest idea of the answer. Seeing my dilemma, he altered it to a more relevant discipline. Fixing me with a penetrating stare from a great height with his pipe quivering impatiently in the corner of his mouth, he asked, "If you have a 2 to 1 and a 3 to 1 double what are the combined odds?" This was easy for me, my Father being an inveterate gambler; "6-1," I chirped up proudly. "Good," said Boss. "No problem with the maths then!"

Since we were incarcerated at Tor House for the first two years of my time at Millfield, we had fun dropping small plastic bags full of water from the top floor dormitory onto the heads of unfortunate hippies making a pilgrimage to Glastonbury Tor, when they decided to rest on the pavement outside the house and play their guitars late into the night. One day we went a bit over the top and dropped a large plastic supermarket bag full of water out of the window. Fortunately for us it missed its intended target; a serious injury would have resulted had it not done so. It exploded on contact with the pavement with a loud bang right next to the intended victim. The poor chap must have beaten the world record for levitation from a cross legged position on the ground.

Being one of the less athletic pupils, I persuaded my long suffering parents to pay extra for me to ride instead. I am sure that this further compounded my academic failure. One spent one's spare time clearing up the dung heap, visiting Point to Points, Polo Matches and Hunter Trials, all of which invariably resulted in frequent and highly illegal visits to the Beer Tents. As a result, we got horrendously tired and emotional, sitting in tack-rooms smoking like chimneys, but never doing any work.

Did I have fun at Millfield? It was unforgettable, incredible, amazing and I loved every minute

Polo players have not always struck me as being aesthetes, but I am revising my view having come across Andrew, in the L6th, conducting a most civilised practice session in the indoor riding school to the strains of Swan Lake booming out from the public address system.

ANNA ARCHDALE (1969 – 1974)

I arrived for my interview with the famously eccentric Boss as a very shy 11 year old showing no academic promise and absolutely no sporting aptitude but accompanied by my highly opinionated, eccentric grandmother. She proceeded to lecture Boss long and loud on the vicissitudes of the army, the dullness of golf and the utter stupidity of cricket, several of the great loves of his life. He listened patiently then took me outside. He threw me a cricket ball which no doubt I dropped, gave me a golf club with which I caused a crater-sized divot and surprisingly announced that I was welcome to start the following year. I never became any kind of sportswoman but I did develop a very healthy respect for eccentricity.

I am hobbling around with one black shoe and one white trainer, having broken my foot. Any claim to gravitas is up the creek. A 3rd year boy surveys the wreckage of my footwear, enquires politely how I am and asks perceptively, "Do you have another pair like that at home, sir?" Later, as I pass two tall, strapping 3rd year girls in conversation, a diminutive boy in their year hurries past on his way to games. The girls watch him with interest, then turn to each other and say in chorus, "How sweet." Thank God he didn't hear this.

PHILIP DICK (1972 – 1974)

It was the spring of 1973, a time of platform shoes and shoulder length hair. The likes of David Bowie and Slade were topping the charts, and the coal miners' strike, the three day week and the two General Elections of 1974 were still only on the horizon. It was a great time to be alive. I was a 17 year old, boarding at Chindit in Glastonbury. 'Brom' was our housemaster. My parents were working in the Bahamas and somehow the distance between us, coupled with the group of fellow Chindit sixth-formers I shared life with day-in, day-out, seemed to embolden me.

For reasons best known to ourselves a group of six of us took to sneaking out of Chindit at weekends for an illicit under-age drink or two in some of Glastonbury's pubs. A particular favourite of ours was, I think, the King Arthur on Benedict Street. We got so carried away with our success in remaining undetected that we even started going there before opening hours on a Sunday morning, when we should have been in church, for a couple of swift pints before lunch back at Chindit.

Inevitably it all came out. Whether it was the glazed look in our eyes or the smell of alcohol on our breath as we sat next to 'Brom' at Sunday lunch I'm not quite sure, but one day 'Brom' swept into the dining room, removed the most current Chindit

House group photograph and disappeared with it. We later learned it had been used to help the landlord of the pub identify the guilty parties!

We were subsequently summoned to appear in front of the headmaster, Colin Atkinson. We feared the worst. However, in an act of human kindness that I remember to this day, and which has also served me well in life, he let us off with a stern warning and reminded us not to go into a pub again until we were 18.

TIM HEARD (1970 – 1974)

It was the summer of 1969 when my mother and I met with Boss and had a walk around the campus. His walking stick turned out to be a golf club and he informed us that as there was no money in swimming, which had been my preferred sport, I should consider taking up golf. I managed to hit the ball a surprising number of times and he thus concluded that I had aptitude as a "natural golfer". There then ensued three years of golf tutorials that proved him comprehensively wrong. I was accepted on the same fees as Bromsgrove. Actually, I think he just liked my mother!

I arrived at The Hollies with a trunk full of inappropriate clothes which at least set me apart until I grew out of them. Colin Atkinson was housemaster, though Shirley, his wife really ran things. I think he only called me a "Moron" once and then it was more of a question than a statement of fact.

Organizing the year's classes with good teachers was a good lesson for life. One quickly learnt the art of negotiation to get the best or most fun teachers and of avoiding those who must be avoid-ed at all cost. Golf and then Swimming were my priorities and everything else fell into place around them. It was important to get classes in the new A & B Blocks – anything rather than the glacial "Nissen huts"

Music, along with Sport, was the bridge between age, senior-ity and women. It enabled introductions that were safe and some-how comfortable. The other day I came across some old blotting paper with "I love Gillian" on it. I looked up Gillian in one of the Year Books and I now recall why. The crushes we had were numer-ous but our confidence in knowing what to do about them was shaky at best! As the years passed crushes transitioned into friendships and a few blossomed into something more. My relationship with Jane began as a friendship when she was head of School and I was head of House. I hoped then that things might progress into something more. However, my dreams were dashed when I overheard her talking to a teacher who was strongly advising her not to be distracted from her studies as I wasn't academically in her league and therefore not worth it. She listened and clearly agreed. Somehow we remained good friends but lost touch after school.

In the Spring of 1970, a group of locals, probably provoked by us, invaded Hollies. Cricket bats and golf clubs were deployed for self-defence. The battle lasted a good hour, but no one was seriously hurt on either side. One unfortunate chap was captured and spread eagled on the dinning room table where he was subjected to a pretty substantial beating. The police investigated but could get little cooperation from either side. The morale of the House improved tremendously.

Boss was such an eccentric optimist that as a student even in the twilight of his stewardship it was hard to imagine Millfield without him. Boss was folk-law. The culture was to strive to be different, to be an individual and not to conform to established norms. The School seemed to thrive on being slightly dysfunctional in the business sense but totally absorbed by individuals who had the ability to excel in sport or academically or who needed some help. It seemed as if it was the folks in the middle ground who got lost or who didn't get all that Millfield had to offer. His lovely, charming wife Joyce always smiled and always remembered your name.

I think we all knew what Colin Atkinson had inherited from Boss and that things had to change. The sound business footing that he began to introduce probably saved the school.

As a housemaster he was somewhat aloof and abrupt. He certainly had no tolerance for fools. With his standards and high demands, he began another era and did it well.

Smoking a pipe was allowed when you were 16 years and eight months – no one knew why. The tobacco of choice was "Yachtsman", some continental mix of tobacco matured in rum and honey, I think. Millfield was probably the single largest market for this product. No cigarettes were allowed and generally this was not abused, but drugs were becoming an increasing issue, and what would now be referred to as "recreational drugs" were readily available.

We had a lot of fun abusing new young teachers – male teachers quickly grew beards in an attempt to convey gravitas and authority.

As a newly appointed Head of House, I received a call one evening from an irate parent who, I believe, was the Managing Director of a major PLC. He wanted to know why I had "gated" his son when they had plans to visit that coming weekend. He explained quite strongly how this was a major inconvenience and that his son could not possibly be involved in anything that would merit such punishment. I was left in no doubt that I was to reverse this decision immediately or suffer the consequences.

Realizing that my reputation in the House was in question, I told him the punishment would stand, explained the circumstances of the infringement and asked for the parent's support. Having heard my side of things he immediately agreed and supported the decision. His son never tried to work around me again.

The most unfortunate instances were those where absence of parental intervention created the problem. One aristocratic member of the house had reached a point of no return and was facing expulsion for a litany of drug and drinking offences. When they were told this, his parents responded that it wasn't convenient for him to be sent home as they were going skiing and could the school keep him for another couple of weeks! They never visited the school and the chauffeur would be dispatched to deliver and collect him. I believe he survived despite his parents.

MIKE MUMFORD (1974)

In my teens, Millfield was my life and I loved it. We swam for two or three hours every day in a very foggy greenhouse. There was always the opportunity to reduce the dictated distance by turning around in the fog if we didn't feel strong. The distances we swam probably don't compare with what they are doing today, but they certainly felt long then. Paddy Garrett, our Coach was a strong mentor for me and the swim team was my "gang". I remember well the many people and events that influenced me but my top ten memories are these;

Meeting with Boss to persuade him to accept me.

A revelation I had at 14 years old. I can remember the exact day time and place, where I realised if I didn't kick myself in gear, start studying and take more responsibility, I would be of no value when I left. That began my drive for personal improvement and growth.

Laughing so much in swim training, I had to stop through fear of drowning.

Winning the School relays with three great friends, Pete Lerpiniere, Simon Meredith and Duncan Goodhew.

Sharing the cricket changing room when it was empty in the winter, and running between that and the pool in our briefs and not much else over icy paths and freezing temperatures.

Riding our bikes to school and back through sun, rain and snow.

Learning that rich or poor, black or white, it didn't really matter, we were all great friends.

Struggling through homework with badly chlorinated eyes, before the introduction of swim goggles.

My first true kiss.

ANTHONY TRAFFORD (1969 – 1974)

For my interview, we were advised not to travel to Millfield by car and especially not in my father's Rolls Royce as that would have been music to Boss's ears, or should I say pounds in his pocket ! We travelled to Somerset by train and went on to Street by taxi.

My first recollection of Boss's office was the pile of Financial Times stacked from floor to ceiling, of which he boasted that he had every copy ever printed. To this day, I don't know why he collected the FT, I am quite sure he neither had time nor the interest in reading the paper, so I put it down to the fact that he wanted to impress the wealthy clients who walked across the threshold.

Once the niceties were over and Boss had subtly established what business my father was involved in, the interview commenced, not with me, but with my father. Thinking back at it now, it was all so bizarre. During what became negotiations instead of an interview, he received a couple of telephone calls. Most people, whilst in a meeting would have their calls held, but then I suppose it would depend on who was calling. He made great strides to ensure that we knew who was on the other end of the phone. The first call was from Elizabeth Taylor and the second, Lew Grade, both apparently seeking information on their offspring.

During the negotiations, my father kept trying to divert Boss from himself to me (the interviewee), but Boss insisted that a parent who is in the concrete business can benefit by supplying concrete to the school in return for a greatly reduced fee. After a suitable arrangement had been reached, we strolled out of the front door onto the lawn. Boss handed me his walking stick (a 3 iron) and told me to hit the ball. Of course I had never hit a golf ball, and I completely missed it. We then strolled to the tennis courts where he proudly introduced us to Mark Cox who was teaching a young girl whom Boss introduced as a Junior Wimbledon star. Little did Boss know, that my parents knew Mark and he greeted us by name. I don't think Boss liked that too much as he was upstaged.

I believe that by that time, Boss had concluded a deal for me to attend the school in return for a few loads of concrete and as far as he was concerned, the interview was over.

Every afternoon I see two or three prospective families together for half an hour after their tour to try to answer their queries about the school. I invariably enjoy these sessions, for our visitors are almost always inspired by what they have seen of us and have no difficulty in appreciating what we have to offer. Today, they wanted to talk about girls' dress, which I admitted was not my top priority, drug education, modular courses, racial mix, criteria for house placements and the range of sixth form courses available. All are entirely sensible and reveal well-briefed people who have followed developments in education for some time. And yet I sometimes long for the good old days when they used to ask whether I was in favour of capital punishment, ("No. We couldn't afford to lose the fees"), and League tables, though no one has mentioned these to me for a couple of years now. The thing I can't say is that their child's development will in large measure depend on who teaches them what at the point during their career, here or elsewhere, at which they are most receptive, and on the other pupils with whom they will make friends in their house. And no parent, however assiduous, can anticipate this.

,

SIMON BECK (1969 – 1975)

My most vivid memories of Edgarley centre around orienteering and maths lessons. In my first year, several members of the class used to poke fun at the teacher, whose name was Nathanial Cook, although the Christian name was a matter of much discussion. Nathanial (or whatever his real name was) used to retaliate by making offenders write out psalms as a punishment. It started with a number in the 30s, then moved up to the particularly long psalm 78, but eventually went 'nuclear' and several members of the group were required to write out psalm 119, which is about 3 times as long as any other psalm. I don't recall whether anyone ever got to the end of it, but I do recall a certain Andrew Jarrett updating this classic piece of ancient literature by including a brief dissertation on Derby County's chances in the forthcoming FA cup competition!

But all this was put in the shade in the final year, taught by Mr Frean. His reputation for throwing chalk, board rubbers or indeed any handy blunt instrument, and for cuffing people was legendary. A sort of indoor battle of the Somme. His real Christian name was Charles, but poor old CF was generally known as 'Cuthbert' or even 'Frean Bean the Cuffing machine'! He was quite an intelligent guy really, and he taught me the lesson that if there's something you don't like doing, the best strategy is to do it as quickly as you can in order to minimise the time you have to spend doing things you don't like. But surrounded by 12 year olds he inevitably became a figure of fun. Indeed we invented a concept known as 'the speed of Frean'. Albert Einstein had apparently determined that the initials CF were determined by the formula C-squared = F, where C is the speed of light and F is the speed of Frean.

Once a week a pupil from each group had the duty of making a list of items required from the stationary cupboard, which was efficiently dispensed by Mr Frean. Pupils in turn would read out their group's list and Charles would repeat the name of the item, pick it off the shelf and slam it onto the nearby table. There was the famous occasion when the prehistoric ink machine, which was used for refilling prehistoric pens, which also lived on the table, was wobbling around on top of a pile of exercise books. Of course, it eventually fell off, smashing to smithereens with an almighty crash in a lake of spilled ink. Frean turned angrily on the nearest child; "Why didn't you catch it, boy?"

Having a lesson from Frean was unforgettable, made all the more so by the predictable course that events seemed inevitably to take. The lesson would begin with the unmistakeable sound of his footsteps along the wooden corridor. Then the door would burst open, and he'd shout, "Sit down will you, sit down will you," regardless of whether everyone was sitting down already or not. He would then walk over to the windows and open one, regardless of how many windows were already open, and unaffected by the temperature outside, whether in deepest winter or hottest summer.

He would then clean the blackboard. This was achieved in one single motion. He would pirouette on one foot, and as he did so grab the board rubber and scrub the board in a white blur, hardly slowing down in the process. But it did slow him down a bit, of course, frequently making him lose his balance. He regained an upright position by slamming the rubber down on the desk, whereupon a mushroom cloud of chalk dust would shoot up, temporarily obscuring him from our view.

To be fair, he was a good teacher provided he was teaching the most talented pupils. His mnemonic "Some people have curly black hair that parts badly" translates to "Sine perpendicular (over) hypotenuse Cosine Base (over) hypotenuse Tangent Perpendicular (over) Base" makes complete sense, provided you realise that it's only going to work provided the triangle is drawn the right way round. But what's obvious to some people isn't so to others, and he could give you a hard time if you were a little slow on the uptake.

Another teacher I didn't get on with was the lady who taught art. She used to bring her dog – a vicious brute - into her classroom, and one day it chased me out of the open door, through the school and onto the lane that runs down to Lower Edgarley Farm, with me screaming my head off. She eventually caught up with me and the dog and accused me of deliberately running out into the road and leading her dog astray.

Another unpleasant experience was entirely self inflicted. There was an assembly when the headmaster, Ben Rushton, complained to the school that the old oil drums which were used to store hockey sticks had been emptied, and removed to a muddy area which had been cut into the hillside that sloped gently down from the main road. Little did Ben realise what had actually been going on. We had been taking the oil drums to the top of the bank, getting inside them and rolling down the bank inside the drums. Once they had picked up speed, there was clearly no way of stopping them. You could only hope you wouldn't be sick before it eventually ground to a halt somewhere on the football pitch on to which we rolled, hopefully without colliding with the goalposts.

Sarah Champion, who is again acting as Head at Edgarley, tells me that she has had to remonstrate with a Korean boy for fighting. "But he hit me first, Miss." "Well you mustn't hit back." "What I do then, Miss? You want I stand there, cry like baby and call Mummy?" Sarah was inclined to see his point and apparently replied, "No, perhaps you should just hit him back like you said."

One of the outstanding characters in the senior school was Martin Craigs. I was awed by his production of 'Joe Egg' which won KW the house play competition that year. Martin was also noted for his iconoclastic attitude to the religious element of school life, bellowing out hymns as if they were chants at the soccer ground, and, when saying grace as Head of House, lowering his voice towards the end in the hope that at least one unfortunate boy would pull out his chair and sit down before the word 'thankful'.

Another pair of characters were Kalvis Jansons and Martin Casdagli, both of whom went on to do maths PhD's at Cambridge.

They spent ages investigating the possible implications of a definition of the exponential of a matrix which one of them had dreamed up, and I'll never forget the expression of utter desolation on Martin's face when we discovered, in a question in an old exam paper, that the whole thing wasn't original after all.

The school computer got rough treatment from us. It was a PDP8E which the school sold off just before it became entirely obsolete. At that time, we believed we were the only school in the country to own a computer, and it had 8k (yes, k!) of memory. There were two teletypes connected to it and it was important not to press any buttons on the teletype that weren't in use when it was configured to be used by only one teletype. I once found out what happened when you do. A fuse blew and the whole of the maths block blacked out.

There were ten occasions during the school day when the bell rang to tell us all what to do next. The most important of these rang at 6.0 pm, when the fleet of buses departed for the dozen or so boarding houses, that were scattered within about an eight mile radius of the school. 6.0 pm in the 'camp car park' was quite a scene. Everyone was supposed to be sitting in the buses ready for departure when the bell rang. However, for some boys it was a sign of machismo to get on the bus at the very last minute, as close to 6.0 pm as possible. The bus drivers for their part did their best to leave such pupils behind. The result was that when the bell rang, there was a mad charge for the entrance as the whole car park disappeared in a cloud of dust with pupils and buses dashing about all over the place. The tutor on duty could only stand impotently by the entrance and say a silent prayer that nobody would be killed.

We knew most of the bus drivers by name. Jack had a new bus and did his best to keep it looking new. Inevitably it wasn't long before the boys took delight in winding up the unfortunate Jack by desecrating his beloved bus. Jack for his part became cross-eyed as he learned to drive with one eye looking at the road ahead and the other in the rear-view mirror, to watch for the least infringement of the rules. The best way to provoke a reaction was to put one's hand up behind the removable covers that protected the top of the seats. This inevitably produced remonstrance, followed by a chorus of "Oooh Aarr Oi'll 'aave 'ee" from delighted 14 year-olds!

Jack used to drive fairly fast, but the king of the road was unquestionably Bob. He was said to be a former racing driver, and everyone's heart leapt with joy whenever they realised Bob was to drive us back to the house. In those days there were no speed limits along the Butleigh road and we were soon hanging onto the seats as we shot along at motorway speeds with Bob inch-perfect in his judgement of the line to avoid colliding with any oncoming traffic. There was one incident when we met another bus in the awkward little dip near where the athletics track has since been built. There was a loud bang that must have been caused by trapped air as the two buses missed by millimetres, but the drivers were mightily relieved not to find any damage.

The only other incident involving single level buses was when, during the traverse of Butleigh itself, a girl shovelled a spadeful of manure at our windscreen as we drove past. We never found out whether this was pure carelessness or whether she was expressing her opinion of Millfield. Fortunately there was no damage beyond a rather dirty bus and a badly shaken driver who thought he'd knocked down an unseen pedestrian.

I mentioned single-level buses, but there was a period when the bus company experimented with a double-decker bus. The local roads were quite unsuitable for this, and the top nearside corner had to be repaired on an ongoing basis as tree branches repeatedly damaged it. The boys, of course, used to gather on the top deck and make the driver seasick by rocking it from side to side. But the double decker was clearly impractical. I remember being on the top deck when the driver pulled over to pass an oncoming car. This happened in exactly the wrong place and the camber of the road sent the top deck straight into a very solid looking tree. Fortunately everyone was already cowering on the floor in terror and no harm was caused, other than to the bus, when two windows broke and several boys were showered with fragments. The double decker disappeared shortly afterwards.

Alex White is 13, Head Boy of Edgarley. He starts his speech on Parents Day to a dauntingly large audience of parents and friends on a splendidly confident note. "As Henry VIII said to his six wives, I shan't be keeping you long."

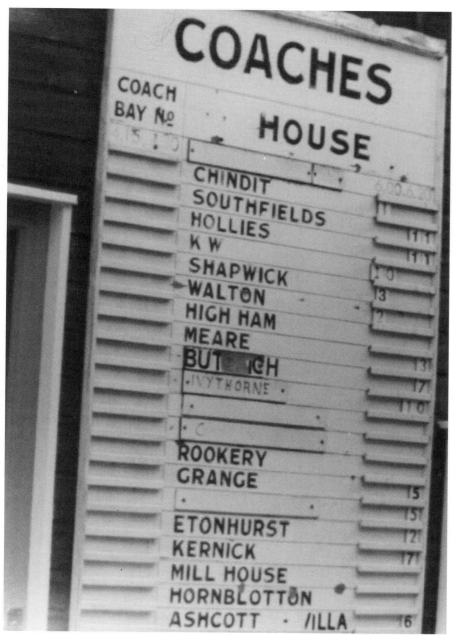

The coaches departure board.

Duncan Goodhew (1970 – 1975)

It was the early 60's and my brother John, who is ten years my senior, had just finished his interview at Millfield. He was waiting in the Bentley while my father polished off his conversation with Boss.

My father had heard what he wanted to hear and that was that his son had a place at the school. However, he had been completely unprepared for what then followed; the request – or was it a condition? – that had come with the announcement. For after the welcome news of my place came Boss's price tag – a new swimming pool for the staggering sum of £100,000. That was enough in my father's view. He said his goodbyes in a good riddance sort of way and on his way to the car I heard him mutter, "Bloody blackmail".

After this encounter it is hard to imagine how he coped with the conversation with Mr Charles, the Headmaster of Windlesham House School where I was then a pupil, when Mr Charles suggested that the only school for me, his bald headed, academically challenged swimming pupil, was Millfield.

We motored down to Somerset again in what would have been near silence had we been in the Bentley. Instead we were in the rattling, bone shaking, cramped Mini Traveller. He wasn't going to make the same mistake twice.

We were ushered in to Boss' study which was an absolute tip. At no time in my life had my bedroom been in such a state as his study. Only once can I remember such a mess, and that was during a three week Easter holiday when it had not stopped raining for the entire holiday, leaving my three bothers and me caged in our rooms.

In the family I was known to be clumsy, so when the Royal Dolton was produced my mother took a sharp intake of breath. I wisely declined tea when it was offered.

Boss asked me a number of questions and then told me that he thought I was dyslexic. I was sent to a room next to his study where I was assessed. I had never heard the term before but when he told me about the condition, I understood for the first time what had always made me feel so out of kilter at school. I knew at once that just knowing about this would make a huge difference for me; after all, you can only fight something when you know what it is you are fighting.

After the interview we were sent to the old swimming pool. The pool was as bizarre as Boss' study was messy. It was really just a Nissen hut with a corrugated plastic roof, reminiscent of a pigsty. This 25 yard liner pool with its teak coping was, as far as I know, totally unique.

Paddy Garrett, the only full time professional coach in the UK at the time, asked me to swim a 4x1 medley. I had never been taught how to swim butterfly, so not knowing what else to do I simply missed it out altogether. This, of course, left me at the wrong end of the pool. Paddy, like all other coaches, seemed to favour one end of the pool exclusively and never ventured as far as the other end at all. When I completed my three lengths, I was of course at the wrong end – the end Paddy never visited – and not knowing how to handle this situation, I just stayed put and showed no sign of moving. Thus Paddy had to walk the whole length of the pool – possibly for the first time – to ask me *why* I was at the wrong end. Sensing disaster, my parents had by now become thoroughly dejected.

In disgrace, I dragged myself from the pool and with my parents and Paddy trudged back up towards Millfield House. Boss intercepted us at the corner of the tennis courts and looked directly into my eyes. As much as I wanted to break the spell cast by his piercing gaze I just couldn't. Against my will, those eyes seemed to hold mine – or was it that I wanted him to see who I could really become? "Paddy, will he swim for the school?" Paddy replied, "Yes, he will swim for the school, and the County, the District and the Country and he will probably even go beyond that."

I was shattered. County, District, Country – but what an earth could be beyond swimming for my country?

Boss suddenly looked away from me and glanced towards my father. Given what had passed between them at their last meeting, I am certain that the deep irony in this situation couldn't have been missed by either of them. With just one question the late, great Boss had sealed my fate and secured my success before I was even enrolled in his school.

CLARE MONTGOMERY (1975)

I have an indelible memory of my first contact with the school and with Boss. I was a candidate for entrance to the senior school aged 10. I had come to the school expecting a battery of tests and a standard question and answer session in my interview with the Headmaster. Contrary to my expectation there were no tests or exams. Instead my parents and I were shown into Boss' study in Millfield House where we were treated to an eclectic and wide ranging discussion covering poetry, philosophy, sport and music. Boss treated my answers as seriously as if I were an adult and seemed to be genuinely interested in my opinion rather than assessing my suitability for entry to the school. I later learned that this was a characteristic display by him. He had a gift for treating each pupil as an individual worthy of his attention.

After the 'interview' Boss showed us round the school. He bet me 2/6 (12.5p today) that I could not hit a hole in six on the golf course. He used my absence to tell my parents that I could come to the school and they should just pay whatever they thought they could afford by way of fees. It was a highly individual start to a highly individual and challenging school environment.

HARRY COWELL (1973 – 1976)

I have been in the music biz pretty well since I left Millfield and have dealt with people from all walks. of life and from nearly every country in the world. I can honestly say that Millfield helped me to be able to do this. The wide range of my fellow pupils gave me the chance to go out there and do what I do best. I really believe that had I gone to a conventional school I would not have been accepted around the world as I have been.

TONY DUBENS (1972 – 1976)

I was not an academic, but I did share a house with most of the school's top tennis players. They would occasionally give me a knock, in exchange perhaps for one of Sly's crispy chicken legs, and I began to think I could handle things pretty well on a tennis court. One day, I walked into my Maths class wearing a track suit and carrying my racket, and I may have had a maths book with me as well. My maths teacher, who expected little from me in class, asked me if I played tennis. Expert deduction, I thought, and told him that, yes, I did and that I was pretty good too.

To me, Colonel MacLagen seemed at least 100 years old. He had white hair and a matching moustache AND he wore glasses. To my astonishment, he suggested we should have a game one day. Well, once I had picked myself up from the floor, laughing, I agreed. I thought I may not be any good at Maths, but I could certainly impress him with my ability on a tennis court. But was it all really worth the effort? He was a delightful man, but so very old, so what possible satisfaction could I gain from humiliating him?

On the day in question we turned up at the Baracuda sports hall, and I felt really guilty that I was going to put this old man through such pain. He was dressed in whites from head to toe, and that included white bandages on both knees and both elbows. The only item that was not white was the brown bandage that was holding his glasses together. His racket looked about 100 years older than he did – a real museum piece. I was now getting seriously worried because he looked as if his limbs would snap if he ran for a ball or made a sudden turn. Was the Medical Centre open? Would I be blamed if he took a tumble?

For the next 45 minutes he stood on virtually the same spot and had me running from corner to corner, drop shots, lobs, making me run around like fury before deciding to end the point at a moment of his choosing. There was no way I was going to get a point from him, let alone a game. I was dripping with sweat by the end, and had had enough. It was only then that he told me that he had once won Junior Wimbledon.

We are hosting the International Flying Disc Championships. Frisbees to the rest of us. There are around a thousand competitors from the USA, Japan and just about all countries in between, and they take it all very seriously. One team from the USA, comprising both men and women who have not scored a point during the whole competition so far, decides to take all their clothes off – an unnerving move for the opposition but entirely legal it seems – and immediately score. I just hope this doesn't catch on generally.

RICHARD FORD (1970 – 1976)

I look back on the canings with hilarity but apart from the wait-ing, the worst bit was knowing that your friends were all upstairs in the dormitory above the housemaster's study. Each with an ear to the floor while counting and silently raising another finger in the air with each swish of the stick.

I fagged for the head of house who was in the first fifteen for Rugby Football. He trained at least three times a week and had a match every Saturday. I had to clean his kit and dry and polish his boots at least four times each week. He only had one Jock Strap and refused to buy another so I had to wash and scrub it after each use. After two terms and a miserly £2 tip for my services, I had great enjoyment in ceremoniously burning his undergarment and pretend-ing that he must have lost it.

Friday meant fish and chips for supper. Max le Chef's special-ity! Nobody said a word until 61 plates were empty.

I recall a friend showing off his new cowboy style boots to us one first day of term. The bell for snacks rang and off we all dashed into the hall to reach the trolley of milk and grab the best biscuits. The new boots were leading but their wearer had not noticed that the floor was recently polished for our return from the holidays. Alas, the leather soles and metal tips had no grip and could not stop him when he tried to apply the brakes. He collided with the trolley and sent 60 poured cups, two huge jugs of milk and about a hundred biscuits up into the air. The sheriff, in the person of St Anne's housemas-ter Neil Chadwick, was not amused.

DEBORAH BEDROSSIAN (1974 – 1977)

A s I begin the process of choosing a boarding school for my daughter, I find myself looking back with nostalgia at my years spent at Millfield. As an American, I was part of an international community of students that made up this diverse student body. My roommate was a princess from Bhutan, a country I'd never even heard of before. The education that we received extended far beyond the pages of our textbooks but was a microcosm of the wider world around us. In today's world where there is so much conflict stemming from religious and cultural differences, I feel so fortunate to have been able to know so many great people from so many different areas of the world. I believe this to be the definition of what was a truly enriching experience which will most certainly remain with me for ever.

Some of my more vivid memories were from Parents' Day. There were multi-colored traditional African robes worn by Nigerian Chiefs blowing in the wind, Sean Connery walking across the field, Omar Sharif speaking with Saudi billionaire Adnan Khashoggi, members of the British aristocracy, Greek shipping magnates, deposed rulers, captains of industry - a virtual smorgasbord of the world's elite. One would have to travel beyond the Earth's atmosphere to find a place where one could not find an ex-Millfieldian.

Visiting Southfields house, we encounter in one room a girl who lives in Minehead and who has never been abroad – and nor, it transpires, has her father – sharing with Evgenia Raspopina who comes three times a year to Street to study here and who lives in Vladivostock. I cannot think offhand of any boarders who live respectively closer or further away than they do.

Today's group of prospective parents who came to grill me turned out to be the sort of coalescence of cultures which could perhaps only happen at Millfield. They are a business man from the Central African Republic with a Pakistani aide, the Kazakhstani Ambassador to Switzerland with an Indian aide and, in the midst of them, a pleasant but bemused English family who, it transpired, had only infrequently left Somerset, and who clearly thought they had mistakenly arrived at the United Nations HQ. Happily, they all found lots to talk about following their tour and all left in high spirits, chatting away as if they had known each other all their lives. I love that sort of thing. Having said goodbye to them outside, I was relieved to see that there were fewer young girls hanging about outside

Reception than there had been yesterday, when Pierce Brosnan, complete with two long pigtails, had pitched up.

RICHARD STRATTON (1973 – 1977)

My memory of life at Millfield is a blur because there were just so many things going on all at once all the time; the six inch rule, of course, and the betting shop in Street, lunch in the chip shop, running up the Tor at 5.00 in the morning, playing pool in Glastonbury, golfing for money, non-stop sport and spending a lot of time in the Dark Room, though not always on photographic business.

Then there was Hughee, the bald Scots driver of the double-decker bus that used to take us in and out of school; and cramming into cabs owned by Don, the private taxi driver based in Street who probably became a rich man on the back of Millfield boys. He was always puffing away on his evil little cigars, so whenever we had been in his taxi, we got into trouble back at school, as we then stank of his smoke.

Mr Fletcher – Flash – was another character who made a big impression on us, though not for any reason of which he'd be proud. He was known as Flash, not because he was a Maths genius, though he was, but because he used to move around the campus wearing a flat cap and a dirty raincoat, checking out all the bins. We never did find out what he was looking for.

I had a fantastic time. I only hope my children enjoy their time at school as much as I did.

RAY FOX, ESQ (1968 – 1992)

I was in charge of examinations for some 15 years and remember being shocked by the conditions to which pupils and invigilators were subjected in the 70's and earlier when exams were upon us. Old Millfieldians reading this will no doubt give a wry smile, but the meteorological conditions prevailing outside were of more than usual interest to those who were beating their brains inside. During the first February exam, there was snow and ice all around, and on entering the Crispin Hall it was evident that there was no heating there whatsoever. Luckily everyone was wearing overcoats, for common sense prevailed in those days. Some also wore scarves and only the incautious or over-optimistic had eschewed gloves. On those bleak winter days, Boss would ladle out a glass of hot punch during break to those invigilators who had survived the arctic conditions in the hall to drink with our freshly baked bun. One day, the geography department recorded 46 degrees Fahrenheit in the Crispin Hall.

However, things were no more propitious for examinations in the summer, for then we were lodged in the marquee. I remember 96 degrees there during one June heat wave. Whatever the weather, the marquee certainly provided variety. Wind often threatened a lift-off, rain provided a continuous patter, and sun – or lack of it – generated extremes of temperature. Rising damp reduced script paper to blotting paper, noise levels mounted as lawnmowers prepared for Parents' Day and there was also the permanent risk of low-level attack by swooping birds. Above all, the thing I found most original was the slope of the ground which literally put the rear four rows of candidates in "dead ground". Somehow, I came to accept that this was Millfield.

GERALD DAVIDSON (1974 – 1978)

My father ran into difficulties and when my housemaster heard, he forwarded a message to Colin Atkinson, who knew me quite well, as I used to be one of his regular squash partners. He then asked me to come and see him. I remember the meeting so well, as if it was yesterday. He asked me what he could do to help me and was kindness personified. In addition he asked if my father needed help with school fees and that if so, I should not worry as it would be taken care of. I know that Colin probably went out on a limb for me and I cannot remember any other time in my life since, when anybody has acted so selflessly.

MIKE DAVIES (1973 – 1978)

One of the daily highlights for a growing lad in the 70's was the morning scramble for the freshly made currant buns snatched from a kitchen window behind Millfield House.

It was a scrum as we all pressed forward; a quick foot up on the base of the wall, an attempt to grab more than one bun from the big wooden tray before taking a whack from an unseen officiant who wielded a large wooden spoon. It was always a race to the main house from wherever the last lesson before break was held, for it was only ever a matter of seconds before there were no buns left at all. The lucky ones could then nurse their bruised knuckles and munch their well earned spoils, surrounded by those unlucky hopefuls looking for a handout from a mate more fortunate than they.

Sadly the practice ended before I left, the victim of some capricious change in the catering arrangements. I can remember to this day the taste and texture of those buns; the dough soft on the teeth and the sharp tang of biting in to the currants. Ah! The simple pleasures of a hungry small boy – now alive only in taste memory.

SIMON HAVERS (1978)(EDGARLEY)

I think it was in 1978 at Edgarley that I took part in a musical based on the life of Socrates, written by our football master, Norman Brook. I remember him principally for his ability to play the piano with an artificial hand, which was of course gruesomely fascinating to a 12 year old. To this day, I find the tunes from the show, and lines like "You've got to be stealthy in Delphi" and "I'm Soc Soc Soc Soc Socrates" leaping unbidden into my head. My father was so impressed by the show that he named his new yacht "Xantippe": the title of the musical. It was surely the best school musical ever written.

Sarah Champion, the Deputy Head at Edgarley who has universally acclaimed pastoral gifts, has passed me a last contribution from a small boy there. He had been naughty in some way and as a detention he had been

required to reply in writing to the question, "What rules would you have at Millfield if you were the retiring Head?" There were some good ones. These, for example;
No. 7 – Intercourse is forbidden in school because after all you are too young.
No. 8 – Cap guns does scare people don't bring them in.
No. 10 – If you see someone fighting break it up.
No. 11 – Do not temp your houseparent get a video overrated in your age.

SALLY HELVEY (NEE KENT) (1972 – 1978)

It was a surprise on arrival to find that our classrooms were either in Nissen huts or in the timber 'chicken runs', luxurious though these would have been for chickens. By contrast, the Biology and Chemistry blocks were considered very plush and were incredibly well-equipped. It was very much like going from the sublime to the ridiculous at Millfield then, depending on what you were being taught.

Being a rider under the watchful eye of Major Burke, I spent a lot of time in and around the stable block which was situated at the back of the coach park. It was here that the CCF would parade for their square-bashing sessions – much to the amusement of us riders who would peer over the wall whilst the NCO in charge had his back to us and try to distract the poor cadets from the serious business of being military. Our taunts were merciless and it wasn't long before the cadets were put out of their misery and were paraded elsewhere on the campus.

The entrance to this coach park was strictly out of bounds to pupils – not just because it was dangerous in the 'rush-hour' but also because it was all too easy for pupils to nip across to Sly's sweet shop on the opposite corner of the road where they sold hot apple pies and sausages at break times. It was always a daring attempt to sneak past either the Chemistry block, risking the wrath of 'Brom', or the Biology block, risking the wrath of Mrs Jackson. Anyone going straight down the middle of the coach park over to Sly's was considered a school hero if he or she came back unscathed armed with all our orders. I admit no shame at having myself broken this rule; it was the best adrenaline-rush ever!

A more serious dare, and one for which you would risk getting gated, or even thrown out as I believe was the case for one boy, was to streak down The Avenue in the lunch-hour. The Avenue then was actually the main drive up to Millfield House itself. It was also out of bounds and only used for visitors – most of whom were prospective parents. One pupil cunningly suggested that he did a sponsored streak in order to raise money for some charity or other. This of course got him all the attention and support he needed to get away with it. A streak was certainly worth turning up for and became a bit of a trend. They were always arranged in secret and usually performed by boys who, shall we say, were more comfortable than girls in their own bodies. Naturally, the girls enjoyed the spectacle the most, and large crowds of us assembled to encourage the streaker. There was soon a danger that streaking was actually becoming part of the curriculum. The Headmaster, Colin Atkinson, was forced to put a stop to it when some unsuspecting – and needless to say surprised – new parents reported passing a boy sprinting down the Avenue in all his glory as they were driving up it.

It was a sad day when streaking was banned.

SIMON JARVIS (1973 – 1978)

Everyone who was in Shapwick Manor will have stories to tell about Barry Hobson and the "harsh" living conditions we had to endure. Whilst our fellow students in other houses had two-man rooms, carpets and curtains and other mod cons, we lived in fairly basic dormitories – not a carpet or a curtain to be seen. Barry ran a very tight ship and gave a lot of responsibility for the day-to-day running of the house to the prefects. Although we never appreciated it at the time, he was exceptionally loyal to his boys and would defend us to the hilt. That is not to say we got away with anything, but he would keep things in-house and deal with us quite severely when we stepped out of line.

Barry used to run a surgery every morning before breakfast for those who were ill, or thought they were. It was rumoured that Barry started taking the surgery because his wife, Rosemary, a qualified nurse, was too soft. I remember one morning waiting in the queue and hearing a boy further up the queue saying he had stomach ache and could he be off games. Barry's response was, "Well, it's not surprising you've got stomach ache, boy, you haven't got any socks on." You didn't get an off-games chit easily at Shapwick!

The strict hierarchy of the bus was another Shapwick tradition. The monitors and senior boys occupied the back seats, and you sat nearer to the front the more junior you were. Woe betide you if you were presumptuous enough to sit in the wrong seats. Every evening journey back to the house involved a singsong, with a variety of old favourites, many of them adapted to include references to Barry or the house prefects. Occasionally, other houses like Etonhurst or Ashcott would have to share our bus, which must have been quite daunting when the singing was in full flow.

MATTHEW MCKAIG (1970 – 1978)

Pure chance took me to Millfield. My father, who was in the Royal Navy, was driving down to Plymouth to take up a new post there. All the family were together. Only the night before was he informed that the prep school I was booked into had suddenly closed. So when we stopped at Mere for lunch my father rang Millfield and spoke to Boss, having heard, from an old naval friend that Millfield was a "good place". He invited us over that afternoon.

There was Boss, sitting on the sofa with Amothe Sankey in the background – sports magazines and other journals in great piles; more like a den than an office and a place to make a nervous boy of 10 feel quite at home somehow, or probably this was Boss's easy manner and avuncular charm. Boss asked if my sister, who was also travelling with us, might come to Millfield. Once my father had said no, she was offered a mouldy pear (or so she said) and asked to sit in the car with my mother, which they both dutifully did.

I suppose I must be one of the last OMs to have been interviewed by Boss and whilst I feel privileged to have actually met the founder of Millfield, I wish I had had the opportunity to get to see more of him. However, I do understand it when older OMs express misty-eyed sentiments about their old Headmaster – he was indeed very special.

In February of 1977 the Great Snowstorm hit Somerset. At

Mill House, we were cut off from the body of the school by 15 foot snowdrifts from Saturday night until Thursday. We spent the days mucking around in the snow, and arranging the mother of all snowball fights with the sporty girls at Kernick, just up the road in Baltonsborough. In the event, we were thrashed and retired wet, bruised and a little scared by the ferocity of the assault. We did ask for it though. Their Amazonian determination to overwhelm us may have had something to do with the fact that we habitually referred to them as the 'Kernick Tanks' – most unfairly, of course.

I remember John Davies trying, at one point, to get us to clear the snow outside the house. This we thought was just plain silly, for we had far better things to do, but I imagine he was just trying to keep us out of trouble, one source of which was the 'Three Old Castles' in Keinton Mandeville. Having battled though the snowdrifts, we could retire to an upstairs room, safe in the knowledge that nobody could reach us there unless they had the same urge to get as wet and as physically exhausted as we had.

A Sea King helicopter landed in an adjacent field, taking away a heavily pregnant woman, the wife of a local farmer. A few hours afterwards, we heard the farmer shouting for all he was worth to anybody within earshot; "I've got a son, I've got a son!"

In the meantime, a JCB digger was working its way gradually along the Brue road towards Mill House, and when it reached us, after three days solid work, we all had to go back to school.

Mill House! What a place, what a location! A rural idyll set against the more urban charms of the Millfield campus. It is hard to believe that when I first went to Mill House in 1973 we still returned to the house, some seven miles away from the main school, for lunch. In fact, we managed to spend much of our school lives at Mill House, at weekends after games on Saturday. It was then that we used to 'sign out' and explore the lanes on our bikes.

One of our most popular activities we undertook was rabbiting, usually very early on a frosty morning and in the company of a couple of friends and some ferrets. The idea was that once the rabbits' exit holes had been covered with nets, a ferret was released down the main rabbit hole. I regret to say that we used to make home-made cross bows for use on the rabbits as they escaped from the holes. Several rabbits were usually caught, which meant that we were able to provide Ivy, the Mill House cook, with a useful addition for the dining room table.

'Signing out' was not always entirely what it was supposed to be. There were a number of illicit destinations involved, apart from the manly exercise involved, of course! Most commonly these trips were used to buy rough cider – "knee-cracker" - from the local farms. The price was 45 pence a gallon if you brought along your own container. I remember, or almost remember getting very happy on the stuff, weak as I think it was, resulting in eventful return journeys and, on return to Mill House, the conspiratorial game of making it known that one was drunk, but only to those without authority. When we got older, these trips often seemed to end up in one of the local pubs - perhaps the Three Old Castles, or the Barton Inn or the Lydford Arms. And for those who smoked – only pipes of course – these trips were pure heaven, allowing those who chose to indulge, to get light-headed from drawing on pipes filled with 'Clan' and 'Borkhum Riff'. Ah, those were the days.

LAWRENCE POOLE (1975 – 1978)

I think I was the first person with cerebral palsy to be admitted to Millfield. My greatest joy was that I was able to play football there – something that I had not been allowed to do at my previous school.

One day when I was 13, my friend James and I took a ladder from the Combined Cadet Force stores and used it to cross a stream. Thirty years ago this seemed the height of daring.

MARK SIEFF (1973 – 1978)

I was injured during a house rugby competition and as a result I had to spend the night in hospital. This was most unfortunate, for the House Hop was scheduled for that evening and I had been looking forward to it immensely. Apparently it was a very good one, so good in fact the whole house was gated for their behaviour and House Hops were banned from that day on.

Being entirely innocent of any charge of which all of my friends seemed to have been guilty, I was promoted rapidly, and the next term I found myself Head of House and a school prefect. From this I learned that lady luck operates in very strange ways and that every cloud does indeed have a silver lining.

> *I toured Etonhurst last night with Sam, the Head of House. He looks 15, is fresh-faced, without guile and is no games player. You would not assume he would cut much ice with the other boys but he clearly has great respect throughout the house. There is silence in prep long before ever we appear on the scene. How does he do it? "Well I don't really know sir. They're all so nice." It strikes me as a good cameo of how liking people seems so often to get the best out of them.*

Stephen Stanley (1970 – 1978)

Peter O'Connell ran the brass tuition and one of his braver initiatives was to put the Millfield brass band together. We would usually practice once a week and occasionally would be foolhardy enough to hold impromptu recitals tagged on to some other event. It would be fair to say that poor old Peter did not have the cream of the Millfield musicians to work with. To say that he was trying to produce a silk purse from a sow's ear might have been unfair to one or two of the musicians, but probably not to most of us. At the time, the Millfield First Orchestra was almost exclusively made up of grade 8 musicians and music scholars, whereas the brass band was made up of players of all abilities and even of none. The best of our group might have been quite musical, but by the time you got as far away from the conductor's podium as the 3rd cornet or the tuba player, well, we probably had less than a year's experience between us.

Up until 1976 our greatest exposure was playing for the Millfield Combined Cadet Force on a summer's afternoon when they had an inspection of some kind. There might even have been a visiting army officer awarding promotions and inspecting the troops. It was probably the first time we had played out in the open air and Peter substituted a big bass drum for his usual baton to ensure that the CCF at least had a regular beat. To our surprise it all passed off pretty well, and we managed to give them some good military tunes to help them all march around the school

1979 A and B Blocks have arrived.

tennis courts.

Emboldened by this, Peter's next act was to enter the band into a much more serious event – a public brass band contest, to be held in Bridgwater. We practised madly to get ourselves up to the performance levels required so as not to disgrace ourselves or the school. Peter's commitment to success conveyed itself to us in a number of ways. We knew it mattered to him, but we were all stunned when, as we went on stage to play our three set pieces, Peter, who was as close to being a chain smoker outside of his classroom as I have ever seen, said that if we didn't come last, he would give up smoking.

Once on stage, however, our sense of mission weakened. Mark Asquith at once pointed out a number of attractive young ladies in the audience and he and I tried to out do each other in attempting to catch their eye while the rest of the band was playing. It must have been interesting for some of the audience to see the first trumpet and first tenor horn winking at members of the audience and trying to obtain a wink in return as proof of success. Fortunately the judges were in a closed cage and could not see our antics.

In spite of this, in the event we came fifth out of eight competing bands. When he heard the result, Peter was actually moved to tears. I'm not sure if he was being sentimental or if it was the thought of throwing away all the cigarettes that remained in his current pack. In any case he kept to his promise and gave up smoking on the spot, destroying his remaining cigarettes in front of us. He was never seen smoking again in my remaining years at the school and is still, I'm told, a smoke free zone.

MALCOLM WELFORD (1973 – 1978)

Even though we encountered a 6th former fast asleep on a bench behind A Block while being shown round by the Tutor for Admissions, Mr Gaskell, my parents still chose to send me to Millfield, where I had many good times. Among them was the time when Mark Reed, son of Oliver, who was in our house, shaved his head as his Dad had just done for a film, and then streaked down the main drive. Later, I was a spectator for a 1st XV match against the Old Boys. We had a really good front row but the Old Boys had among others Gareth Edwards and JPR playing for them. At half time the school had the audacity to be winning, largely due to our front row. JPR had had enough of this and watching him take out the offending player was simply amazing. Nothing personal, just business.

VICKY WILLISON (1976 – 78)

My Maths tutor was Major Noakes – he may have been a Colonel and I apologise if my memory has demoted him. He taught a ragged group of eight boys and me, the honorary female, in one of the wooden huts. We were a straggly, emotive, fractious and frankly bored band, incapable of achieving 'O' Level, but his enthusiasm to drag us through basic maths to gain a CSE was commendable. He achieved this by instilling in us sheer fear of his heavy walking stick, which was his preferred artillery, but he always had an endearing twinkle in his eye.

He fondly nicknamed me his 'decorative piece', the artist in him creating a permanent hangman/woman picture of me in the corner of his blackboard – hair flying out in schoolgirl pigtails with bulging eyes and flailing limbs. Whenever I succumbed to the toilet humour of my fellow Maths victims, he would tap menacingly at his chalk effigy with that wooden stick.

One day I fell asleep, such was the stupefying effect Maths had on me. As my nose drifted towards the graphs in front of me, I failed to hear the warning tap, tap, tap on the board.

That stick came down so fast and so close that I never had a chance. The hairs on my upturned nose quivered with the force of the descending weapon, which landed with a mighty crash on my textbook. I left my seat in a nano second, flying backwards into the arms of Ashraf – that gorgeous Egyptian bloke – taking with me 2 other boys plus one trestle table. Stunned, we all lay in a tangled heap on the floor. If he had been a millimetre closer with his aim – well, who knows/nose what might have happened – but at least I learned my decimals.

He was a very fine and effective tutor!

VICTORIA BISHOP (1978 – 1979)

I had just five terms at Millfield but, having left a school that had once been a huge success and had suddenly gone downhill, Millfield was a bright shining light for me. Everyone seemed to accept me for what I was, and I was certainly not a sports fanatic or an academic wizz kid. I just loved the fact that everyone appre-

Abbey pupils admire Elizabeth Frink's statue.

ciated every effort – so I made lots of friends and was the fittest I have ever been in my entire life!

My art lessons were absolutely typical of the way in which

Millfield was so untypical. Since my choice of A Levels did not fit in with the regular timetable, I had my own 1 to 1 lessons with Gyr King and we chose together what I wanted to study. Those five terms of modern Art history really opened up my eyes and ever since, on all my travels – and I've been lucky enough to do a good deal of travelling – I have hunted out Art galleries and really enjoyed so much more than I could have imagined. The practical side of my course was pretty alternative and I created some rather off the wall pieces of 3D stuff, whilst those in the other groups were drawing & painting, where I would never have succeeded. So thank you Millfield – not just for a great experience but for opening my eyes to the whole world of modern art.

Max in the 4ᵗʰ year comes up to me on the athletics track and tells me he likes my portrait hanging in the current summer exhibition. "A really good composition," he says with feeling. "Oh good," say I. "Have you seen the other picture there by the same artist?" Max looks blank. "You know," I prod his memory. "The one of the girl in her bra with a bloke standing close behind her?" For a moment then I realise I have his complete, unadulterated attention, and even I suspect, his respect. His mouth opens. Breath comes out, and then, "Was that you as well, sir?"

I took a visiting sculptress round the exhibition of Elizabeth Frink's sculptures, which has graced the campus all summer. "All the heads look like her; they have her chin," she said. I asked her whether this also applied to her water buffalo. "Less so, but a bit." It was rather touching, when the term was under way, to see two third year girls sitting quietly on the grass by the eight foot high, well endowed male nude, fashioning a sort of loin cloth for him out of ever-green branches. When I enquired why they thought this necessary, they suggested that they thought he looked chilly. What, in mid summer? "Well, you never know, sir, do you." There's no arguing with that.

CHRISTOPHER GALLOP (1974 – 1979)

I was more than fortunate to have, in Mike Cole, a biology tutor who was both an evident enthusiast and an inspirational and encouraging teacher. One day, reading around, I happened upon an algorithm for calculating the likely size of a population of wild mammals, which depended on the technique of trapping the animals alive, marking them with a biologically neutral pigment, and releasing them again. Over time, the changing proportions of new and previously captured animals found in the traps would indicate a closer and closer estimate to the actual population size when fed through the algorithm.

Excited by this practical application of mathematics to the subject of which I was most fond, I showed the text to Mike Cole, who immediately suggested that I try it out by assessing the size of the local mouse populations. Within days he had sent off for and obtained four Longworth small mammal traps and handed them over to me. For half a term through a hot Summer, I worked the traps at two sites, in amongst the discarded machinery and rubble behind the maintenance workshop, and in the brambles and other undergrowth down by the duck-pond, where Mike had shown me how to detect the presence of mice by setting out flat tiles covered in a thin layer of soot so as to show up their tracks. Each morning, after the coach arrived on campus from Etonhurst and before first period I would visit the traps, decant any occupants into a plastic bag, and then struggle somewhat to get a line of blue paint onto the back of a wriggling field mouse without either getting bitten or covering myself with paint, until gradually the algorithm began to reveal a likely population of four mice – most likely a single family group – behind Maintenance. I had less luck at the duck pond; all I ever caught there was a shrew. Upsettingly, because shrews' metabolism runs so fast, my usual 24 hours between visits was far too long with nothing for the shrew to eat besides the bait in the trap and it was dead when I found it. Still, practical field-work on my own at 16; tremendous stuff.

My next project was slightly different. Having developed an interest in psychology, I suggested to Mike that I could try training a mouse to run a maze. Wisely, he pointed out that it might be more sensible to use an animal which was already used to laboratory conditions, rather than rely on training one of the victims of the Longworth traps.

Behind the display of vivaria on the ground floor of the Biology block there were a number of prep rooms, ordinarily the domain only of the teaching staff and technicians, but into which access was permitted to those few others with good reason. I discovered that there was a tank in there in which lived a snake of some sort, belonging to another boy. Since the snake lived on live mice, a supply of which was living in another tank, I was able to persuade the snake's owner to lend me one of the mice as an experimental subject, provided I promised to return it for consumption when I was finished with it. Once I had built a simple maze out of cardboard and secured a supply of cheese to reward the mouse with, I was in business and spent many happy hours amidst the sharp smells and soft humming machinery at the back of Biology, teaching my loaned mouse to distinguish left from right.

Captain Maslen, housemaster at Etonhurst during my last years there, had a more than relaxed view of drinking. As an ex-naval man he actually encouraged the house prefects to spend Saturday nights at the Ring O' Bells up the road next to the church in Ashcott, and provided large tankards of evil-coloured rough cider for everyone at Open Weekend, but he would seek to have expelled anyone he found smoking. This took a bit of getting used to for those of us who had arrived at Millfield in the days when prefects were allowed to smoke pipes, and for that matter to grow moustaches if they were hormonally capable.

The first Saturday after my eventual promotion to house prefect I was duly escorted by my now fellow prefects to the back bar of the Ring O' Bells, but I have never been an enthusiastic drinker of beer in volume, and certainly wasn't when I was 17, so after two pints I began to grumble that I was full and besides was beginning to feel a bit less than sober. Never mind, said my minders, switch to shorts and you'll feel better, at which they began to provide me with bacardi and cokes.

On the way back to the house, for some reason the significance of which escaped me at the time, they seemed very keen to impress on me that, whilst we should have to present ourselves to the Captain on our return, I should resist any temptation to speak. Outside the Captain's study I was propped against the opposite wall of the corridor and reminded to keep stumm. Unfortunately, the Captain addressed a direct question to me – how had I enjoyed the evening? I beamed. Surely a direct question required an answer? "Well Sir", I said, expansively. I may even have gestured to indicate my fellows, the vicinity and the world in general, "I have had a *very* enjoyable evening", but, leaning forward to meet him eye to eye, and screwing up my face against the corridor light which suddenly seemed extraordinarily bright and uncomfortable, and lowering my voice for confidentiality, "I *may* have had a *little* too much to drink". The Captain grinned at the rest of the party, who were standing thunderstruck. "See you take care of him"...and vanished back into the study.

I was a rotten prefect. Captain Maslen eventually confessed that he had only promoted me in the first place because I had turned out to be such a failure as a house monitor and the only way he could think of to lessen the degree of contact I had with the 'troops' was to promote me to the relative isolation of prefecthood and the sanctuary of the Prefects' Common Room. When I came back for my seventh term in the sixth form, for Oxbridge entry, I would have been Head of House by virtue of seniority had the Captain not persuaded Salim Bahwan to stay on as well. Salim was a full School Prefect to my Deputy and so became Head of House. Salim, who was essentially an adult man by then must surely have been conscious of why he was there, although we never spoke of it. It was hardly as though he was trying for Oxbridge himself; I had been instrumental in helping him to survive his Maths prep assignments two years earlier during which time he had insisted on paying me a pound a time for my trouble, and in turn I had salved my conscience about taking his money by insisting that he sit with me and listen to my explanations instead of my just writing his prep out for him. I was deeply saddened when a few years later he was killed in a road accident.

But I had absolutely no air of authority, and once, when Deputy Head of House, I was out for a stroll after dark, I ran suddenly into two of the other house prefects outside House Grounds, both of whom were smoking crafty cigarettes and who were terrified at first as I rounded the corner of the wall behind which they were leaning, because they thought I was the Captain and that they were finished. Their response to this mistake of their own was to burst into my room later that night when I was in bed, jump on me and give me a good pummelling in order to teach *me* not to sneak around quietly at night.

I was an even worse Deputy School Prefect. By the time of my final elevation to the "birdshit" tie I had essentially decided that the whole prefectorial system was a waste of my time. This was largely because nobody I particularly respected or liked amongst my contemporaries had themselves achieved promotion, with the honourable exception of my (still) life-long friend Andrew Last. Andrew's family home was a short walk from the campus, opposite that of the Atkinsons, and Andrew's parents, in common, it seemed with several of the parent body, took a fairly relaxed view of some of the school's own precepts and requirements. The Last's mild contribution to misrule was to connive at Andrew's and my own loose interpretation of our turns of Town duty, which was supposed to consist of wandering the streets looking for ISP miscreants, and which we chose to regard as being satisfied by sitting at the Last's kitchen table drinking tea and chatting. We always reckoned that if CRMA were to see us from his own house he would fail to spot our delinquency since we were by then such semi-detached members of the community of prefects that he wouldn't recognise us, and since we had little or no interest in sport we reckoned that he would never have known who we were anyway. I don't believe I had a single one to one encounter with CRMA during my entire time at Millfield.

This was certainly in part because of my difficulties with sport. I was spectacularly poorly co-ordinated as a teenager and had profound and genuine difficulty with most of the large-scale movements associated with mainstream sports. "Smiler" Kemp, whose main interest appeared to be in ensuring that we turned up to tennis lessons during PE periods on time and dressed correctly ("or I will say to you: 'Tennis Defaulters' and you will smile and say 'thank you, Sir' ") had to admit defeat with me. At the end of a term's tennis coaching we were all supposed to take and pass a very basic LTA competency test, serving, returning and playing a short game, which proved entirely beyond me. However, anxious to preserve his 100% pass record, "Smiler" fiddled the results and I was awarded the certificate anyhow.

I was a lost cause to most sports, but, particularly at

Etonhurst there were kindred spirits, fellow Nerds I suppose we would be called these days. After my first term, in which I made the serious mistake of signing up for Soccer as my team game, leading to many afternoons spent running alone around the perimeter of the pitches for "not trying", I settled into a pattern of Hockey Leagues in Winter and Spring terms and Cricket in Summer. Hockey involved seeing how many clothes we could get away with wearing underneath our games kit, especially if we were allowed to keep our tracksuits on, more or less guaranteed if Ossie Simes was in charge, less so with anyone else, and competitions to see how long we could keep a hockey stick balanced upright on an outstretched palm. Cricket comprised a gratifying amount of lying on the grass in the sunshine listening to the Alan Freeman show on the radio whilst waiting to bat. But this harsh regime relaxed as I moved up the school and I eventually managed pretty much to escape from taking exercise at all, other than on my own terms. I did go for long bike rides round the Somerset Levels on Sunday afternoons for instance.

> *Wednesday afternoon is games afternoon. The sun came out, and with it a sense of optimism. I don't think I saw one glum face all afternoon. I watched a bit of tennis, fencing, judo, squash, climbing, weight-training, badminton, riding, aerobics and an U14 girl's hockey match. Our coach, whose Irish humour never deserts her, was shouting our girls on from the touchline. "Oh, unlucky," she called as the ball is driven past our goalkeeper to give the opposition a lead. Then sotto voce to me, "It's bad play really but you have to encourage them or they cry." Leaning over the railing watching them, one mother said unprompted, "My daughter's nicer since she came here. She's more considerate. That's what boarding does for you, I suppose."*

The first move was to take up .22 rifle shooting. One of the great benefits of Millfield was the chance to try out minority sports, and having dabbled with fencing and canoeing (on the River Brue, so hardly white water and I even managed to get stuck on top of a tiny weir so slowly was I generally moving) I discovered that I was quite a passable shot, making the school team. That took care of two of the three games periods a week and apart from other advantages such as not having to get changed I genuinely enjoyed the sport and the challenge of reaching the Zen-like calm necessary for success in competition. Then Morris Gould, who was in the year above me at Etonhurst, managed to get himself appointed as scorer to the Athletics Squad, and invited me to agree to being appointed as his deputy. For most of a Summer term, when we were not at Athletics meets taking down the results for Millfield, we were in the computer room, supposedly loading the figures into the school computer for storage but actually playing a primitive moon landing game.

Eventually some sort of administrative process coughed up an allegation back at Etonhurst that we had been missing in action but we escaped punishment and I developed the distinct impression that by the time we reached the Sixth Form nobody really minded if we were strangers to the world of active participation in sport.

Teddy Birnberg was a great man. He always wore a grey pin-striped suit to lessons, with a maroon v-necked sweater in winter, and, slightly scarily, clearly knew all his charges pretty well. Those of us who took 'O' Level French a year early had the option of staying with Teddy for another year in which we would start the 'A' Level course with the prospect of eventually taking the 'A' Level early as well. I signed up, although only for the year as once I embarked on my Lower Sixth year I couldn't find room in my timetable for French any more. But in that extra year we read, amongst other things, L'Etranger. Astonished by what I saw as Meursault's pointless and disastrous refusal to conform, I delivered myself in class one day of a diatribe to the effect that the novel was stupidly unrealistic, people didn't behave like that in real life and that nobody would suddenly develop principles so profound as to be preferable to continued existence without there having been more sign of them beforehand.

Teddy blinked at me through his glasses. "You're quite wrong about that, Christopher", he said, quietly. He was the only member of staff who always called me by my full name without it sounding like a rebuke. I stopped, expecting Teddy to embark on some sort of personal revelation. After all, as a middle-aged single man, and a Jew, he probably knew something about being an Outsider. "People do behave just like that, and what's more you will yourself, one day". Now I was blinking at him.

"Oh yes", he said, nodding and softly picking up momentum, "I know what will happen. You'll leave here, you'll go to University, you'll put on a suit and get a job, have a wife and a family no doubt and lead an ordinary life. And then, one day, something will take place. I don't know what it'll be, but something will strike you as wholly unacceptable. *Wholly* unacceptable. And you'll fight it, no matter what that takes, no matter what it costs you, you'll fight it, *because nothing else will make any sense to you*". I was completely speechless, because I could see that he was right. I still can. I haven't had my Teddy Birnberg moment, yet. But I shall, one day.

Morris Gould formed a punk band, the Ripchords, with three other friends: Mike Trei, who was also at Etonhurst, and Sean Dromgoole, and Jonathan Collins aka Jonathan Jetlag, who were Day Boys. With help and backing from Mike's father, they recorded, cut and marketed an EP, featuring pictures of the band on the sleeve in a gritty urban environment. Actually, the gritty urban environment was the outbuildings at the back of Etonhurst House, with the use of some careful camera-work. CRMA had to give his permission for the enterprise, which involved handing him a demo-tape of the three tracks on the EP for him to listen to. One track, "Peace Artist", which Morris claimed was about me since it denounced the 'anything for a quiet life' attitude which Teddy Birnberg had detected and pronounced ultimately temporary, needed editing. It contained the line "fuck off the world but don't upset the apple-cart". Stung by the implicit accusation, I tried to persuade Morris that since CRMA was highly unlikely to listen to the demo-tape at all, it would be quite safe to leave the line on the track in unaltered form, and a heated argument ensued in the music hut at Etonhurst where the band used to 'rehearse'. Eventually wise counsel prevailed and Morris and the others recorded a version in which the line appeared as "forget the world", permission was granted and the EP was released.

As far as I know, it was played on radio four times, twice by John Peel, once on Radio Bristol, and once, fantastically, quite without warning, late one night on Radio Luxembourg when I just happened to be listening under the bed-clothes. The Ripchords played one live gig, at a school hop, to which I turned up in week-end punk gear, consisting of hair rendered spiky with gel, badges and safety pins stuck all over shirt and trousers, and a tie with a ridiculously small knot, the ensemble topped off with a silk dressing gown worn open and held down with two belts. Hops during the year or so at the height of the punk era were fun. Normally, hops were socially challenging events in which my friends and I would fail to get off with any girls and would be left watching the slow dance at the end in a mood of grim frustration.

Hops at the height of punk were quite different as we could dance to *our* music, which the rest of the school seemed to find completely baffling, dress on *our* terms, and huddle superciliously whilst some of the surviving 'dinosaurs' music was played. There was one remaining problem in that there were only about three girls in the entire school who were into punk and they were a bit intimidating, so we still tended to have to sit out the last dance, but at least we could do it scornfully rather than wistfully.

One of the aspects by which Millfield's progressive character was supposedly illustrated in those days was the absence of a book of school rules or indeed of any written rules at all. There were rules of course; we were meant to memorise them, together with the colours of the various Houses and the names of the Heads of School as part of our New Bugs test. In Etonhurst at least that had degenerated somewhat when I joined, so that the major element was the singing of a song, preferably a rude one, whilst standing on a table in front of the whole House. Because I joined in the Spring Term with only one other person, called Stephen Browning, I felt a bit exposed, especially since I didn't actually know any rude songs. Browning went first, having summoned up one verse of some half-remembered rugby song and climbed down to thunderous applause. I had decided to go for the novelty approach, if not sympathy vote, and had memorised "How Much is That Doggy in the Window", to be sung backwards. The applause when I finished can best be described as 'polite', but I can still remember easily how it goes backwards, more than thirty years later.

As for the school rules, there were only two on which everyone seemed to agree. One was about only prefects being allowed to walk up the drive. This was eventually dealt with when the drive was dug up and turfed. The other was the Six Inch Rule, which was the one about members of the opposite sex having to be no fewer than six inches apart at all times. Nevertheless, there was always room for doubt about a rule, which like the British Constitution, was unwritten.

I managed to get myself elected to the School Council at one point, I don't now remember exactly how. Most of our meetings, like those of School Councils everywhere, were relatively innocuous, though we were permitted to redesign the House Colours tie, coming up with a design in black with a diagonal slash of the relevant house hue on a white background, with a black windmill in a white oval above. Even that was a bit controversial, quickly becoming known as the "Hitler Youth tie". But we excelled ourselves when it came to the Six Inch Rule. I can't recall how it started, but at one meeting we embarked on a philosophical discussion about the nature of rules and whether or not rules in a society such as a school could be said to have the status of obligations or indeed any validity at all if they remained unwritten. Straying into deeply revisionist territory, we took the Six Inch Rule as an example and passed a resolution stating not only that the Six Inch Rule did not exist, but more importantly, that it *never had* existed.

Sadly, the School Council was presided over by Mr Newman, who, if nothing else, had learned from his work with the Conservative Party the importance of taking control of events rapidly. There appeared on House notice boards the only reference I ever saw to a School Rule in written form, namely that, contrary to whatever the School Council might have resolved, as far as the school authorities were concerned, the Six Inch Rule did exist, had always existed, and probably always would. Furthermore, if it were broken, retribution would follow swiftly and decisively. Nevertheless, hops were a kind of licensed environment, and I recall enthusiastically breaking the Six Inch Rule at my last hop to the extent of reversing my partner heavily into a table and knocking several glasses off it to smash on the floor without any of the nearby staff taking very much notice at all.

Three pupils in quick succession this morning; one who wants me to agree to his returning to Saudi against his parents' instructions; answer, no. Then a posse who want to set up another Young Enterprise group with

*four different projects; answer, yes; and finally the irre-
sistible Zoe with a new charity request for a non-uni-
form day; answer, yes, as always. A grilling followed
from two sets of efficient and well-briefed parents with
children in tow, and then straight into the School
Council, all 60 of them, who have prepared a long list
of ingenious questions which they put with incomparable tact. David Rosser, who chairs the meeting with
unflappable good humour, manages to concede half
their points, while ensuring that no real ground is given
where it could never be reclaimed.*

*At the Junior hop, run by one of the girls' houses,
there is the usual racket, war paint, miniskirts, too
many bare midriffs, flashing lights, dry ice and ear-split-
ting music. They all seem to be having a ball. Bellowing
into my ear as we watch from the sidelines, a senior girl
on duty shrieks, "I'm so glad I'm not young any more,
sir."*

I was talking to an OM friend recently, and we agreed that whilst
we were both very sure that it had been the right school for us, and
that we had certainly been happy there, as non-sporting, relatively
academic offspring of non-wealthy parents, we had both felt at the
time, as well as in retrospect, that we were members of a kind of
minority community within the school, and that maybe even the
school's collective attention was to some extent focussed away from
us. Now, that's not entirely fair, and probably over-states the case,
but that's somehow what we felt.

*A mother comes to see me to explain that she wants to
remove her son after just one term. She insists that she
has nothing but admiration for all that we have done for
her boy already, but it turns out that he has always
wanted to go to Eton, and has rightly deduced that we
are not it. She says he feels "different" from the other
pupils here, but I wonder how he can feel more "different" than, say, those who come from 54 different countries to be here, and who make the most of their difference. Anyway, her mind is made up and she will take*

him tomorrow to Sherborne where she hopes that he will feel less "different". But what a terrible shame it is that he should flee difference when we should all revel in it. Is this our fault? His? I am really depressed by this interview. The Brassens song that I have introduced to countless classes in my time springs to mind. "Tous les braves gens n'aiment pas que l'on suive une autre route qu'eux." Vive la différence!

WILLIAM LOUEY (1973 – 1979)

I was sent to Millfield at the age of 13. Being a complete stranger to the British boarding school culture, I found everything so different and interesting that there wasn't really any time to be homesick. By any standard, to a city boy from Hong Kong, the school was huge and it took me days to get myself fully orientated in the new environment. My seven years at Millfield were fun-filled with occasional interludes of distress from examinations, failures and injuries on the sports ground, including the fracture of one of my limbs while trampolining.

My ties with Millfield were renewed in 1995 when I started sponsoring talented students from China and Hong Kong to study there. So far, all my scholars have been doing exceptionally well both academically and professionally. Like myself, they are all true Millfieldians who extracted the full benefits from all that Millfield has to offer.

JAN RICHARD (NEE PETERS) (1972 – 1979)

Initially I was billeted at Greinton (near Ashcott House) and one of my first impressions is of a long coach journey to this vast campus which felt totally overwhelming. That, plus having to milk Alice the goat for milk in the morning and spending rather a lot of time cleaning shoes in the boot room as penance for some misdemeanour or other. And the swimming pool seemed to have been built inside a greenhouse with rusty pipes on which we used to cut our feet, and yet we kept going back for more. How I loved that pool!

My 1st year highlight was being blue lighted in an ambulance down the main driveway after my house mother had mistakenly fed her three billeted students poisonous mushrooms that she had picked in the field and we were all rushed to hospital with a helicopter on standby to take us to a major London hospital if we took a turn for the worse. We all recovered of course and enjoyed being celebrities for a day or so, so it did have its advantages.

The following year I went to Southfields with Mr and Mrs Kirkwood. What a glorious place that was! We would go into school in the morning, race back to the coach car park to go back to the house for lunch, change to another outfit, then return to school. Life was a whirl of lessons in wooden huts, which we loved, dashing between the bells from one classroom to another, sitting in biology whilst the master fed rats to his pet snakes and a continuous whirl of sport.

One summer evening when we were all outside near the cottage, in response to some cheeky comment that I had made, my brother suddenly picked me up and slung me over his shoulder. Behind me I heard this booming voice. Mr Atkinson had seen the whole thing. 'PETERS, PUT THAT YOUNG LADY DOWN!' My brother calmly replied, 'Sir, that's no young lady; that's my sister.' I think it was the only time I ever knew Colin Atkinson lost for words.

I left Millfield as Head of Southfields and took so many memories with me that it would be impossible to put them all down on paper; funny ones, such as watching smoke billowing from the sides of wooden classrooms while we all stood and watched in the prefects common room as students genuinely believed they hadn't been seen smoking; of hours spent getting ready for 'school hops', all of us practising dance routines to show off and as we got older the joy and sadness of Leavers Balls, wearing dresses that we had proudly made.

Most of all the memory is one of a very happy time and although eventually I was ready to leave, I regretted having to do so. The dining room had been built and we no longer ate in the houses at all, the library was being built and, as always, the school was moving on, as indeed we had to ourselves. When eventually I went back, I admired all the new facilities – but it didn't seem quite the same. But then again, why should it be?

Roland Rudd (1974 – 1979)

I arrived at Millfield in the autumn of 1974 in the belief that I had secured a good pass in the Millfield transfer exam – still below the common entrance pass mark but not bad for a chronic dyslexic. My moment of satisfaction proved short lived when, to my horror, all those who had taken the Millfield transfer exam were given a spelling test. My heart sank in the knowledge that this was going to be a disaster for me, and so it proved. I was promptly placed in the lowest set a year below my contemporaries, behind even those whose scores in the transfer exam were lower than mine.

I was determined to do better. My first battle was to move up into a higher set than the one in which I had been placed. In this I elicited the support of my housemaster, and it worked. But once I achieved this goal it left me with an overwhelming desire to move up a full year, which would put me back in line with most of my age group. This proved a much trickier battle to win, and the master in charge of General Studies understandably warned me that over-confidence was not an unalloyed positive. Nonetheless, the school was willing to accommodate me once more and I was duly promoted.

The following year I was back in my housemaster's office. "Sir, I need to move set again because I must learn French". My bemused housemaster was at a loss to know why I should want to learn French before I had even mastered English. "I need it for Oxford". "Oxford polytechnic?", enquired my housemaster tactfully. "No, the university Sir", I replied. Since my housemaster had been to Oxford he knew a thing or two about what was required, and supportive as he was of me, he clearly felt I was now setting myself up to fail. But I would not budge. So in the end he persuaded me not to try and move set for the third time but to come back to French later if I achieved sufficient grades to take the Oxbridge exams. I was happy with this compromise and in the event I got a place to read theology, and took French O level in my gap year.

I don't believe any other school would have first allowed a pupil to move up twice within the school and then give him an opportunity to try for Oxford when his academic record was not promising enough to warrant sitting an exam for one of the best universities in the world. But then Millfield was always different.

SARAH FINCH (1970's)

In my first term there was the annual play competition. Our House group, Etonhurst, had already decided to put on Noel Coward's play, 'Hands Across the Sea'. As I was entirely new, there was really only one part left which had not already been auditioned and allocated, and this was the part of a maid. Altogether, she had eight lines to say, so it seemed unlikely that, even If I were to get this part, I would be able to make much of an impression on the Millfield theatrical world. However, undaunted by this realisation, I auditioned, along with various previously disappointed aspirants, and got the part.

Rehearsals started immediately, although I was naturally not much involved. Then one day out of the blue, the girl who was playing one of the key roles, that of Mrs Wadhurst, left the cast. It was a thespian moment of high drama, involving loud shrieks and floods of tears. I think she had been the director's girlfriend, but they'd quarrelled and he'd broken off the relationship. In any event, suddenly the play was heading for the rocks and only finding the right person to play the principle part could save it.

This was my chance. I read in at the next rehearsal, and was offered the part. As it happened, the adjudicator of the competition that year was Robert Bolt, the author and screen writer of *The Man for all Seasons*. To our dismay, he placed our play seventh out of eight and then started to discuss in front of a large partisan audience the various merits and defects of each. When he eventually came to ours, he mentioned that it had been a poor choice and then to my amazement, he said, "I am only going to talk about one character, and that's Mrs Wadhurst."

I was on the stage with the others behind the curtain, while he was speaking from in front of it. All I could see were his shoes as he spoke about me and paced up and down. He was very complimentary and encouraging. I had always wanted to become an actress, and that night decided me. I went on to drama school and have worked as an actress ever since!

Yesterday was the staff panto, "Cinderella", directed, produced, lit and staged by the L6th in a unique reversal of roles which we had all enjoyed in rehearsal immensely. Dan and Mia had done a splendid job of making us learn our lines, turn up punctually and give the whole enterprise what style we could produce. The invisible lines between teachers and pupils were rendered delightfully fuzzy by our drag and their direction. Jenny, my incomparable secretary, with a solution to every problem, lent me her leotard, Suniti produced my tutu, and made me up as a fiendish Fairy godmother. We did two performances, a matinee and an evening performance, to 800 enthusiastic pupils and raised £1600 for African children suffering AIDS in Nairobi. Between the two shows, I had to rush home and host a dinner for a number of Governors to discuss the future constitution of the Governing body. I managed to hide the leotard under my suit, but traces of Fairy godmother make-up shook my guests visibly as they arrived. As Sir Robin said in his incomparable fashion afterwards, "Christopher, this is the sort of thing you can do in your last year, but not in your first." Too true.

DOROTHY SHAW (NEE GIACOMIN) (1976 –1980)

My first memory of Millfield was coming for my interview with Boss when I was eight years old. As we were walking round the tennis courts, a group of girls came running past saying "Boss, there's a swarm of bees coming – you'd better get in the pavilion!" So we did, and had a very nice cup of tea and biscuits. I chose the only Bourbon biscuit, being my favourite at the time and Boss said "Oh, they're my favourites too!", so I broke it in half and gave him the other half. I always think this was why Boss said I could start at Edgarley straight away.

I spent my Oxbridge term at Burleigh Cottage, which was the most wonderful homely atmosphere and where we used to sit huddled together watching horror films late at night and having midnight feasts of condensed milk, honey and bananas! We also got together a singing trio to record some of my songs – I've still got the tapes.

There was also the enormous number of piano practice rooms where I used to spend nearly all my free time and once became famous for being locked in! I always think it was because of those practice rooms that I became a pianist.

Of course there were bad memories too, not least of which was discovering I couldn't do riding because I didn't have my own pony, but all in all I think it enabled me to have as broad an education as possible and experience another side of life that I wouldn't otherwise have known about.

ROY TJIOE (1978 – 1980)

One day, in a demonstration more of machismo than of science, our chemistry teacher, Mr Bromfield, poured concentrated sulphuric or hydrochloric acid on his hand, and said, "Now, this is something you should never, ever do." He had positioned himself carefully by the sink before he did this, and turned on the tap immediately, intending to wash off the acid at once. Alas, nothing came out of the tap. The water had been turned off for some reason, and he spent several very anxious and increasingly painful moments seeking relief from another basin in another lab next door. Was there a lesson here for us? If there was one, it had little to do with acid, and more to do with checking your escape routes before doing anything really stupid.

There was a 3rd former named Mark Schlessinger who had a pet python. It was felt generally that the best place for it to be kept would be in one of the biology labs. He would feed his python with a white mouse every day. I once witnessed the spectacle where the little mouse would be dropped into the glass tank. Once the snake realized it was there, he would raise his head and stare right at it. Behind his head, his body was coiling into a spring and then, like lightning, it snapped its jaws on the poor creature and swallowed it whole. We'd watch in amazement as the lump got smaller and smaller as it made its way through the snake's body. Mark was always delighted by our reactions.

NIGEL PAYNE (1978 – 1981)

Syd Hill was my Housemaster. Everyone knew his most famous saying, just three words, which we would hear every time there was bad news, especially when this involved any of his charges stepping out of line. "Oh bloody hell." His eyes would then roll up in search of some sort of inspiration from his own private Welsh heaven. Under Syd, JK was run like a family home.

FELICITY WATERMAN (1979 – 1981)

I remember not really wanting to go out at all. It was raining very hard and it was dark. I could find no one willing to come with me. However, it was our house's duty to pick up all the litter between Slies and the main gate and I was the Prefect on duty, so I had to venture forth.

There is something beautiful about lamplight in a storm and, all bundled up against the wind, I was happy. Stooping again and again, I dropped soggy wrappers into a black plastic bag. It was very peaceful out there, away from the commotion of post-prep toast and fudge making and squabbles of what to watch on the television. I let the evening wrap around me, calm me down. I relished the feeling of insignificance in the silence of night – emptiness – school.

With my back turned toward the road, I didn't see him approach and jumped, gasping with the shock of interruption from my solitude as he questioned me gruffly about being out of the house, at night, in the rain and alone. When he saw what I had been doing, he relaxed, almost smiled and stood a moment with me, quietly in the rain. I felt he too knew the peace of the lamp-lit storm. Then off he loped, Mr. Atkinson, going home after a too-long-work-day, without a backward glance.

The security guard told me this morning how last night he had watched as a vixen had led four fox cubs out from under the Bolts and let them play in the moonlight on the Headmaster's lawn, right in the middle of the campus.

Give the bulbs a chance.

ELSPETH MCPHERSON (1977 – 1982)

For those of us fortunate enough to experience the Music Lodge under Geoff Keating's tenure, memories of Millfield are full of eager wind, brass and string music, ground and polished for performance. Here, techniques took second place to fly tying and sailing, with Geoff's eyes firmly set on the season's sport. He created an atmosphere of excellence, huge camaraderie in the Lodge 'set', tucked happily into the eaves in the A Level and O Level common rooms, and on hand for performance calls.

In the third year we had arrived and watched the Sixth Form scholars in absolute awe, setting standards we never believed we would attain. As new kids on the block, we suffered the horrors of the first Prom concert under the critical gaze of the old hands. The Lodge staff were exemplary, creating a unique environment, a retreat from the School into our own world of music. Pre-eminent amongst these were Peter Bond, Chris Mahon, Tony Pooley and Pat Benham. We won't ever forget Peter for releasing us on a Headmaster's Discretion to sing madrigals outside, nor Stewart Woods in his Paddington duffle coat. Were there marmalade sandwiches in the pockets, we always wondered? As an organist, Chris Mahon remains my inspiration. He was the driving force behind the first organ students at Millfield, and acquired the first organ. Practising above the judo dojo was positively surreal. At 17, playing Howell's epic 'Paen' at Wells Cathedral was unbelievable. And most of all, of course, there was Geoff. His departures to 'tie flies' were the best preparation I had for subsequent Oxford tutorials: "Carry on with the sequences," he'd say. And we did.

Three concertos in a single evening; Emily Crump played a Mozart flute concerto, Kate Rees played the Bruch violin concerto and Isabel Claisse the Dvorak cello concerto, all accompanied by our 40 piece orchestra, only six of whom are leaving this term. To manage this at any stage in the academic year would defeat most schools, let alone in the last week of term in the post-exam limbo.

DRUMMOND MODLEY (1980 – 1982)

There were summer evenings of blissful contentment playing in the nets. The mystical backdrop of the Tor must make these the most exotic cricket nets in the country. Colin Atkinson spent hours out there with us. Crowded around him, we listened, we practised and we learnt. Then of course we had to put it all to the test in matches, and out there on the square, though well prepared, we were on our own. But that, of course, is exactly what schools are supposed to do; prepare you for the real thing.

JULIAN SHELBOURNE (1972 – 1982)

In the 5th Year, after I'd given up full-time swimming on Paddy Garrett's swim squad, Gyr King's sculpture room became my social and creative centre. I would hang out there after school working on my sculptures with exotic titles like "Grief", "Mrs. Lopez Makes the Breakfast" and so on, and various friends who were also working towards Sculpture or History of Art GCE exams would drop by.

It was like a kind of "Salon" where people would just come in and chat, and often we'd get into quite philosophical discussions. We also created a few impromptu works of art which had nothing whatever to do with the syllabus on which we were supposed to be working. A memorable one was "Digestion" – an abstract piece involving smeared blue and yellow paint, with a nice brass plaque underneath which we decided to hang on the main dining room wall. This was a source of amusing mystification and general fascination, until someone realised that it wasn't an "approved" work of art, and it was summarily removed.

Another non-approved piece of art that we developed around this time was a large, white, plaster snail, which, for some reason, found its way on to the low wall running up the main drive, sometimes in the crook of a tree, or peering out from under the long grass, depending on which of us got there first that morning and where he determined it should hang out that day.

Meanwhile, at some point in the mid-70s, the boarding houses had all planted House Trees. These small saplings were all planted in large, round flower-beds, along the pathways leading in and out of school, with large wooden stakes positioned to support them as they reached their anticipated height. The Joan's Kitchen tree seemed to suffer from generically stunted growth and eventually died, leaving just a large, eight-inch diameter stake in the middle of a four-foot diameter hole.

At first, as a joke, we just planted a single bull-rush in the middle of the hollow, and came to regard it as our "JK Tree". This never struck us as entirely satisfactory, however, and so we decided to go for something altogether more impressive. We "borrowed" a 15-foot ladder, which we propped against the stake, making the ladder appear to levitate, leading nowhere. A sort of 'Stairway to Heaven' motif.

We then took the levitation theme one step further. One Sunday afternoon, we made off with one of the school park benches, brought it into the sculpture room, bolted struts to its underside, and then, in one bold manoeuvre, carried it out to the JK Tree site. There we screwed the struts onto the stake, and left it apparently hanging in mid-air, levitating. Double English was much more entertaining the following day, as we watched several senior Masters struggling to remove our structure from the stake, lending it briefly a new and rather satisfactory kinetic quality.

I'll always look back to these days as being some of the most creative and fun times.

The sculpture project by Charlie Hadcock has now arrived. It's a large cast iron version of his original polystyrene packing cases, observing the Golden Ratio, on which Charlie will talk to the pupils – or anyone else – at the drop of a hat. He quotes Vetruvius from the 5th century BC. "The definition of good architecture is that it does not claim more of the space we all share than it should." It will go in the quad and be wonderfully controversial.

And indeed that's how it turned out today. I took Sir Robin Buchanan, Chairman of Governors, to view it. He studied it carefully for a while with that whimsical smile that I have come to enjoy, and then said, "Christopher, if I had a scrap heap, and this was next to my scrap heap, I'd move my scrap heap."

DICKON THOMPSON (1981 – 1982)

Coming from a private boys' school in Vancouver, Canada, had prepared me for only some of the things I would learn at Millfield: that the individual was valued for himself as much as for being part of a team, that diversity was more important than homogeneity and that any spark of ability would be encouraged. And that having girls in class was not only beneficial but also quite a positive change.

Another key tenet I acquired here was the notion of balance – the importance of both work and play. Of work, there was plenty. On walking into my first morning of Modern European History I was presented with a yard of books "to catch up". This, no greater than the number of books to "dip into" for English History, was an indication of how seriously academe was taken. For the athletic side I was introduced to the rigours of Paddy Garrett's swimming regime, and was fortunate to be demoted to the B Squad almost immediately!

I wish I could have spent longer at Millfield. There were so many things to do, so many exams to sit (mock and real, after only two terms!) and so many people to meet, over a thousand individuals, each encouraged to excel in their own terms, while still being part of the team. It's a school of opportunity for those who will take it – a source of unexpected pleasure and knowledge, of tolerance and high expectations. I hope that everyone will think back and remember our school with happiness.

NICK APPELL (1980 – 1983)

I had been moving around various schools prior to Millfield, so rather than doing any form of entrance exam, I was interviewed for a place by the Deputy Headmaster Mr Gaskell and the Headmaster Mr Atkinson.

When I went in to the Headmaster's study he asked me who I had just seen and I told him I had been with Mr Atkinson.

"No you haven't", he replied.

"Yes I have."

"No, you definitely have not seen Mr Atkinson."

Now getting a little irrated as a rather impatient 12 year old, I said firmly "Yes I have. I was with him for the last fifteen minutes, over there," pointing in the direction from where I had just come.

"Well, do you know how I know you have not just been to see Mr Atkinson?"

"Why?" I enquired with less conviction.

"Because I **AM** Mr Atkinson."

I think I was lucky to get in.

GUY BLYTHMAN (1977 – 1983)

My perception of public schools having been coloured by Billy Bunter stories, I expected ivy-covered walls and masters sporting gowns and mortar boards. I felt somewhat cheated by the reality, for the only part of the school which remotely accorded with my preconceived notions was Millfield House itself, a Gothic affair which although still rather hideous was nevertheless considerably more attractive than the other campus buildings. Visually, it was a rather depressing environment of wooden huts and concrete blocks, but considering the youth of the place, this was perhaps not surprising. However, I can say with pride that I was never really homesick in it.

One thing Millfield did for me was to prevent me from ever becoming a racist. Some 20% of the pupils were foreign, quite a few of whose decency put one's English peers to shame. I know I was shown great kindness when going through a bad patch by a Jordanian prefect, with whom, sadly, I have now altogether lost touch. To be honest though, one's attitude was somewhat ambivalent because some of the foreign pupils did throw their weight around, causing considerable resentment.

Her Head of Year has gated Polina Yumasheva for various minor infringements. Subsequently I receive a phone call from the Kremlin, asking politely but persuasively if I will waive this punishment temporarily to allow Polina to see Tatyana Yeltsin during her visit to London over the weekend. Having just read of Mr Yeltsin's influence with

Saddam Hussein, I am tempted to contrast Iraqi and Millfield approaches to the implementation of our respective rules, but refrain. My refusal to comply is taken with good grace, for which I am grateful.

Discipline was poor at times. It was thought to be worst in Kingweston House, whose inmates were regarded as semi-literate thugs. The running joke about Kingweston concerned the damage done by a fire in the house library. Both books were totally destroyed and a spokesman for the house reported that people were particularly upset because they hadn't finished colouring them in.

Life in those days would have been much less bearable without the famous Maxwell Edward Falconer Milligan, the scion of a famous Millfield family, who kept us constantly amused with his irreverent Monty Python-style humour, thus performing a psychologically valuable service. Humour is a major antidote to the misery of what are wrongly supposed to be the happiest days of your life. Max lightened many a lesson with his impromptu Basil impressions, exaggerated body language and facial contortions. He had very distinctive features, another comedian's trait, and it was said that you could be made to laugh just by looking at him.

There was a certain group of girls, all friendly with one another, who formed a sort of *coterie*. I always had my eye on them for they were the subjects of my adolescent sexual fantasies. Proper relations between the sexes were governed by the Six Inch Rule, which meant that you were to keep outside that distance of a female at all times, unless it was simply unavoidable, which most of the time it was. The SIR – an appropriate acronym – was difficult to police and frequently broken. Those who remember me as a sedate and scholarly paragon of virtue will be scandalised to learn that I broke it once myself. One day on the way to class, a rather strange young lady decided to slip her arm into mine. I did not resist, probably because I did not know how to react. We walked quite a distance without anyone challenging us, which seems to confirm my opinion of the rule's efficacy.

In my last year, wishing to spice up my c.v. a bit, I became more involved in extra-curricular activities. In particular, I joined the Debating Society which in November 1982 organised a debate on the motion, "Women are Subordinate." Of course the whole thing was meant to be a joke but I took it seriously and voted against the motion, the only boy present to do so. For this, I was subsequently regarded by my male peers as being rather odd, but I became President of the Society shortly afterwards, largely because of the female vote.

KARIN SINNIGER (1980 – 1983)

I do remember Christmas time when we were all bussed to Wells Cathedral for the Carol service before the end of term. The Cathedral was lovely but as cold as the "garden sheds" in which we were taught History and Maths. But I had a solution. I would troop off the Grange bus with the other girls, find an aisle pew, enjoy some of the carols and excuse myself after ten minutes by saying I needed to find the loo. I'd then repair to the nearest pub, order a half pint of cider and read the newspaper for half an hour before nipping back to the freezing cathedral for the end of the service.

Sadly, I never discovered an equivalent tactic to get me through the raw English winters during History lessons.

Helen, in the U6th, and I find ourselves walking across the campus together, and I ask her how things are in her House. She is worried because, while she wants to help her juniors with their prep, she's not sure whether she should. And she has a further worry. "I know what the real answers are in their History prep for instance, but I've forgotten what the 4th year answers are supposed to be."

STEPHEN GOULD (1981 – 1984)

S ummer term,1983 at lunch in the dining hall. The scene is set. Sitting at a table with a few mates, when Walder (Julian Walder-Smith) joined us. He casually turned to a junior on the table behind, picked his plate up, held tight to the rim on both sides, and at the top of his voice shouted two fantastic words. "FOOD Fight!!!" All hell broke loose. All I recall was jumping out of a window...one of many great escapes I had in three fantastic years at school.

Mrs C. arrives in my room, unannounced, with her entire family comprising five and seven ninths children, one of whom is with us. He has been involved in a fight in his House and has lost a tooth. Sadly, it transpires that this is the same tooth that was fixed at great expense very recently. Mother, heavily pregnant, is furious and it's easy to see why. One can make all sorts of allowances for anyone in her current state, especially when she is confronted by renewed expense and what looks like an unprovoked attack by another boy. However, she quickly becomes hysterical and from then on there's no possibility of getting to the bottom of things. She is going to take out a prosecution for assault on the other boy. I know this chap quite well, and find it hard to see him as a natural aggressor. Mrs C. has no doubt at all, however. "My son has told me everything. He never lies. It was an entirely unprovoked assault." She tells me repeatedly that she is a born again Christian, but in this case she wants a tooth for a tooth. She has spent three hours on the phone to her son's long-suffering Houseparents and expresses amazement when I tell her that she has reduced her Housemother to tears. She assures me that she has written a six page letter of complaint to me about the "fact" that we have a more relaxed disciplinary policy for the sons of the wealthy than for those of more modest means. I try to tell her it's bunkum but she is utterly sure of herself. She will come back for a pound of flesh tomorrow.

Tomorrow dawns, and the post brings her letter, as threatened, which thuds on to my desk along with the report of the investigation into the incident. Thus I am well prepared for her subsequent visit. It is now clear that her son "who never lies" (how often have I heard that from parents?) had been making a string of racist remarks at his aggressor until patience had snapped and the blow was landed. Her wretched son admits it, and his poor mother implodes. From a position of incontrovertible rectitude to one of abject apology is a hard journey for anyone, and by the end I feel for her. Her hapless son deserves all that she is undoubtedly going to give him.

181

THOMAS BELL (1983 – 1985)

I spent two years in Georgian Cottage. During that period, my house mates included a Sri Lankan golfer who never practiced, because of the weather, but still managed to come 4th in the British Junior Open championships; a tennis player ranked 24th in the world at junior doubles; a soccer player who captained the England schoolboy squad, a junior national judo champion, and a very charming fellow, something of a late developer, who now squires Liz Hurley. That's some peer group. Millfield is an odd place.

Nineteen entries in the diary today. The best moment was when Penny Vincenzi, an elegant, cosmopolitan woman and best selling author visiting as a prospective parent, met in my room another prospective parent, a plasterer from Bristol, both with excellent daughters, and discovered that they had a kibbutz in Israel in common – one born there and the other with another daughter there. Further meetings with Jonathon Mindu, a visiting teacher from Uganda, Mr. Badr from the UAE, the Green Council debating our environmental policies in school, pupils back from suspension, promising, predictably and properly, not to err or stray again. Finally a visit with Mike Gilfillan and the Chaplain to select the electronic organ for the theatre at an unlikely organ shop in a private home near Weston-super-Mare, far enough away from neighbours for Mike to be able to let rip with all the decibels he could elicit from a whole battery of likely machines.

THE GASKELL YEARS

1986 – 1990

Brian Gaskell.

BRIAN.

Group Tutor, Head of the Maths Department, Director of Studies, Housemaster, CCF Officer, Deputy Headmaster – such was BG's c.v. as potential Headmaster of Millfield, to which he acceded in 1986. Totally trusted by CRMA, he relieved his friend of the day-to-day problems occurring in a large boarding and day co-educational school and enjoyed the many successes achieved by the pupils. Colin continued to wrestle with the finances without the assistance of a bursar, and found time to be Chairman of the Cricket Committee of MCC, Chairman of Somerset CCC of which both he and Boss had been Captain, and Chairman of HTV (West).

They had agreed with the Governors that they would resign together when Colin reached the age of 60, but, sadly, it was not to be. The cancer returned and Brian chose to retire with Colin in 1990, leaving the school in a flourishing state.

Tony Ng (1982 – 1986)

Even after 20 years, studying at Millfield remains the best time of my life. I acquired 2 A's and 1 B for my A-levels and my sweetheart at the time still remains my best friend. However, it was not exactly a piece of cake. For a start, there were the bullies, and for a quiet and polite child like me, I had to pick up bodybuilding so that I could stand up to their threats. The administration at the time did nothing to help me.

Jenny Brunt, who did not get on well academically at school, was seen by everyone as an ugly duckling. But I saw her unique quality and I was her first ever photographer. All she wanted from the 4th form was to be a model and when she left without finishing the 6th form, she very quickly became one of the top 100 models in the world. In fact she didn't like school that much, not unlike many others at Millfield at that time.

It is not an easy task to write about good events without writing also about the bad. There were some excellent teachers, such as Mr. Godfrey, who managed to teach me within four hours during half term everything that I needed to know about calculus and pure maths. Mr. Roger Whyte taught me engineering drawing and even allowed me to talk him into teaching me driving after school.

While in the US to visit the OM's in New York and the Virginia Fellowship administrators, I look in on the University of North Carolina to discuss the Morehead scholarship scheme, for which I do occasional interviews here. While there, it is good to learn that the first woman President of UNC is called Molly Broad, and that her Vice President is a Mr. Hooker. It reminds me that we have appointed at Millfield Miss Foal as Director of Riding, and that she joins Joy Ride who teaches Biology.

E. JOHN PLANK (1983 – 1987)

Neil Harper helped me to carry my trunk up the fire escape stairs of Millfield House. He was the new head of house and seemed very pleasant. (My Mum took a shine to him in any case). His physical presence was impressive. "Gotta be a sportsman!" I thought. For me at that time though, sport was a very narrow field, comprising rugby. It certainly did not include swimming which was... well, something you enjoyed on holiday, in a pool in Spain perhaps. You might, if pushed get a little "puffed" but that was it. When I found out that Neil Harper was a swimmer – worse still a backstroker, I was devastated!

A short while later I was standing outside Taff's (ie Alun Ford's) office. I needed to find out who my guide was to be. I was suddenly joined, by a rather gangly boy, who, I wasn't surprised to discover, was also a swimmer. Here I was in the original Millfield House, where Gareth Edwards developed into a rugby legend, and I was surrounded by fish!

Mark Foster, as he was called, was to change my attitude towards swimmers. He soon became the swimming captain and arranged the house swimming trials. I was "off games" with an injury which prevented me from running, but I was fit for swimming. Taking this excuse to get off prep early, I went along.

I was in the first heat and at least made it to the end of the pool. I remember being surprised at how considerably puffed I was. Mark Foster stood very officially with a clipboard and from time to time jotted things down. It was obvious that he hadn't thought about swimming himself and it was only after a bit of teasing from the rest of us that he agreed to take part in the final race.

It was like a cartoon clip. His dive alone took him three metres clear of the others. And, with the exception of his hands, that was the last time he touched the water! He beat most of the other swimmers by more than half a length, then very casually climbed out, grabbed a towel, picked up the clipboard and continued to write notes – only slightly puffed!

At 7.0 a.m. I am en route to a meeting with the Counsellor and the doctor when opposite the pool a taxi draws up and four bleary-eyed boys from Etonhurst spill out. "We've come for recreational swimming, sir. Our first time." "What, now?" "Yes sir, look, it says so here; 6.00 to 8.00." Only then did they realise it was p.m., not a.m. However, when the elite swimmers, who of course had been at it for an hour already, began to appreciate the enormity of the sacrifice made by these poor guys, they kindly squeezed up and made a spare lane for them, so virtue was rewarded after all.

We have won a third consecutive senior water polo match, where conditions were described in the match report as "Wet under foot."

MATTHEW FEATHERSTONE (1983 – 1988)

I remember the very first day I walked into Millfield with my father feeling very nervous for my interview. There was an amazing feeling of happiness and warmth given off by the other students walking around the campus. They seemed both calm and energised at the same time and I had a very strong feeling that they really wanted to be there. There was a colourful mix of clothes and races that gave off a real glow. Before even entering Colin Atkinson's office, I knew this was where I wanted to be. I can only assume that he sensed this and that for this reason, if for no other, he offered me a place.

ROGER PARSONS ESQ. (EDGARLEY)

THE OFFGAMES ENGLISH ROAD
By TR Glover Esq
(with apologies to G.K.Chesterton)

Before the Romans came to Street or out of Millfield strode
The Edgarley offgames walkers made the English offgames road,
A reeling road, a rolling road made by the legs that ached
And blistered feet on bog and peat, in gumboots thickly caked.

A painful road, a mazy road, such as they did tread
The days they went down to the Brue by way of Beachy Head.
They all went walking down the lane with grumbles in their teeth
The days they went to Glastonbury by way of Cowdenbeath.

May God forgive the tutors for making babes to rove
From Edgarley to Kensal Green and back by way of Hove;
Their blisters were appalling and many shed a tear
The day they walked to Weston by way of Brighton Pier.

But offgames tutors all agree that fresh air does us good
And boys and girls who hate to walk must realize that they should
And if to Western Pennard they're offgames walking bound
It's always best to reach that goal by way of Plymouth Sound.

And this today the tutors teach although their feet are sore,
And so they're bound for Paradise by way of Glaston Tor.

(Note: the Offgames Walk provided exercise and fresh air for those not fit enough for Games.)

Barry Hobson "A History of Millfield"

The antipathy which arose between Boss and Colin, his own appointment as his successor, festered unhappily for 20 years, but on 12th February 1989, within 18 months of both their deaths, Colin wrote Boss a note, accompanied by a small gift.

RJOM

Some sustenance – with every good wish.

If you could bear it, I'd much like to come and see you: and I'll phone Joyce first to see how you feel about that.

I'm very sorry your lungs are in such poor condition. By the way, I agree with you re. S. Africa. But counties are running scared of TCCB money (not that it's a lot anyway!)

Regards, Colin.

The card was carefully filed, but neither knew there was so little time left and Colin's award of the CBE undoubtedly stuck in Boss's craw. Rumour had it, however, that the great man was seen watching a 1st XI cricket match from his car in the summer of 1990, 55 years since he had first seen the ground from a taxi window on the road from Castle Cary. Christopher Martin invited him to return to the school the following term for the Remembrance Day commemoration. That was to be Boss's last moment at Millfield.

Romla Walker (1982 – 1988)

When I was in the 3s, my friends and I had to do "Orienteering" for MAP. After a term of unsuccessful

Snow releases new energies.

tent erecting, the culmination of the course was that the four
of us were dropped somewhere in the middle of Somerset (or so
it seemed), on a Saturday afternoon, with the target of locating a map reference point to set up camp. Being four teenage

girls, the camp site chosen was actually in Overleigh's back garden. It was a lovely hot, summer's day and, after little more than an amble through the countryside, we arrived. The only thing to dampen our spirits was the fact that we were missing the junior hop that night. To the rescue came our wonderful housemaster Paul Wootton who drove out to pick us up, took us back to Johnson's in time to get glammed up and saw us off to the hop. Mindful that we endure the hardships of surviving our outdoor challenge, he waited for us to get back from the hop, wipe our make-up off and change before driving us all back to our tent. Roughing it, Johnson's style.

A letter today from a current parent, whom I have met, starts, "Dear Sir or Madam." This is bad enough. Have I really been so long at this job that I have become unsexed? But it gets worse. The signature is incomprehensible so I don't know if this is a man or a woman writing, much as s/he apparently can't tell this of me. The substance of the letter is a bitter complaint about an "illiterate" circular concerning the Duke of Edinburgh's scheme arrangements for next term. I studied the circular carefully and could only see one typo and a misplaced comma. Our correspondent failed completely to acknowledge, let alone to express gratitude to the Tutor in charge of D.of E. who is willing to put in countless hours at weekends accompanying the expeditions listed in the original circular. I enjoyed composing my reply!

KIM RIDGEON ESQ

It was September 1989, the first day of term and the first full day of my life as Houseparent in Southfields. During the course of the evening I ventured to the top floor but, on arrival on the small landing there, found entry denied me by my helpful Head of House. She informed me that Houseparents did not need to patrol that particular area of the house as she was doing the supervision there herself and had the situation fully under control. I could see the sense of this from her point of view but nevertheless I replied that her senior smoking and drinking club could remain open for one more evening only and that the establishment would then be closed on a permanent basis. Welcome to the real world. A Houseparent's education starts immediately he takes up post. Thus my first two diary entries read;

Day 1. The girls all came back in high spirits. What a charming and delightful lot they are.

Day 2. Surrounded the House with barbed wire, set alarms on all doors, fixed CCTV cameras on all walls and mantraps on the drive. Am thinking of acquiring a Doberman.

But of course, inside all lovable devils there are lovable angels.

CHARLOTTE CORNWALLIS (1988 – 1990)

If it hadn't been for the likes of Mr Driver, Mr Chamberlain and Mr Smith I'm not sure I'd be where I am today. I am now a World Champion at Real Tennis and an international hockey player. Millfield was the key to this and I will always be grateful for that. The tutors were always willing to give me training time on the pitch, providing my work was up to scratch of course. They made my future possible, even though I chose on a number of occasions to completely ignore their advice. The facilities were second to none at the time, but now they are quite incredible. I wish I were 16 again.

Talking with one of our hockey coaches, she comments that at all the tournaments we enter, our girls seem both individually and corporately to be so much more vibrant than our competitors. I know exactly what she means, but how does one explain this? Self-selecting genes? School atmosphere? Porridge, perhaps? Maybe a bit of all three.

THE
MARTIN YEARS
1990 – 1998

Christopher Martin.

CHRISTOPHER

Service with the 10th Gurkha Rifles in Malaya, a Modern Language degree from St. Andrews and a housemastership at Westminster led Christopher Martin to Bristol Cathedral School as Headmaster for 10 years. Then in 1990 he became Millfield's first Head to be appointed from outside, whereupon he had to resign his Chairmanship of the Choir Schools Association and his membership of the Headmasters Conference. The Governors hoped that he would reapply for the latter, carrying the now more conventional Millfield with him, and this he successfully did a few years later.

The deaths of both Boss and Colin in 1991 cast a shadow over his first year but he went ahead with various projects including the Fine Arts Centre, the equestrian centre, the hockey pitches and the indoor tennis centre, together with the construction of the first new boarding house on the campus. The opening of the Meyer Theatre and its attendant Maths Block and the Olympic-sized Swimming Pool were probably the highpoints of this phase of the school's development. Paul Oddie, the Bursar, who had been appointed with Christopher, played an invaluable part in managing these projects.

Christopher did great service to the School and the OMs by visiting Jack Meyer at home in Wells and persuading him to visit the school in his last year, and by helping to resuscitate the OM Society's flagging fortunes.

SARAH LEWIS (NEE CASE) (1987 – 1991)

I was a rider at Millfield and I was lucky enough to be able to go foxhunting during my time there. The Millfield horseriders, escorted by Major Burke, were welcomed at one of the most elite hunts in the area. I had never hunted before and found the whole experience thrilling. I took a small fence, one of many on an exhilarating day, and was congratulated by those who followed me because of the excellent line I took over the fence. I was very proud as these were seasoned fox hunters who welcomed us so warmly on their hunt.

The house singing competition in my fourth year. I was a

reluctant participant but Mr Wilkes insisted that all third and fourth formers should attend. Practices were held after prep. I soon realised it was a great way to get out of the house in the evening and socialise with the boys from the houses with which we were linked. The sixth former in charge chose Billy Joel's 'Longest Time', to our great disgust. We really wanted to sing something more of the now! However as rehearsals progressed we found something out – we were really good. I don't think we won that year but that didn't matter. It really was the first time I discovered that it was the taking part that mattered most.

> *Today Hung-Jong Lee, newly arrived from Korea, who speaks almost no English but who after only one month is already deeply popular here, played his clarinet in Chapel and was rewarded by an entirely spontaneous round of applause. It was extraordinary to see him later in the week singing in his House choir in the House Song competition – extraordinary only because it was the Anvil Chorus from "Il Trovatore" and because they sang it in Italian, as did nearly 1000 other singers. The following day, the crowd watching our 1st XV doing battle with Llandovery suddenly launched themselves into the Chorus again, word perfect and in harmony. It must have shaken our visitors more than a little, especially when it's normally the Welsh with whom one associates passionate community singing at sporting events. . I am brought back to earth later by a mother of a new 13 year old. She tells me that, when she asked her son what they had sung, he had replied, "Something from Verdi's rectum."*

ALISON MOVERLEY (1989 – 1991)

If I were given the chance to go back and start my two years at Millfield again I would do so at the drop of a hat!

As captain of the tennis team, probably my fondest and proudest memory is that of winning the Aberdare Cup both of those years, but I was also very inspired by my teachers and will be ever grateful to Mr. Mnatzaganian, who taught Arabic but who also taught me French. He spent countless hours giving me extra help and is responsible for the fact that I am now a teacher myself.

Millfield had a profound impact on my life and the multi-faceted education I gained there has been invaluable.

Talking with our Arabist, I realise for the first time, and late, how hard it has been for Sattam Al Saud and the other Saudi princes to try to adapt to life here, where we expect from them the same level of effort that we would of anyone else. At home they have power of life and death – literally – over their teachers. A teacher who had the temerity to reprimand a royal pupil would be open to physical attack and the sack. No wonder poor Sattam found everything here so perplexing. A few years back, one of his cousins had shot a local Councillor, who happened to be passing his house where he had thoughtfully placed an air pistol target in the window. Needless to say, the gun was illegal, and he had missed the target. Fortunately, the Councillor was wearing a thick fur coat at the time, but the consequences could have been much worse than merely getting the Sun on the phone at midnight. In the light of what I have just learnt, no wonder he was so surprised that we took it all so seriously.

Mrs Sarah Champion, (Edgarley)

I remember as a real privilege having a young Linda Bramley in the school. She was a larger than life, loud, heart-of-gold cockney who was lethal with a hockey stick. She had the enviable knack of saying what we all want to say but usually don't, because discretion overcomes us at the last minute. On this occasion, while driving Adrian Harwick's old green minibus back from a match, I misjudged the width of a gate, and we ground to a halt. Clearly damage had been done. There was a deathly silence from the girls for a moment, which Linda broke in characteristically expressive terms. "Cor Blimey, Miss Studley. I wouldn't wanna be in your shoes when old 'Ardwick sees this."

Later in the season, Linda asked me who all the other matches would be against. I started by naming All Hallows, to which she interjected, "Cor bleedin' 'ell Miss Studley. What, all of 'em against Allers?"

In fact it was Linda's colourful, even contagious language that was responsible for the only time I was reprimanded by my Headmaster. Ben Rushton was not amused by my report on Linda's hockey, which read simply; 'Ockey. Bleedin' good.

Sadly Linda died soon after leaving school, trying, perhaps, and failing just that one time to be larger than life. And yet the very fact that we are still talking about her now means that in one sense she is indeed larger than life. The magic of the Millfield mix is hard to beat.

RICHARD HART (1987 – 1992)

B radley Fincken was the archetypal pillar of Millfield sporting excellence and he knew it. You see, to a timid soul like me, he seemed to have everything I didn't – height, strength, speed, broken voice, confidence and, of course, like every groupie cool kid, 'pulling power'! 'A' team for rugby and football, with national credentials for sprint hurdles and javelin, whatever he touched turned to gold. Fincken – no messing with phoney nicknames – had an irreversible 'big' spiky, black bouffon hairstyle. His needle-gelled hair only accentuated his razor-sharp qualities.

Then there was me. Looking back I didn't have a chance. Re-Christened 'Beaker' on entering the third year – after Dave Hopes and Simon King spotted a cruel resemblance to Dr. Bunsen's skinny assis-tant on The Muppet Show – my first term was a blubbering blur. Quite frankly, like many new boarders, I struggled to cope with home sickness and sheer inferiority. To coin one of Hopes' analogies, Millfield was like a new world held in a briefcase being carried around by someone else in a different world. Reality seemed far away, and I do thank my Houseparents, Chris and Kath Page, and 'guide', Tristan Forman for helping me find my feet again as time went on.

But I had one thing going for me; I could run. My dad used to say, the sporting fields are a great levelling ground and so it would prove that second summer at Millfield. Before I had even got to the track for pre-season training, I was inspired with burning ambition. Listening to the Seoul Olympics, I was astonished at Ben Johnson's drug-assisted 9.79 seconds to win the 100 metres. I remember wondering if there was some legal super potion I could take to beat the rugby giants Fincken, Grafftey-Smith and the fast-improving Demetrius Agiostratitis, or if I would simply have to rely on my own starting blocks (few had them back then) for that all-important psychological edge.

I had never raced Fincken during the third year so our sports day encounter of 1989 was hailed as a potential classic. If memory serves me correctly, Grafftey-Smith, who, with Orchards' orange vest coupled with blonde flowing locks resembled a fleeting, flickering flame [alliteration not harnessed since my 'A' level days with TRN], ran the 200 metres instead. This lowered the odds against failure and left just Fincken and me.

To add extra significance to the occasion, David Hemery was opening the new all-weather track, so by the time we lined up I was petrified. The usual throng of Fincken's female admirers clustered round the track, and to me they looked more certain than ever that he would prevail.

Mr. Harding called us to our marks and on the 'B' of the bang I reacted and tore out of the blocks. A quick starter, I would often fade at 60 metres and so I was surprised to find myself throwing one arm and extended finger aloft a good 10 metres from the line as I won in 12.1. Fincken closed only marginally towards the end, and Agiostratitis was a whole second back in third. It was good for morale that Mark Smeed took the senior boys' race later that afternoon in the same winning time.

After that day, I never raced Fincken again, but I shall never forget the day a bit of quick running down a pimply red track led to the highest of highs. As for Fincken, I wonder if he ever had someone to look up to, a legend to topple.... I hope so.

CORDELIA ROBINSON (1988 – 1992)

My first day, arriving at Southfields, was the worst, having cried the entire journey from home which was three hours down the road in Cheshire. I had never been away from home before, and the whole experience was very traumatic for me. I was greeted by the head of house, Natalie, who showed me round. I had had nightmares about huge dormitories, with rows and rows of beds, high ceilings, and nasty girls. She showed me into what was to be my dorm, and there they were... rows and rows of beds all with the same pink duvet covers on them. I hated pink!

Then I met my room-mates, all of whom seemed lovely, genuine people. I particularly remember meeting Thalia Lane, who showed me pictures of her beloved chinchillas. However, despite the chinchillas, I continued to be very home sick, waking at 5 o'clock every morning and sobbing quietly – I hope quietly – until it was time to get up.

Of course, I ended up loving my time at Southfields. The Ridgeon's were outstanding houseparents, very hard working, and always fair. When it was time to leave, I wanted to stay with them – and cried all the way back home again!

The leavers ball was something to remember – just! First, we were asked to have a glass of champagne with Miss Longbottom, our assistant houseparent, and then another glass of champagne with the Ridgeons, before climbing onto the coach into school. We were all given tickets, and each time we had a drink, a corner was ripped off our ticket. We were thus allowed four. To cut a long story short, I got drunk for the first time and was subsequently very ill over night.

The following day, I felt dreadful, didn't manage any breakfast, and decided to head straight for the surgery, being ill on route, an event kindly camouflaged by my friends! The nurse took one look at me, and said, "You were at the leavers ball last night, weren't you? Take this tablet, and by lunch time you will feel 100%". To this day, I have no idea what that was, but she was right, I felt just fine by lunchtime, though the fact that I missed my mock word processing exam that morning still rankles.

A quad from Kim Ridgeon lightens my day. He tells of a parent of a girl in his house who thoughtfully left £50 with him in safekeeping for her daughter's pocket money, but omitted to tell him that she was slipping £650 to her daughter in cash, "for those little hidden extras."

Peter Mason (1988 – 1993)

It was the Friday afternoon Sixth From Lecture. Having just been made a prefect in the summer term of the L6, I was invited to join the Headmaster and a few other L6 students for lunch before the talk with the speaker, who was a distinguished astronomer. Simon Whitehead, the Head of School was chairing the session and Richard Watkin was going to wrap it up. I had no specific role, but was looking to make an impression, nonetheless.

Sitting next to the Headmaster and opposite the speaker, I noticed that the three of us were all enjoying our spotted dick and custard with equal gusto, and so, in an easy points-scoring manoeuvre, I offered to collect three lots of second helpings, a suggestion which was received with enthusiasm. Coming back to the table clasping the tray with the extra portions, I squeezed past my envious friends, handed the plates round and was starting to feel pretty pleased with myself.

Then things went pear-shaped. As I reached across the Headmaster with the tray, he put out his hand in what I thought was a gesture of congratulations. Not really believing my luck that Mr Martin was going to reward my efforts with a handshake, I determined to respond in kind. As I moved my hand confidently through the air, a puzzled look spread across his face and, to my surprise, he began to retract his hand. But I was committed. Grabbing what was left, I managed to clasp two of his fingers tightly. I realised the situation was not as it should be, but nevertheless, filled with nervous energy, I waggled his arm vigorously up and down by the two fingers I had captured. "What are you doing?", he asked, clearly in pain.

"I thought you wanted to shake my hand sir," I responded.

"No, I didn't. I wanted to take the tray," said the Headmaster. "Let go of me!".

I broke into a teenage panic sweat, but fortunately the awkward silence that followed was broken by the announcement from the teacher in charge that it was time to set out for the lecture, and that when we were ready Simon would lead us over there. The speaker piped up in a helpfully cheeky tone, "Oh, we're under Simon's orders, are we?".

Sensing redemption, I blurted out in like manner, "Yes, and if you don't watch out, he'll drag you out by your hair." Looking straight at the speaker for a response, it was only then I noticed that he was as bald as a coot.

I had to wait until the summer term a year later before I was made Head of School.

MATTHEW SMITH (1990 – 1994)

I had been made a prefect in the third batch, if I remember rightly – nothing to boast about. When I was on lunch duty, I got increasingly fed up with juniors bunching right at the door of the old dining hall. I had quickly got wise to their requests to visit the toilet (just inside the door) and was adopting an increasingly tough approach, when I was distracted by an incident on one side of the door. I saw out of the corner of my eye two people slip past into the inner queue. I went after one of them, grabbed him by the shoulder pad of his jacket and spun him round. It was then that I realised it was a visiting speaker from Eastern Europe.

I had problems with my bowling run up. Joel Garner, the great West Indian fast bowler, was attending our net session on one particular afternoon. (I loved the fact that we could play supervised sport four times a week). I told Joel about my run up issue and the great man – great in every respect - focussed all his considerable attention on me for five wonderful minutes, before Mr Curtis interrupted to take him off to coach the 1st XI. I had played in the 1st XI when two years young at my previous school, but I could not even get into the second XI at Millfield! Mind you, there were some junior county players who also couldn't make the 1st XI, so I didn't feel too bad.

One of my worst memories was hearing with horror from my parents that I was on my last warning before suspension. I wasn't even aware of having received any warnings in the past – in fact I had never even been house gated! Given that there were 250 pupils in each year, and sharing as I do the most common surname in the English speaking world, there was another Matthew Smith in my year, and a warning letter had been sent in error to my parents rather than to his.

It was the night before my English History A-level paper and the comparisons and contrasts between Gladstone and Disraeli were still too hazy in my mind for my liking, so I phoned up Mr Kelly, my History teacher, at around 9.0 pm to ask for some clarification. He was not at home, but on his return immediately phoned my houseparent, also a History teacher, who came into my room after returning from the pub, ready to help. Great staff support just when needed at any hour of the day or night.

It was lunchtime on Christopher Martin's first day as the new Headmaster. He had collected his tray and by chance decided to sit at a table with 4th year pupils. He asked their names and when he came to Galahad Clark, clearly couldn't believe his ears. "Galahad!" he said. "You'll be telling me next that your father's name is Lancelot." "It is, sir," came the reply.

Whenever my parents and little brother Nathan visited me at the school, Mr Martin always lowered himself to his knees to talk with him. I much valued that, as I also did that he seemed to get to know every person's name in the school.

One of my profoundest moments was saying good-bye to a friend in the year below at Shapwick who had just been expelled for smoking cannabis. His mum had come to collect him and his stuff and I remember thinking what a waste it was – him leaving such a great school. This experience was made all the more stark by hearing that some rugby lads who had been involved in a fight in a local pub were just given a warning. Obviously I didn't know the circumstances, but I just remember thinking which is worse – fighting or smoking an arguably peace-enhancing drug?

Cannabis is found behind the bed of a boy in Kingweston house. He tests positive. It is profoundly disappointing, for he is one of three boys whom I have so far allowed back, following admission of a first offence a year ago. He now leaves. Then his room mates have to be questioned. One is a very pleasant chap who is easily led, easily distracted, finds work hard and struggles to keep up. To my utter dismay, he admits having smoked cannabis last weekend. Had he not shared this particular room, he'd never have been questioned, and might never have been drawn into smoking in the first place. I am going to allow him back after a two week suspension. He writes me a long,

*painful, fairly legible letter, which I find very touching.
"Although I am not very good academically, nor very
sporty, I have a good heart."*

On Friday afternoons, you could choose between about 100
things to do for the Millfield Activity Programme (MAP). I
chose to do Social Services and was so privileged to be able to
visit Mr Wheatley, an elderly ex-Fireman from Bristol, who
lived near by. I visited him each school week for a year and we
built up a good relationship. Millfield could become claustro-
phobic sometimes and so it was really good to escape for a
couple of hours each week. I still remember where I was when,
having just returned from my summer vacation, I learnt that
Mr Wheatley had died. He was one of the first people I had
known to have died, and I was quite upset, especially as one of
the last conversations I had with him concerned his local
church. "I'm not interested in church," he said. "The only time
I see them is when they come to ask for money." That remark
has stayed with me, and always will.

And lastly, who can forget Peter Mason's magnificent speech at
Parents Day in July 1993? I had gone into his room at around 2.0 am
and he was still in the middle of writing it. It was an incredible speech
and I still remember having tears in my eyes at the end.

HELEN WINTERTON (1992 – 1994)

There we were, full of anticipation and looking hideous in out-
fits borrowed from our mums. We had just landed in Amman,
as part of Millfield's Jordan exchange programme. We had no idea
what to expect from this experience. Mr. Mnatzaganian had
enchanted us with tales of Arabic history and culture. Mr. Cramb
had urged us to dress modestly as this was a Muslim country. But
really we were shamefully ignorant about life in the Middle East.
Would it be safe? Would we be staying in houses with modcons?
Would our exchange partners seem very sheltered to us?

Nothing could have prepared us for the shock. Lined up to
greet us at the airport were the most glamorous and confident girls
I have ever seen! Short skirts and lots of make up, we felt ridicu-

lous in comparison... Fortunately our exchange partners forgave us our wardrobes and we had the most amazing holiday. We met the late King Hussein and Queen Noor at an education reception. We explored the Roman ruins at Jerash, the crusader castle at Ajlun, and the rose red city of Petra. We swam in the Dead and Red seas, and learned Arabic dancing in the aisles of the yellow school bus. Most importantly, we experienced life with ordinary Jordanian families and made some really good friends. The Jordan trip certainly changed my own career path. Two of our group spent gap years teaching in Jordan, others went on to study Arabic at university. Years later my job has taken me back to the Middle East, and last year I was there when my exchange partner Lubna got married. I still think of Jordan as a second home. In today's political climate I really value this link, and am so grateful to Millfield – and especially to Abbi Mnatzaganian – for such an opportunity.

PAUL GILMON (1990 – 1995)

I believe it was during first lesson after break. It was my first year in the senior school and we were in the middle of a French lesson with Mr Harper Holdcroft. Suddenly a strange message was relayed over the school Public Address system. All teachers were asked to check their classrooms, rubbish bins and corridors for strange looking objects. Innocently, we all set about doing what the tannoy had asked. Shortly afterwards, we were told to evacuate all classrooms and gather on the grass in the middle of the campus.

There was no sense of panic from either staff or pupils, but as we gathered outside, rumours began to circulate and before long, talk of a bomb scare was rife. We soon began to realise that this was quite a serious business. Police arrived and a cordon was set up around the technology building. I approached one policeman who was standing guard to ask what was going on. He said that a suspect package with wires hanging out of it had been discovered in the technology building. There was also a rumour that a hoax bomb threat had been received by the school.

Suddenly the bomb disposal squad arrived in an armoured vehicle and things got really serious. The cordon was extended. One of the bomb disposal men entered the building wearing his protective mask and full body armour – the works. But at about this time it also started to become clear to a group of us that the whole thing could be explained quite simply. My good friend Luke Sutton had been working on a project in technology which involved designing a timer device of some kind, and he had left his project in a box outside his tutor's classroom. Luke was laughing with us as we discussed how funny it would be if it was in fact his project which was causing all the fuss, though none of us really believed that it was. By then, a high powered pressure hose had been wheeled up by the bomb squad and from a safe distance, one of the officers zapped the suspect package with a jet of water. There was no explosion, the bomb squad withdrew and we all went back to class. It was all rather an anticlimax.

Later that day, after the excitement had died down, Luke was summoned by his Head of Year. It turned out to be true. It was indeed his project that had been mistaken for a bomb and subsequently destroyed. We all found it hilariously funny, but Luke was outraged. "I spent a lot of time on that project and now look at it. And it cost me money, too." I don't think he realised that the bill to the tax payer would have run into several thousand pounds.

Luke was – indeed still is – a fine cricketer and once said he had two ambitions; to play for England and to play for Butleigh. He achieved the first, but sadly never caught the selectors' eye at Butleigh.

LIBBY MOURANT (1993 – 1995)

The Dance Extravaganza was coming up and yet none of us in Tor house were involved. There were 13 of us in the sixth form and this particular Saturday night we were all mooching around in our diminutive common room, feeling vaguely disgruntled about this and indeed more broadly about life in general. It was raining. Sunday beckoned with nothing planned in it to raise the pulse rate. Was life passing us by? The mood was bleak and getting bleaker. Simone, Cathy, Elsa, Valeria, Jenny, Louise, Helen, Sophie, Alex, Olly, Marie and I gazed at each other in gloomy silence.

Suddenly, as if by common assent, we all knew we were going to be part of that Extravaganza, even if we all expired in the

1995 The Art Block is in place.

attempt. All our decisions came in a rush. We were going to be the Tor House Flappers. We were going to do the Charleston. We were going to be drop-dead gorgeous, a well-oiled team of immaculately rehearsed dancers. And we were going to be dressed to kill.

But there was a snag; in fact, there were two snags. We couldn't dance and we couldn't sew. None of us had much of an idea about how you actually did the Charleston, though each of us had picked up some small smattering about it. We pooled our meagre thoughts, found some music which seemed to fit, pushed back the furniture and started rehearsing immediately. We worked practically non-stop for 24 hours, snatching sleep and something to eat between rehearsals, all in our tiny common room. During the occasional break, we found a sewing machine, contributed bits and pieces of clothing, and started to rustle up our costumes. We got quite a factory going and in no time everyone was covered in frilly bits, sequins and feathers. Given that none of us knew how to sew or dance, in that one day we taught ourselves a great deal about both.

Come the night of the Extravaganza, we were the only House entry, the only self-rehearsed entry, and the biggest team entry. And we wowed 'em. The thunderous applause was cream on the cake. It's amazing what you can do in a day if you really go for it.

CHARLOTTE LESLIE (1996)

In retrospect, I must have been quite antisocial. I can say this with some certainty since for the term I was privileged to have an Acacia room all to myself, I adopted a resident blue-bottle and called it Wendle. Wendle and I would spend many a happy evening not watching Eastenders but instead rampaging through the Tacitus text I was required to know in some absurdly short space of time. My parents had given me a very small bottle of Harvey's Bristol Cream sherry, which I stowed beneath my underwear, and to this day, Sherry reminds me of Tacitus and Tony Morrison's "Beloved".

So it must have been due to these two preoccupations that Mr. Mantell caught me running down the Acacia corridor having set off the burglar alarm at 1.20 in the morning, shortly before my A-levels. I remember thinking through a haze of rather liberally chaplain-administered red wine that Mr.Mantell could never POS-SIBLY think that I'd been bad, given my strange propensity to bury myself in Latin texts. If I stick to my story hard enough, I told myself, he'll HAVE to believe me. I don't think he did believe that I'd spent the last six hours looking at the moon, but his incredulity paralysed him long enough for me to make my escape. And for some reason, from that night on, I have never forgotten the smell of Acacia carpets.

Before the space-age structure of The New Swimming Pool landed on Millfield soil, we swam in what can only be described as a wide ditch which sustained an extraordinary variety of wild-life. It was in this ditch that I would plough up and down, morning and evening, thinking of the large stodgy pudding which I would consume, shoveled out with gusto from those clattering metallic pig-dishes at supper later. The pool had a distinct smell of chlorine and the water had a fascinating way of adhering to the walls of your mouth, in a way I have not encountered before or since, in all my wide experience of swimming pool waters.

But the most memorable part of the Millfield Swimming Experience had to be the mad dash between the changing rooms and the swimming pool, in the open air, through all that the Somerset Climate had to throw at you. Which was usually rain and occasionally snow. I never quite got over the incongruity of the gleam of the great Millfield Machine, and the old fashioned public school sadism of the Changing Room dash. I wondered at the time if it was something to do with 'discipline' and 'fortitude', and indeed I wonder if these have suffered under the aegis of the New Swimming Pool?

This evening it was the regional round of the English Schools team swimming championships. We won all 12 races, most of them very easily. At first I began to feel guilty; the others must hate us. But then I remembered the immense dedication of our people, down in the pool at 6.00 most mornings, and at lunchtime, and again for the evening sessions and I finish by just basking, as usual, in their reflected glory. It is magnificent swimming – a joy to watch, as even our competitors graciously concede.

MARK PALLIS (1994 – 1996)

I bumped into Mr Speed, the Head of Games, at some point during my first week at school. After telling me to cut my hair, he commented that I was a 'big lad' and that he looked forward to seeing me on the rugby pitch. (Clearly, anyone athletic looking and over six feet tall had only one logical place to be on Mondays, Wednesdays and Saturdays). I said no. School sport for me wasn't running, or swimming, or fencing. It was what was commonly known as 'dossing'.

I loved dossing so much that I went as far as cheekily to propose that compulsory games on Saturdays should be replaced with 'personal time'. This was met with derision by the sport-mad senior prefects in my House who, regrettably, vastly outnumbered the dossers.

So, there had to be some sport. I had two main activities. The first was the fantastic fitness class. We were an unlikely bunch made up of smokers, artists, and of course, those few who, rather surprisingly, genuinely wanted to improve their fitness. I would chat, meet new people, take it easy. The biggest plus though, was that at only half an hour – or 20 minutes if you were, as we used to say, sly – it was the shortest class on the curriculum.

My other foray into the world of sport was Croquet Club. Led by the dilettante and all-round charmer Mr Valentine, assisted by a literature teacher on exchange from the US, who rejoiced in the unlikely name of Fleming Pucket, this was my kind of sport. Relaxing in the grounds of Kingweston on deck chairs, with a picnic and a cool drink, chatting, we would, if all else failed, sometimes even discuss the odd croquet tactic.

I met Olivia this afternoon, one of life's enthusiasts, but by no means a sporty girl. At some point I asked her in all innocence which games she was doing this term. "Chess and shooting, sir," she replied amiably. Her concise reply impressed me, but also raised the shadow of a doubt in my mind. Was this combination strictly allowed? Did one of them constitute a team game, for instance? I pursued the point with her tentatively. "Why those two, exactly?" I asked. "Well sir, you only have to use two fingers for each."

Jo Beadsworth (1992 – 1997)

Wednesdays in the U6 were particularly busy for me. I would finish lessons at lunchtime and go straight to Self-Defence for an hour or so before spending the afternoon fencing. On one particular Wednesday our Self-defence instructor Jeremy decided that we had progressed far enough to be able to learn how to defend ourselves against rape attacks. As most of the group were 3rd years he thought it more appropriate to choose me to demonstrate on. At the time, Mr. Dovey was the Master in Charge of Games and he used to turn up a couple of times a term to check that the various sessions were running as they should. It came as something of a surprise to him to walk through the door and find me lying on a mat, legs akimbo, with Jeremy on top of me, surrounded by a group of politely attentive 3rd years. As Mr Dovey hastily backed out of the room, Jeremy paled and said, "I think I'm going to get fired!"

Later that afternoon after we had packed away the fencing equipment, my fencing coach, who is also a fantastic dancer, was trying to teach me to waltz. We had all been sent to compulsory ballroom dancing lessons so we wouldn't make complete fools of ourselves at the 6th form Ball but unfortunately they weren't having the desired effect. So with my coach in front of me and the boys' captain behind me we tried slowly moving around the Salle. It was all going well until we tried to turn a corner, and inevitably got our legs tangled and collapsed in an undignified heap of limbs. It was at that moment that Mr. Dovey decided to come and check on the fencing session. He took one look at us and asked, "Jo, why is it that every time I see you today you've got a man lying on top of you?"

In my 6th form tutor group we had one of the 'Brunei Scholars', an elite group of geniuses who came over each year to show the rest of us up for the dimwits that we were. Fakhri was a lovely, quiet, law-abiding guy who one day became the hero of the 6th form for getting himself gated. Internet terminals had only just been installed in the library and the librarians guarded them zealously. Before we could use them, we had to fill in a form giving the exact address of the website we were going to visit. Surfing for information was not allowed, and we had to sign a waiver saying we wouldn't use the facility to look at anything lewd or licentious.

As a result most of us only used them to look at university online prospectuses, which didn't differ much from the paper copies in the careers hut just outside the library, but these were the only websites we knew. One afternoon, while flicking through the Leeds University website Fakhri found a link to the new Kylie Minogue album cover and out of curiosity clicked on it. No sooner had the picture begun to download then the librarian came charging over and frogmarched him out of library. For this Fakhri was gated for a week and his 'rep points' soared!

The year I won the U18 National Championships the team were all getting nervous after the preliminary rounds, so to try to motivate us our lovely Master in Charge of Fencing, Phil Cooke, said that if one of us were to win, he would buy us a bottle of champagne. We asked "What about if one of us comes 2nd?" He said that for that he would buy wine with dinner. Not feeling very confident we asked, "What if one of us makes the top eight?" He smiled and said that he'd buy that person a beer. That year we came 1st, 2nd and 7th and, bless him, he stuck to his word, although he did say that he would never make such rash promises again.

When we joined in the 3rd year it was decided that as we might be intimidated by the older pupils we would be given our own common room in one of the old huts that were slowly becoming disused. It was made up of the two classrooms at the end of a row that had been connected and it contained a drinks vending machine and a TV. Despite the good intentions of the teaching staff this building became the hatching site of every St. Trinians-esque scheme we could think of. On one occasion someone was accidentally pushed through the cork partition wall so that his head got firmly stuck and it took until the end of the break for his friends to be able to get him out.

Then there were the general studies lectures on Friday afternoons where, if you were careful and draped your hair across your face, you could get a good hour's kip, without being caught, before having to go back to lessons – a skill which served me well at university during some of the more boring lectures!

Or the hours spent stumbling around in what looked like radiation suits creating the replica of Henry Moore's Sheep Piece for our GCSE art project. I believe it is still there by the cricket pavilion to this day.

Or turning up to afternoon lessons in the summer soaked to the skin because we'd had a water fight in the lunch break. Or always being on the top floor of A or B block when the fire alarm went off. Or the mad crush of trying to get to lessons while the Theatre was being built, when the only way of getting from one end of the school to the other was through a 3m wide gap and you had 500 people trying to come the other way. Or of course the way you could buy Doc Eagle off with a Fruit & Nut bar if you hadn't done your prep.

ALAN CLIFTON-HOLT (1991 – 1997)

In the first week at Millfield we were all asked to fill out a sports form to say which sport we played and to what standard. At the time I had just come from a very small prep school in Kent, which had a pretty good rugby side, being undefeated for the previous two years. I thought that I could play to a decent standard and said so on the form. When it came to the first training session I was picked to train with the A's which I thought was only right. By the end of that first training session I was feeling bruised and very silly, as I had been dropped from the A's to the B's. I was told that it was more to do with my size than my skill, but it did little to repair my pride. Further damage was done later that term when I was again dropped to the C's.

When I got home that Christmas I complained to my father that I should at least be playing for the B team. He laughed and asked me who I would rather play for – the C team of the best rugby school or the A team of the worst rugby school. I took his point and never complained again.

Rob Wadsworth is to be seen practising football skills by himself on the astro for hours on end. He can bounce a ball on his feet, his head, his knee, his shoulders apparently endlessly. No wonder he has offers to compete for Southampton and Sampdoria. But it's his body swerve, which is his secret weapon. He can convince his opponent, the spectators, the referee and even his own side that he's going one way, and then he goes the other.

211

Paul Schwarz (1995 – 1997)

Some time after the old theatre behind the Fencing Salle had been decommissioned and just before it was to be taken down, a friend and I concluded that it would be necessary to liberate some of the expensive lighting for use in our next theatrical production. It seemed a shame to let it all go to waste. The retrieval of these lights took place very late one evening, and to expedite matters, we took the precaution of securing the assistance of an unsuspecting member of the campus security staff, whom we managed to convince that what we were doing had been authorised at the highest level. Convinced that we had all the bases covered, we set about our task with enthusiasm.

When all was successfully accomplished in the small hours – lights taken down and transported to a holding base – we crept back to our boarding house. There I was shocked to find my house-parent waiting up for me. I was asked to wait in the office while he made a telephone call. It transpired that our absence had been discovered, and since we had naturally left no clue as to where we were headed, our parents and the police had been alerted, and posses sent out to scour the countryside to try to find us. The seriousness of the situation began to dawn on me, and indeed it was made clear that there could be grounds for my suspension. I was becoming extremely nervous, not to mention embarrassed, and asked what the punishment would be. To my surprise, I was told that I would be choosing my own punishment. Naturally I chose the most lenient activity I could think of – I think it involved washing up teacups.

The point is that I learned my lesson. My actions had repercussions for which I would have to be responsible. I realised then that the nature of the relationship between a pupil and his house-parents is truly unique and it is a friendship that I will remember and treasure for the rest of my life.

A quad from a Houseparent. "During Sunday playtime, David thought it a good idea to cover his dorm-mate's face with chocolate and to try to wash it off with a fire extinguisher. Shades of David Mellor, but unlike the politician, this David is to be gated for a week."

MICHAEL ABSALOM (1993 – 1998)

Istill believe that my first year, or 3rd year as it was known, was by far the best time of my life. There was a great opportunity to make loads of new friends, including for the first time girls, there were no serious exams to worry about and enough sport to shake my hockey stick at. I often didn't sleep at night because I was so excited about going to school again the next morning. My Tutor Group (3 AHD) was the best blend of personalities, comprising as it did nine girls and four boys – a perfect recipe for disaster. The ratio was definitely in our favour. I worked out that if the boys played their cards right, we could end up with two and a quarter girls each.

During one of Mr Hill's Saturday morning English lessons, he told us that this would be a silent reading session. This was a challenge. Indeed for 13 youngsters, most of whom had only a limited attention span, it was to prove impossible. Still, it was only fair to give it a try.... Two minutes later heads were popping up from behind our books. We started trying to make each other laugh by pulling silly faces but the girls proved surprisingly good at maintaining their composure. The boys, by contrast, were completely useless and it was not long before Mr Hill had his first victim; Chris Lees.

Chris was generally the first to crack under pressure so it was no surprise that he was caught and eliminated from the game so early on. *The Little House on the Prairie* just wasn't thick enough to muffle his laughter. Mr. Hill had no hesitation in sending him out and telling him to stay out until he had pulled himself together. I suspected he would be out there for quite some time. From outside the classroom, Chris kept appearing and disappearing at the door like a phantom in the night. He pressed his face right up against the glass panel and this proved too much for me. I was the next to be sent out, replacing Chris in the draughty corridor.

I tried several times to come back in with a straight face and eventually succeeded. I apologised, made it back to my desk and was once more back in the game. I noticed that some of the girls were so bored with our childish games that they were actually reading their books. Anyway, I prepared to perform my favourite stunt which involved my school tie, in the hope that I could get someone else sent out. Here's how it works. First, suck in air through your mouth like a vacuum cleaner. Second, flick your tie up towards your face. The result? Due to the laws of Physics (I don't know which ones) your tie sticks to your face in a comical way.

Once we had all grasped the basic concept, it was just a matter of time... Next out was Johnny Lang. Three down and one to go. With 15 minutes still left in the lesson, we all worked hard to eliminate Will Jones in what had become a monster contest. I decided to stick with another tie trick, which disappointed the girls because it meant they could not join in. Or could they? First, gather your tie in your fingers so that it is stiff enough to stand upright. Second, with your free hand make the shape of a gun. Third, fire your "gun" and at the same time twitch your fingers which are supporting your tie. Result? Your tie should fall in a dramatic simulation of death.

But Will was in a different league from the rest of us. At first his face never twitched. It was not until Chris and I started shooting down each other's ties that we got any reaction at all. The *coup de grace* came when Leila Hughes, Nicki Sparks, Helen Havercroft and Jo Hepworth all joined in as well. It was like some sort of saloon bar in the wild west. Fortunately there was only one casualty and that was Will, caught in mid-draw by the Sheriff, Mr Hill, who sentenced him to ten minutes in the corridor. A full house at last!

After a long hard day at school there was nothing better than the ten minute walk down the hill back to Hollies. It gave me a chance to unwind and to reflect on the day's events. I shared the house with 23 other boys, six of whom were in my year. On this particular afternoon, my best friend Matthew Scaife was waiting for me with his golf clubs at the ready. It was clearly time for Dorm Golf.

The rules of dorm golf were very simple. Playing with air-flow golf balls, you just had to make it from one dorm to the other with as few shots as possible. Scaife explained that the fairways – the corridors – were tight and did not allow for much of a back swing. Then there were the hazards which he had thoughtfully placed on the course in advance, namely a hoover, a fire extinguisher and several kit bags from surrounding dorms. He thought this would make the game much more exciting, and so it proved.

He jumped onto the first tee – Mark Stringer's bed – and prepared to tee off. "Dorm 3, par 3," he shouted and smashed his shot off the bed, against the door and down the corridor. A very good start indeed. Scaifey was very competitive, and had already decided to become a pro-golfer. We had made a pact earlier that term while playing on the course outside Millfield House that if he did in fact turn pro, I could be his caddy. This was a great offer and probably my best chance of ever getting on the tour. Unfortunately for him when he was just 19 he had to have an operation on his wrist and was never able to play to the same high standard again.

But back to the game. I sliced my first shot straight into Donald Asprey's cupboard. According to Scaife, my back swing had come very close to the overhead strip light. It was lucky I hadn't touched it for it smashes into a million pieces if touched with a golf club. Or so I'm told...

I've always been a positive person, and slowly things got better as the game progressed. I chipped my ball out of the locker straight down the fairway and dorm golf started to feel good. Yet at the first hole I still found myself four shots off the pace. My only chance came much later on the 15th hole when I nailed my approach shot right down the fairway. Unfortunately it nearly took Mr Page's head clean off his shoulders. Our Housemaster had come up to see what all the noise was about. Caught red handed with my club still swinging, we had no excuses, though Scaife did try something about helping me to improve my swing. Mr Page didn't buy it for a second, and we were House gated for a week. Perhaps it would have felt worse if we had not had a taster of it the week before. We had decided to wolf whistle Mrs Page as she wandered through one of our House meetings in her netball gear.

I wasn't aware of it all those years ago when we played dorm golf for the first time, but it was back at the house where people let their guard down where true friendships were made. Funnily enough, the punishment we got from Mr Page actually brought Scaife and me even closer together. It seems that life-long friendships are made every day by pupils at Millfield. It's that sort of place.

JULIAN BRYDEN (1996 – 1998)

There was a team of cooks at St Anne's who filled us with food, ranging from rather bland to extremely flavoursome and apparently healthy! A particular favourite was the Sunday roast lunch with fantastic roast potatoes. Some of the best I've ever had. Life at St Anne's was worth getting up for, most of the time, but especially on Sundays. One of my favourite periods of the day was the morning coach journey into school. It gave me time to wake up and I could simultaneously enjoy a first class view of the countryside, though on weekdays sadly not on a full stomach.

DOROTHEE DEGER (1996 – 1998)

As a German student visiting the UK for the first time when I came to Millfield in the 6th form, it was the sense of community binding people together which first struck me as special. One of the moments when this struck me most was the rugby match against a team from Canada. I am still not too interested in this game, but it seemed to me that it was not just the game, which was attracting all these people to support the school team. It was, in my opinion, the unity of the school. Having only attended state schools in my country till then, this unity was for me a whole new experience, which impressed me very much.

Another wonderful thing about Millfield is that you never found yourself alone. If you had problems – and which young student does not at times have problems? – the first people to realise this were probably your friends, of course. Then there were the kind and very friendly cleaners in the House, who we all came to know really well. Then the Houseparents at Overleigh, Mr and Mrs Cole, and also naturally the teachers. So there were always plenty of caring people around to help. I do miss this support a lot now.

SUNITI DHUPELIA (1996 – 1998)

Millfield, land of the impossible! Where else would you find a cast of teachers, mostly men I might add, dressed up in their finest dresses, hair pieces and make-up? Indeed.

Come the spring of 1998, the Millfield charity committee came up with a brain wave. We would produce a panto, with the added attraction of the staff playing all the key roles. The production would be Cinderella; the location, the Meyer Theatre. Anticipating a real struggle to fill the roles, the charity committee turned model students: handing in prep on time, being extra co-operative in lessons, avoiding dress defaulters and so on, until we summoned up enough courage to pop the question. Please Sir, will you be in our panto? The roles were surprisingly easy to fill. Mr Speed and Mr Warne paired off as two rather Ugly Sisters and our very own Headmaster turned into a Fairy Godmother, complete with tutu and magic wand. The production was a huge success, played to packed houses and made a lot of money for African AIDS victims. I think the images from that production will be ingrained in everyone's memory for quite some time to come!

PATRICK FORBES (1993 – 1998)

Expressing my memories of five very happy years at Millfield in a single paragraph proves much too difficult, and so a simple stream of nostalgic consciousness will have to do instead: terrible jitters while walking through the quad during my first week (in a bright red jacket); the struggle to make a sports team at practice during the week and thinking it would be nice to be in my older brother's shoes; being moved by the raucous singing at the back of the bus every Friday on the way back to Kingweston; and losing House singing competitions five years in a row; a spell-bound French class with Abbi Mnatzaganian in full flow telling his stories; wondering which books one had to read to be able to quote and make references the way Mr Martin did during his beginning of term talks; the wall of aftershave that hit you when getting on the bus headed for a hop; and returning empty handed; the pride of being able to wear another coloured tie; and looking around at faces during the final Open Day and wondering how it could all go so quickly, and how much I would miss it.

FORBES HENLEY (1996 – 1998)

"Back or the front of your head," was the choice I was given my one of the upper sixth, this being the choice of where he would punch me, since I didn't want to sell him my jacket. He then obliged with my option of the back of my head. There's a memory from the worst two years of my life.

BEN NICHOLS (1997 – 1998)

'Sly's'…The bags of 'millions' are the outstanding memory of this shop, which every Millfield pupil can't fail to have tasted. Then the house laundry duty, which involved shifting those huge laundry bags up or down the stairs, seemingly taking an eternity as the sixth formers used to push them back down the stairs again as soon as we'd got them up. During those barmy summer evenings, we used to go down to the Astroturf to have water fights with the other houses and we'd come back absolutely drenched. Each summer or winter ball that took place I remember the sixth formers warning us of the wolf whistling that would take place when the housemaster's gorgeous sixth form daughter left for the ball. This ritual was known to us more than a week in advance! The 'Butleigh monument' was also carefully planned in advance so that those who would get involved were fully aware days ahead of what the plan of action would be.

> *A note from a Head of Year. "Alison, at Grange, found in possession of fireworks. Claims she did not know the word "banger" meant firework – a perfectly under-standable error. She thought they were sausages. One week school gating."*

NATALIE PRICE (1996 – 1998)

Millfield is a sporty school by tradition. It is also fantastic for art, music and drama, but at the age of 16 I was much more interested in the latter than in the former. I joined the school as 'an all-rounder', which meant that I was basically up for everything but would not excel at anything in particular. Millfield is a school where most people excel at something. At the end of my first year I had this concept tested. I was in Southfields, a house renowned for being 'all-rounders' at the time, and I was given the task of putting together a team for Inter House Athletics – a day when the entire school congregates in the sunshine to watch their peers compete from the grassy banks around the athletics track.

No one wanted to do the 1500m race. After much debate I finally put my hand up and said I would do it. After all, how hard could it be? That morning I walked into breakfast and bumped into a friend, Vicky Edwards. She asked me if I was competing that day and it turned out she was running the 1500m as well. However, the difference was that Vicky was a highly accomplished County Netball Player. I was not. Anyway, we both decided it would be a laugh and that we would run around together and not take it too seriously.

After lunch the whole school was ushered down to the athletics track where there were photographers and reporters waiting for the track races to finish so that they could catch Olympic training Carl Myerscough throwing the shot put into the Guinness Book of Records and Ed Willers setting a new high jump record.

By this time, I was getting a little bit nervous. I became even more nervous when I realised that Amelia Doran, Commonwealth Games trainee, was in my heat. Unfortunately, the rest of the heat was made up of swimmers who were renowned for being in peak physical condition and who were often better runners than the trained runners! That just left Vicky, me and one other, a polo player who looked even less fit than we were. Looking at her, Vicky whispered to me, "Look mate, at least we know we won't come last!"

Finally, it came to our race. Amelia Doran had a steely look of determination on her face, calm but totally focused. The swimmers stood ready, but relaxed waiting for their marks. Vicky and I stood a little bemused but as yet unfazed by the whole thing. It was the last track event before the eagerly anticipated major events, so everyone was now firmly in their places, ready to cheer on the last race and get it over and done with.

On your marks. Get Set. Go. Off like a shot Amelia goes, off the swimmers go. Vicky and I leisurely start our jog. Amelia disappears into the distance like a gazelle and laps us in no time, the whole school cheering her on. I remember her being one of those people who it was a pleasure to watch running. In no time the swimmers were gaining on us as well, but our safety net was still behind us so on we jogged. As the swimmers over took us, Vicky started to gain speed a little, willing me on. "Come on Nat, you can do it, we can't get lapped twice!"

"I'm trying Vic" I replied through pants and puffs, realising that my asthma was kicking in and that I was suddenly finding it very hard to breath.

Amelia lapped us again. The swimmers gained on us and out of nowhere the other girl over took us. "Come on Nat, we can't get lapped by her, that is just embarrassing." Vic tried to instil some competitive edge in me.

With her apologies, Vic shot off. I was now loosing the will to live and definitely could not breathe very easily, but on I went at a very slow jog. Amelia had long finished the race by now, as had the swimmers. Suddenly I realised that I was the only one left on the track still running. Slowly but surely I became the centre of the entire school's attention. I started hearing shouts from the banks, "Come on Price! Come on, you're nearly there! You can do it!" I had a sudden burst of energy; I was not going to give up. "Come on Price! Come on you're nearly there! You can do it!" The entire school was willing me on. People who did not even know me, teachers who had never taught me, people I had never even spoken to.

I finally fell over the finish line, and promptly started pulling away at my inhaler, but I did finish the race. Naturally, I spent the next week getting sharp comments from all corners. "Could you just run over there and get that for me, Nat?" But the cheering by the whole school not only for athlete Amelia and also for me, the straggler coming in right at the end, embodies for me the camaraderie at Millfield that I will always remember fondly.

VICKI TURNEY (1993 – 1998)

They were casting for the production to celebrate Millfield's 60th anniversary. "60 Not Out" was to be a major musical extravaganza and as a wee girl of just 13, in the first year of a-vast-world-of-a-school, being confident yet secretly anxious and ever enthusiastic and intrigued by the theatre, my school career felt somehow complete when I won the role of "Lorna Lush". Lorna the tarty, dappy PA to "The photographer!" Wow!

To play alongside all those "adults", I gasped. To perform with all those talented, mature and impressive actors of the 5th and 6th years, I thought. To be involved in such a thespian feat made me tingle with excitement and pride. I can still picture myself as "Lush", clambouring intentionally indelicately up and down the theatre steps and weaving clumsily through the audience, subserviently and mindlessly following my "snappy happy boss". At each of his bellowed cries of "Looornaaa!", I'd leap to attention, swaying my hips melodramatically beneath a mere suggestion of a skirt and tottering about madly in a pair of precarious pink stilettos. Such was my repetitive repertoire throughout the entire show! My exaggerated efforts to keep up with his strong, long male strides were the sum of my first attempts at comedy! Lorna had no lines to say and was ultimately a ridiculous two-dimensional chauvinistic creation, yet I revelled in my embellishment of such a caricature.

I remember hearing my friends and acquaintances giggling and whooping, "Go Vix", as they caught sight of my decorated physique wobbling up and down the stairs time and time again throughout the musical. I still chuckle with delight and satisfaction at the thought of it all. The whole school came together in a myriad of magical, artistic and supportive ways to create a fabulous dramatic celebration. What an achievement! These warm memories have had a tremendously positive influence in promoting my accomplishments and contentment today. That is one of the many marvels of Millfield.

THE
JOHNSON
YEARS
1998 –

Peter Johnson.

PETER.

R obert Bolt, Head of the English Department in the 1950's chose a phrase "A Man for All Seasons" as the title for his famous play about Thomas More. More has been canonized by the Roman Catholic Church, and while Peter Johnson would hardly claim sainthood, he does have a wide experience to call upon as Headmaster of Millfield. An Oxford University Degree and a commission in the "Parachute Gunners", 4th Regiment, Royal Horse Artillery preceded his teaching career at Radley where he became Senior Housemaster under the Master, Denis Silk, who was a friend and admirer of both Boss and Colin, and a Governor of Millfield. He was then appointed Headmaster of Wrekin School in Shropshire from which he joined Millfield in 1998.

The building of the boarding house "village" has been Peter's biggest project, along with the new dining-hall and "Springbok", the Headmaster's house, placed very suitably amongst the playing-fields and overlooking the pool. Peter was an all-round sportsman, an Oxford "Blue" at Rugby and Judo, and is probably the best supporter of Millfield teams on record. His support too for the Old Millfieldian Society has been outstanding, attending almost every event that has been held.

MIA COLLIS (1994 – 1999)

I had just arrived as a thirteen year old foreign student from Kenya. It was my first week ever outside Africa. I was thousands of miles away from home and flung head first not just into a new school but into an alien culture so different to what I had ever known. One week in to term we had our first photography class with Mr. Harper, a silver haired, gentle looking teacher, very softly spoken and sporting a distinctive white beard. I was petrified! He spent twenty minutes explaining the aperture, f stops and general functions of a manual SLR and then handed us the cameras and assigned us to the school grounds to capture three pictures each. "Look for composition and lighting," he urged, "and make sure the shot is focused!" After this we were instructed to return with our footage where we would have our next lesson in the dark room making prints from our footage.

"Composition, lighting and focus," I repeated in my head and nervously, with no confidence, entered the school grounds, task in hand. Totally unsure of where to begin and what to do, I wandered the playing fields for twenty minutes not once lifting my camera. Time was running out, when suddenly I caught a glimpse of a large Zimbabwean sculpture peeping out of the leaves on a mound in the trees. Shakily lifting the lens, I twisted some dials with no idea of whether they should be going clockwise or anti, did my best to focus and clicked. Immediately afterwards I remembered 'composition, lighting and focus.' But by then it was too late. We had to report back, time was up, I was late and embarrassingly had only got the one shot. In fact I had this horrid feeling I hadn't even captured it! My inability with the aperture and speed I was sure had secured a failed attempt altogether. Mr. Harper collected our film and told us that next week we would be developing the negatives in the dark room.

A homesick week passed before we entered Mr. Harper's class again. I made myself as inconspicuous as possible. "I have developed the negatives," he started, "and have been sorting through the good from the..." he paused, "not so good." I sighed under my breath. Having explained in some detail the reasons why and what went wrong he picked up one single negative that actually made it to image. 'The good news is, that we have one picture to work with. It's crisp, well composed and lit perfectly." He held up the strip to the light. "Put up your hand who took the photo of the Zimbabwean sculpture?"

My stomach churned! I scanned the room nervously to see who else had captured the sculpture. No one raised their hand. No one volunteered. "Well," he said. "We can't have a phantom photographer?". I raised my hand gingerly. "It's very good," he said directly. What a lucky fluke I thought! I genuinely smiled the first smile in two weeks. We used the print as the example throughout the lesson and Mr. Harper quietly told me that I had a good eye.

Now in my mid twenties photography is my chosen career.

More and more in recent years have I come to realise that such little boosts of confidence from the right person at the right time, whether it be a teacher or a parent, can be hugely powerful in shaping who you become and what you do in later years. In this domain teachers place themselves on the frontline. Undoubtedly my one photo was an incredible stroke of luck but what I really got from my photography teacher that day was a morale boost. The next lesson I strode out into the grounds, camera in hand with perhaps a completely false notion that I was actually good! With practice however this pretence became a reality and that one day I was good. Thank you Mr. Harper. Thank you Millfield.

> *I bump into Ben, who is in the 5th form, and who decides to get something off his chest. "I really want to succeed here, sir. I've tried hard in classes. My games are going well. I think I might even make the 1st XV next term, and in the House I volunteer all the time and I've taken Mr and Mrs Gabb's children to the shops and everything. And now they are moving to the new House, sir, and I've got new Houseparents. It's not fair. Three years of creeping wasted!"*

NATHANIEL COMER (1994 – 1999)

My most fond memory is the honour of singing at Christopher Martin's last Open day in the marquee, to a crowd of over 2000, most of whom would have been used to watching professional performers rather than the immensely nervous 17 year old standing on the stage in front of them.

The musicians of the then Lower Sixth in 1998 were asked to perform a tribute for him and we decided to do "You'll Never Walk Alone". At the appointed time I stumbled nervously on to the stage. After the first few shaky bars I relaxed and gave, what I remember to be, one of my favourite performances of all time. An actor to the end, on the last chorus I turned to the Headmaster who sprang up and instinctively joined in, which culminated in a huge cheer and standing ovation from the crowd.

There have been very few chances in my life since to sing in such a grand and auspicious setting. That was for me my best Millfield memory and one that has greatly impacted the way in which I remember my time at school.

> *The last Lower Sixth assembly gave me more pleasure than they will ever know. There was acting from the actors, music from the musicians and dancing from the splendid dancers – and all for me this time. Venetia gave a speech extolling the virtues she was kind enough to say she had observed in me and Nat Comer sang a solo for me. This got a wild reception from his 300 peers but at the end of term anything would have worked well. Which is not to disparage his voice at all. He has the lungs of an opera singer, even a Wagnerian one, and the figure to go with it, too.*

AMY GROVES (1994 – 1999)

It was the afternoon of the inter-House cross-country races. I was injured and couldn't run and so was reduced to the role of mere spectator. Half way through the race, the heavens opened and it began to pour with rain. I spotted a large umbrella under a tree and limped over as fast as I could to share it with its owner, only to discover that this was Christopher Martin. As we sheltered from the storm, we got talking about running and why I was not doing any that day. I told him that in fact I was thinking of giving it up altogether, because most of my pals had already done so, and, reasonably enough, I was wondering whether to follow them into a less demanding sport. As we gazed from under his brolly at the sodden figures stumbling by, this seemed indeed to be quite a good idea.

He had seen me run and sensed that I was at a turning point. He gave me a bunch of arguments as to why I should stick with running, not the least of which was that he thought I was good at it. Anyway, his encouragement did work for me, and the next year I took up the biathlon and came 2nd in the South West and qualified for the Nationals in cross country and athletics, captaining both school teams. And now I'm a secondary school PE teacher. It's

This weekend our debaters were in action at the Oxford Union, Millfield sides won four Rugby Sevens tournaments, the 1ˢᵗ Soccer team beat Cardiff University's 1ˢᵗ team (last year's national champions), and the 2ⁿᵈ team beat their 2nds (this year's national seconds champions). The girls Hockey team beat Bromsgrove, last year's national schools champions, and we hosted the national IAPS Hockey championships. On top of this the U14 hockey boys beat the favourites in the national schools championships, 10 - 1, to qualify in style for the final. It is particularly good to hear that Kirsten and Allie, our two star violinists, came first and second in the Mid-Somerset string section of the Music Festival, beating the Wells Cathedral School music specialists. Triumphalism is a sin I know, but nonetheless, what a weekend!

ALEXANDRA TOHME (1993 – 1999)

I joined Millfield in 1993, having been at Edgarley for 5 years before that. In fact, my parents had moved from Saudi Arabia where we had been living, just so that I could come to the school, such was its reputation. I cannot remember a single time when I wasn't having fun. Since children are changing into adults, school between the ages of 13 and 18 is probably the most difficult time anyone has to go through, but there was so much going on – music, sport, field trips – that this time for me passed painlessly. I didn't have much contact with the headmaster, but I am convinced that had he not been doing something right, my friends and I would not have had the positive times and good experiences that we did. The teachers were exceptional. Whether that was due to a good recruitment system or because the school attracts talent, or a mixture of both, I don't know. I have to say I feel proud when I say I went to school there.

NEVILLE VAZIFDAR (1997 – 1999)

I lived in Georgian Cottage and arrived straight from India where I now live. Millfield was a great school with amazing facilities. It set a solid foundation for the future for me. It taught me to be independent but also how to follow a discipline. The friends I made are the kind of friends you make in childhood – true friends. I think that apart from the education for me the most special part was going to the Golden House for Chinese food. Even though we were not allowed to go there I'm afraid we did; sorry! For me, that gave me the best education for food as today I am the owner of two of the most popular Chinese restaurants in Mumbai. The headmaster and staff gave the school great values.

ALEX WOOLLCOMBE (1994 – 1999)

The last half hour of prep would always take forever, as we adjusted shell suits, stretched eager limbs, and refilled water bottles. After what felt like hours Friday Night Football would roar through the wastelands of Street, windows down in the minibus. Slowing for the drive-by of the Jubilee shelf, the deafening beats of the 'Rhythm of the Night' synchronised magically with the silhouetted top halves of Grange girls as they elegantly went nowhere, bouncing serenely on running machines. While getting the goals out, we all enjoyed a certain satisfaction in knowing that we were having the best Friday night in Millfield: football and girls in lycra.

Friday night was girls' night in the Gym making the timing of our football almost as inspired as the MAP badminton coach who witnessed a surge in attendance after rescheduling to coincide with girls' trampolining in the Barracuda.

More stretching exercises, furtive glances to the Jubilee shelf to see how many Grange girls had left the gym to come out to watch us, and then we'd be lined up against the wall and captains chosen. In situations like this it isn't necessary to be good, but it is important that there is someone worse than you. Having one person with a bit of a belly and the disadvantage of being French narrowly spared me the ignominy of being forever referred to as "The Pieman". Usually the deadwood was equally spread.

The main thing was to recognise your limitations. The occasional turn of skill, or even better a goal, would lead to a fleeting hope that maybe one of the girls' had noticed; the scales had dropped from their eyes and they were now wildly attracted to this outwardly unremarkable but inwardly fascinating young man. The hope was fleeting because invariably female eyes were fixed on the torsos of swimmers who always seemed to be on the team that played topless. As the rest of us had to endure hours of exposure to mutually admiring half-naked swimmers back at house, we weren't so bothered. We recognised that without the six pack which was the passport to Hop success we would probably never enjoy such drooling admiration from the Jubilee shelf, or anywhere else.

As a teenager who had difficulty getting into PG's on his own, I soon learnt who it was imprudent to tackle. Going in goal was an exercise in maintaining the appearance of wanting to stop the ball without risking the loss of any vital organs. Renars was a menace. Stocky, and the son of post-Communist capitalism, he was used to getting his way with most things, including footballs. Listening to discussions during the Ashes of what facing a 95 mph cricket ball must be like, I thought, "I know". When Renars bore down on goal, as a goalie, you prayed he'd aim for the corner, or at least far away from you. The face of a third year, who foolishly tried to stop one of Renars' shots with his body as he, and the ball, flew together into the goal, will remain with me for ever.

People who say school days were the best of their lives obviously went to the wrong university, or Durham. Some people thrive in institutions while others find the petty rules they spawn like sores unendurably frustrating.

A decade on, it's the microwave that we weren't allowed to use to cook things; the deeply sad, daily battle of wills to see how close to 7.46 I could arrive in the Common Room without it actually being 7.46 which would lead to a defaulter; seeking refuge in the closed tuck shop on cold, wet Sunday afternoons because we weren't allowed to stay in house, watching the living death that is the Eastenders Omnibus; the horror of having to choose between the Daily Mail and the Express to read in house: all of these experiences could be described as "character building" – a phrase old people use to assuage young people when we have to do something that is crap. Such a multitude of small irritations sometimes allowed the bigger picture to be lost. Millfield imbues confidence in industrial strength levels to anyone who can thrive within its confines. Often this becomes the arrogant, posturing public school boyishness that makes Chavs' seem appealing; but it can be a very positive thing.

It is not mentioned in the prospectus and there are no classes dedicated to it, but probably the greatest thing I got from Millfield was a belief that, all things being equal, I would back myself to do anything as well as anyone else of a similar ability to me in a given situation.

Football with Under-18 and 21 international sportsmen, my housemaster's eight year old son, third year sporting prodigies, terrifying Latvians, academic Asians and overweight Frenchmen was brilliant. It was the highlight of our week. Even though we weren't as good or as old as the brilliant ones we could still play football with them.

The trick was, and is, to get out of the way of the balls you can't stop.

RORY CHAPLIN (1995 – 2000)

I recall coming for interview at Millfield, approaching the school with a mixture of trepidation and excitement, keen to delve into the two most fascinating landmarks that I saw as we headed for reception: the Meyer Theatre and the Art Centre. Walking past these stunning buildings, both seemed to radiate a sense of prospective excitement which I still remember vividly.

It was to these two buildings and the teachers who shared their wisdom that I owe a Scholarship to the Bristol Old Vic Theatre School and the career which followed. I remember the Headmaster towering above me as I left his office that day, beaming from ear to ear, excited as to what a boarding house called 'Joan's Kitchen' would resemble, with his words ringing in my ears; "May fortune smile on you, Rory."

PHINEAS PAGE (1995 – 2000)

Breathalisers were introduced for use by house parents when I was in the 5th form. This conversation took place at 8 a.m. one Monday morning, between Mr Ford, Head of Year, Ed Fromson, my room mate – a notorious hard man – and myself.

AF: You two were breathalised by Mr. Mills on Saturday night and you both failed. You both know that you will be punished for this?

Me: Yes, Sir.

EF: Sir, the breathaliser does not always give a correct reading.

AF: Mr Fromson, the breathaliser said you were drunk, and Mr Mills said you had obviously been drinking. So don't argue, you are both school gated for 2 weeks.

EF: Sir, I admit I went down to the pub, but didn't drink, but I know I can get gated for that, so I won't argue anymore.

AF: Ed, you are on dangerous ground as it is, and lying will get you in very serious trouble. Both the breathaliser and Mr. Mills agree you were drunk.

EF: Well Sir, if that's the case, I admit I was drunk as I don't want to get into more trouble, but I didn't drink sir.

AF: No Ed, you don't understand, you are denying something that your houseparent, a senior master, has stated happened.

EF: Sir, this isn't a court of law, but I admit I'm wrong and won't disagree with you anymore, I admit being drunk.

AF: Both of you get out and report here at break time.

LUKE VAGGERS (2001 – 2003)

Since my only link now with music is through my CD player, its rather funny that my greatest memory is when Shapwick house group won the House Singing. Practices were a real hassle. I used to dread them and avoided them at all costs but the night itself was unforgettable. The Sports hall was packed and we performed with all the energy and enthusiasm we could muster. We were the absolute outsiders with no particular musical expertise in any of us, but oh what a performance it was!

I don't think I've ever heard such a roar as when they announced us as the victors, and I've seen England play at Twickenham. We sang all the way back to the boarding house and with a few beers inside us, continued well into the night. It was a night when strict bedtimes were certainly not observed. No house parent could have controlled us, and to think all this was for winning the house choir, when originally not one of us had been interested.

Jo Allen (2004)

My A level music class with Mr. Anselm Barker consisted of four girls, including myself. As there were only four of us, Mr. Barker regularly made us cups of tea and coffee. In this particular lesson, I was slurping my coffee quite noisily and this was remarked upon by a classmate. To our surprise, Mr. Barker commented that he could easily out-slurp me any day and promptly demonstrated this unlikely skill! Music lessons were never the same again.

Henry Sands (1999 – 2004)

I used to be asked to take prospective parents on school tours. These seemed to get longer and longer as the facilities available multiplied. One mother I showed around stopped after 20 minutes when I had shown her the library, and said, "God, this place is terrible. It's like a comprehensive school. I don't think I could ever be seen to send my children here." I remember replying to her something along these lines. "Well, madam. I understand exactly what you mean by that, but try for a moment to appreciate whilst you're here what actually goes on within these classrooms. Don't limit yourself to judging how effective they are just from the outside."

I saw the same woman a good time later at her son's first open day. She told me how she had decided to "cut herself a slice of humble pie for the sake of the child's education!"

I just laughed to myself.

There seems to be some sort of social stigma attached to the school. Millfield has more to offer than other schools in the country by a long way, but it will never be thought of in the same way as Harrow or Eton, given the snobbery that seems to prevail in our country's social system.

The first full Monday of term; seamless appointments from 8.00. Teaching a new 6th form set is a treat – some Heads would call it an indulgence – and more than compensates for the extraordinary parent of a new arrival

*who comes to see me. He comes straight to the point.
"I'm sorry, Mr Martin, I know this is wrong. Alex
enjoys the school already so this is not his decision, but
I'm going to remove him today." Why? "It's just that
when I left him in his House last week, I did not like the
look of the other parents." And he takes his poor, resist-
ant son away. It reminds me of the time when an
experienced houseparent was confronted by a military
parent sporting the rank of Major on the first day of
term. "Mr Cole, my daughter appears to be in a room
with three foreign girls," he complained. "Don't
worry," replied my colleague. "I'm sure they won't
mind."*

OLIVIA LITCHFIELD (2002 – 2005)

It was my final assembly at Edgarley. Much to my disgust, I had
never won a prize, never gone up in assembly, and never received
an award in front of my year, let alone the whole school, the parents and the faculty. Then out of nowhere I was called up, to
receive a commendation for an award I had won on the French
horn. I remember sitting back down again afterwards, with people
clapping around me and a feeling that I had been accepted into the
Millfield family. It was then that I had a sudden epiphany and saw
for the first time the closeness of the community of Millfield. From
that day forward, I never again took for granted the huge family of
support I had around me.

2003 The theatre and dining hall completed.

POSTSCRIPT

In February 1993, Millfield was admitted to membership of the Headmasters' Conference (HMC). This followed a detailed inspection by a team of HMC Headmasters to determine whether the school met all the criteria for membership of that body. One of the Inspectors, Tom Wheare, Headmaster of Bryanston, later Chairman of HMC, wrote this sonnet to me at the conclusion of their visit.

MILLFIELD IN HMC

My heart leaps up as I explore your school.
It is a glorious place where children may
Lead lives in which achievement is the rule:
Loved, guided, they make progress every day.
From Boss's first adventures until now
It's offered education of the best:
Excluding none from courses that allow
Low-fliers to feel cherished with the rest.
Do other schools appreciate how much
Is possible for those in such a place?
Not just the pupils but the staff can touch
Heights that could be described as states of grace.
My sonnet sounds admiring hymns of praise.
Chris, here's a school worth serving all your days.

* * * * * * * * * * * *

LIST OF CONTRIBUTORS

THE MEYER YEARS

THE ATKINSON YEARS

THE GASKELL YEARS

THE MARTIN YEARS

THE JOHNSON YEARS